THE BOLLINGEN SERIES XXIX

文賦

余每觀材士之作竊有以得其用
心其放言遣辭良多變矣妍
蚩好惡可得而言每自屬文尤見
其情恒患意不稱物文不逮意蓋
非知之難能之難也故作文賦
以述先士之盛藻因論作文之利

The Art of Letters

LU CHI'S "WEN FU," A. D. 302

A Translation and Comparative Study
by
E. R. HUGHES

With a Forenote by I. A. Richards

BOLLINGEN SERIES XXIX

PANTHEON BOOKS

TABLE OF CONTENTS

Table of Contents

LIST OF PLATES

vii

FORENOTE

"Look in thine own heart and write," wrote Sir Philip Sydney, whose name may well stand near Lu Chi's. We look; and commonly it is a very dark well we look into, and we cannot guess its depth.

> I've looked as far as I can see,
> And that's not far, down into me . . .
> Tell me it's a pretty sight!
> Look again and take a light!

as Ralph Hodgson advises. Much depends on the kind of light. The lights of the Western tradition show us things to be supremely afraid of; knowledge, if it can be achieved, is condemnation. Chinese lights, by contrast, are reassuring. There is nothing much to fear and no good reason to doubt: "This is not difficulty in knowing. It is difficulty in being able," Lu Chi says as early as the sixth line of his preface.

As for the famous Dweller in the Depths, "This thing which is in me, but which no efforts of mine can slay," its release through words, when and if it comes, is preceded for Lu Chi by "the blocking of every kind of feeling. . . . It is like being the stock of a sapless tree, being empty as a dried-up river." This blocking comes, it seems, even after "the lightning release of Nature's spring" and the wonders of growth in the dark. Then, even though "the will [to create] be gone, the spirit held bound," then is the time to "lay hold of the mutinous soul by sounding its secret depths" till "thought come screaming, forced out from the womb."

So much for the creation of meaning. But there is also the making of the form. "Keep the two distinct and both will be to the good, deal with them together and both will suffer." Lu Chi's account of the writer's quandaries will make the least and the greatest of us wince and grin: "We are constantly grabbing the tail to wrest the head in the right direction." A strangely diverse confraternity can enjoy these things together, for it is a mind quite candid with itself that has such searching humour. And as his "record of the superb artistry of the former writers" achieves what it describes, so his diagnoses are prescriptions too; in noting what is wrong he points out each cure.

He covers all modes of writing from the lyric down to the school essay and the doctoral thesis: "Memorials to the throne should be easily intelligible along with their polished elegance . . . expositions of theories are very illuminating—and deceptive." He treats them with a model brevity: "Since it is essential that the language be understandable and reasoning well maintained, there is no point in being long-winded. "

If such advice, so exemplified, were to be learnt by heart and "hugged to the breast," there might well be a "tiger change." The Western world could owe as much to this "axe grasped to cut an axe-handle" as to anything in its own tradition of literary criticism. Who knows? Letters might again "give aid to governors and generals when ruin is impending."

I. A. RICHARDS

Harvard University

PREFACE

Natural scientists, when they conduct a controlled experiment, not only do that experiment under controlled conditions with the materials with which they work, but also are at one and the same time experimenting with their minds with a complementary set of conditions operating there; and it is by this combined process of experimentation that they arrive at their results and conclusions. It may be that this is a well-known fact in the scientific world. If so, I apologize for mentioning it in this simple fashion. But I let the observation stand, for it were well that my readers should learn at the outset that I am a very ignorant person, and do not know all sorts of things which they and the scientifically learned know so well. Further, I am shameless to the degree that I obtrude an observation on the field of music, where again I am a stumbling, purblind hierophant. Is it not true that in musical composition, say in Beethoven's and Schubert's symphonies, there is also a double experiment under controlled conditions? I envisage a theme coming to the composer, as an idea to a scientist, and he proceeds to work it out within the compass of the dominant key, the keyboard, and the strict possibilities of harmonic orchestral combinations. There was the material, and there alongside was the musician's mind, absorbed in—that is to say, controlled by—the medium in which he was working. Then both in the field of science and in the field of music, since in both cases the experimenters use media of communication, whether in equations, narrative of consecutive events, or in the wordless definitive utterances of musical sound, there is a third experiment being prepared—an experiment on the minds of those who come within the range of those communica' tions and take the time and give the necessary concentra' tion of attention to grasp what is being communicated to them.

I preface this small book with these suggestions, for to me it has been in the nature of a controlled experiment. The data, the material, consisted of a certain Chinese docu' ment, dating A.D. 301/302, praised by teachers of litera' ture down the ages in China, but very much a problem to the modern student. In a word, there was a difficult prob' lem of meaning attached to it, since it was written in a style which to later ages has appeared extremely recondite. Since the subject'matter of the document dealt with the great and highly controversial theme of the art of letters, here presumably were data which might prove very re' warding to exploration, just as the scientist sees uranium and its little'known properties calling for elucidation. A preliminary survey of the work made in Kunming in 1943, while the guest of Tsinghua University, convinced me that here was material which touched on many prob' lems in literature, problems dating from classical times and Aristotle's treatment of poetry and prose, and problems which have only come alive in this stormy, iconoclastic age of the twentieth century.

On my return to England late in 1944 I was immediately plunged into a sea of academic duties, and it was not until 1948 that freedom from these, plus the magnificent re' sources of the Chinese library at Harvard University, enabled me to get to work on assembling the apparatus of my experiment. There were various sections to that apparatus. At one end of my laboratory was the apparatus required for assessing the relative honesty of mind and poetic competency of the document's author. At the other end was the apparatus required for pitting the outcome of those qualities, namely, the document under examination, against the outcome of similar trains of thought in the West. For that was the basic nature of the experiment, to see whether and how peoples speaking alien tongues under alien conditions could get to close quarters with each other's minds. So in the last resort only the first part of the experiment has been conducted in the pages of this book. My task has been to elucidate and draw attention to certain facts, theorizing about them as little as possible. The final part of the experiment, the really illuminating part, must come from those who have not come under the influence of the Chinese language and Chinese ideological patterns as I have, from those who are deeply versed in the poetic traditions of the West, and from those who have a sense of new directions in the mimetic arts, those arts which today are proving themselves more than mirrors hung up to nature.

In this connection I might do well to explain one aspect of the problem I have been facing for some years. It is that a large number of thoughtful and educated people are prepared to put the Chinese philosophizing tradition alongside their own Western tradition, but when they try to look clearly at it they find that apart from a certain fairly clear-cut set of Confucianist aphorisms on moral obligation, the rest of Chinese thinking seems intolerably blurred. The main cause for this, I surmise, is that attention has been so predominantly focused on the earliest era of Chinese philosophizing—that is to say, when the Chinese language was very much on the march, and its grammar and syntax had not yet reached the point of instrumenting the new sense of logicality which was reaching into the dark inside cupboards of unconscious presuppositioning. In those circumstances we cannot expect to get conceptions and judgments which are mirror-clear. The state of the language—to which must be added the uncertainty there is as to the exact forms in which those concepts and judgments were inscribed at the time—precludes the critical historian of thought from getting more than a wavering approximation to the meanings expressed. That being the case, the only sensible method of clearing up these blurs in the mind is to acquaint ourselves with the writings of the Han and post-Han writers, the men who became self-conscious on the art of writing and set up standards for distinguishing good from bad writing. For all their dependence on the past, they made the grammar and the syntax. If we are to get clear communication we must look to them. Unfortunately, the translators have not got down to this except in the field of purely lyrical and elegiac poetry. I would not for a moment minimize the intrinsic value of the work done there, but I do urge that it makes an essentially unhistoric appeal. It is not semantically sound. Also, it appeals so much to the heart and so little to the head. It largely ignores the fact that without the work of the prose writers and *fu* writers between 100 B.C. and A.D. 700 there would not have been that lively consciousness of composition as an art which made T'ang poetry possible.

The result is that the sympathetic but judicious Western reader is left with the suspicion that in T'ang poetry lies the essential genius of the Chinese language and in the last resort that genius is incommunicable. We are, therefore, very little nearer to *understanding,* unless we are to assume that all the best Chinese minds worked by blind intuition and not by arts of self-conscious reasoning. I can only say that the more I read of China's great literature the more I have come to doubt that so wild a generalization has any but that amount of truth which attaches to similar generalizations that might be made about the course of Western literature.

Thus, for the enlightenment of the said sympathetic but judicious minds, minds which Milton described as "of a quick, ingenious, and piercing spirit . . . subtle and sinewy to discourse," this experiment had to be made, elucidating the texture of a late third-century Chinese mind. That learned modern critics such as Professor Ch'en Ching-to should regard the writings of that era as something of an aberration from the true Chinese spirit makes the experiment the more crucial and the more illuminating, one way or the other.

It remains for me to express my profound gratitude for the help which I have received in the various stages of my experiment. First of all there was Professor Tschen Yin-k'o, who in 1943 encouraged me in my nascent conviction that the early masters of parallelistic writing knew what they wanted to say and showed high genius in saying it. Then in Kunming there were the professors of the evacuated Lienta University, Wen Yi-to and Chu Tzu-ching, now, alas, both passed on into the Silence. They were always ready to discuss problems. So also were Professors Shao Hsün-cheng and P'u Chiang-ch'ing good enough to guide my steps. Then when I came to the United

States in 1948, the Harvard-Yenching Institute liberally availed me of its library, and, if I got stuck, that prince of librarians, Dr. Ch'iu K'ai-ming, was ready to make fertile suggestions about useful material. Mr. John Sweeney, in the Widener poetry room, was so kind as to open the door to my knock out of hours and provide the Western books I needed for comparison. An experiment has to keep moving, or those baleful futilities, attractive side paths, lead you down blind alleys. There are such paths, enough and to spare, in Chinese art, and with the Fogg Art Museum and the Boston Fine Arts Museum at hand I might have been led far astray. What is it in America that makes curators so generous in the time and trouble they will take to put right into your hands precisely the material you want? But Mr. Langdon Warner of the Fogg did more than that. He would show me in two minutes if I had gone astray, and then be willing to take an hour in helping me find the right road in relation to that wrong one; and all the time he would make me feel he was learning from me! I have refrained from quoting from Professor I. A. Richards' works. I do not always agree with him in his answers, but he has the rare genius of asking the right questions. Today I am more than ever in his debt, for he and his friend, the late Professor Theodore Spencer, not only criticized but also gave me much practical encouragement. Lastly, after coming to California I have had Professor Ch'en Shih-hsiang's generous criticism, and, in making the final revisions, Professor Ch'en Shou-yi's teaching in relation to some of my tentative interpretations. To the latter I am also much indebted for tearing his mind from his history of Chinese literature and writing the learned and perspicuous note on the Lu Chien-chih transcript. (See Appendix 4 and the frontispiece.)

As to the Ku K'ai-chih landscape (Plate III), it may strike the connoisseur, familiar with the original in the British Museum, as going rather far in increasing the visibility of the landscape detail. However, every possible precaution was taken to minimize the risk that color reproduction inevitably entails. Further, I was actuated by the same educational motive that induced Laurence Binyon in the first instance to take equal pains in getting a highly expert Japanese wood-cutter to make a woodcut. It is from an impression of that woodcut, not from the original picture, that our reproduction has been taken. With regard to the authenticity of the painting under Ku K'ai-chih's name, I am, of course, aware of the many doubts that assail the art historian; but I attach considerable weight to the following two considerations. One connects the fact that Ku K'ai-chih had a strongly marked vein of humour and the plain evidence, in this and the other paintings in the scroll, of a similar vein. The other consideration is that close examination of the relevant evidence points to the conclusion that in the fourth century the sense of graded perspective in landscape and the tentative techniques required for delineating the same had just about reached the stage of development that this picture reveals.

In conclusion, my wife has never failed to give shrewd criticism and never refused to retype a revised chapter. And through her friendship with Mrs. Tabor Low we received her hospitality in that eyrie at the end of Cambridge Common. There I was near the pulsing life of the university and town and yet above it; and my pen flowed. And when I paused in the night, there was Concord Avenue stretching away to the winking lights of the television power station. At this time—of all times in the history of Sino-American relations—to explore the range and significance of congruities between Western and Chinese minds, to get evidence of hidden electrical forces of the spirit as well as of the air, sparking in men's minds on both sides of the world, was an inspiring business. And if in the pages of this book I have sometimes let the frivolity of my mind run away with me, the benevolent reader will, I trust, forgive, for surely no man can afford to take himself too seriously.

E. R. HUGHES

Claremont College
March, 1950

Acknowledgment is gratefully made to Geoffrey Cumberledge, Oxford University Press, London, for permission to quote a passage from *The Note-Books and Papers of Gerard Manley Hopkins,* edited with notes and a preface by Humphry House, 1937.

THE ART OF LETTERS

vation is a poem, the first point to be dealt with is the matter of "poetry." "Poetry" calls up the image "winged words," a very clear image, one universally understood. Of course, no one has ever seen words, spoken or written, with wings, but none the less there is a peculiar quality about certain combinations of words which makes a large number of people think of them as having wings. For instance, to turn to history, the man (commonly known as "blind Homer") who coined the phrase[1] coined a great many other such memorable phrases and altogether made such an impression on the Greek-speaking peoples that some hundreds of years later those two highly intelligent and rationally minded men, Plato and Aristotle, were quite persuaded that Homer's speech was winged, and regarded him as the great example of a poet; i.e., *poiêtês,* maker. It is self-evident that in a real sort of sense Plato and Aristotle, and all the Greeks of that time along with them, were right. Homer's words had winged their way down those centuries and had made very deep impressions upon their minds. Plato, in consequence, the reader will remember, had grave doubts about the advisability of having poets about in a well-run state. However, at the present day there is a widespread belief that the "winged words" of poetry in particular and of good literature in general are of very great importance to the community. In fact, the educational authorities in America and England spend colossal sums of money in seeing to it that there are competent teachers who can bring home to the young that words have wings; and if any Member of Parliament or Congressman were so foolhardy as to denounce this expenditure as waste

---

[1] My Hellenist friends assure me that "winged" in the original did not refer to birds' wings, but to the feathers that enabled an arrow to fly to the mark. This interpretation gives yet more point to my reflections here.

of public money, he would not remain a Member of Parliament or a Congressman for very long. What better proof
than that can you have in a democracy?

On the other hand, there is definitely a qualification to
be made. The very people who would be shocked by the
action of our hypothetical Member of Parliament or Congressman are the very people who in a large number of
instances seldom or never read poetry, although the busi-
nessmen and politicians among them appreciate the power
of winged words in another field. They are the first to
recognize that a good advertisement or a good party slogan
is an important thing, since it has a quite miraculous power
of winging its way from one person to another. The literary highbrows have to recognize this, whether or not
they like it, as also that a considerable number of people get
a considerable poetical kick out of, say, a set of blueprints
in which the parts of a new machine are skilfully imaged
from one angle after another. So, too, the more expert
mathematicians get an almost mystical feeling of aesthetic
delight out of a "beautiful" set of equations. There is every
reason they should, because 1, 2, 3, . . . and $x+y+z$ and
all the rest of the mathematicians' box of tools are pure
abstractions—that is to say, symbols, images. It is by their
means that the minds of these experts get wings to what
they are trying to express; and very beautifully balanced,
i.e., equated, wings they are.

So the literary highbrows have no real ground for being
contemptuous of a scientist whose taste in verbal poetry
may be very simple or very bad or who may even have no
taste for it at all. These phenomena may quite well come
from his having had poor teachers at school—one, the
teacher of literature who tried to ram flowers of speech

5

down his throat, and the others, teachers of history and science and mathematics who were just gadgrinds. Let the highbrow cease being an unimaginative snob and the scientist an illogical Philistine, and we shall all come to understand the real nature of winged words better.

The main trouble about the controversy is that the poets (the makers) are almost universally supposed to be preternaturally talented creatures who, by virtue of an essentially non-rational genius, are able to produce sublime pictures of life and nature in relation to eternity, or vice versa. So they often do, as also they paint these pictures in language which has a high power of creating emotional response. But that is no reason for supposing that the poets have a monopoly of the rhetorician's gift of persuading or that they are the only people who use intuition and imagination, the gifts commonly assigned to poets and artists. The plain fact is that a set of equations or a set of blueprints is designed to express something to those who study them, and the makers of those equations and prints could never have made them had they not used intuition and imagination as well as the particular logical tricks of their respective trades. If only the admirers of poetry could recognize this and on their side would help us all to realize what the logical tricks of the poet's trade are, we should all be more clear-minded in the matter.

One point of controversy between the two camps is the use of figures of speech. For instance, "winged words" is classified in *The Oxford English Dictionary* as a metaphor, and "metaphor" is defined as "a figure of speech in which a name or descriptive term is transferred to some object to which it is not properly applicable," and "proper" is defined as "strictly belonging . . . accurate, exact, correct

6

. . . normal." So there we have it. The adjective "winged" is not one strictly belonging, etc., to the noun "words." Far be it from us to impugn the authority of *The Oxford English Dictionary,* but that triplet of quotations would seem to be misleading in this case. As the argument above about Homer, Plato, and Aristotle, and British and American educational bureaus and Members of Parliament and Congressmen demonstrated, it is historically accurate and normal and even "strictly belonging" to associate wings with certain types of word communications.

This conclusion has, however, a touch of sophistry about it, because it is quite plain that the scientists and the philosophers, the high priests of logic and reason, can present quite a case against "arguing from analogy." One is compelled to agree that metaphors and analogies are dangerous things, traps for unwary feet. Take, for example, those potent terms in logic, "induction" and "deduction," and the unassailable historical fact that for the Romans they meant "leading or taking in" and "leading or taking out" in the physical sense of taking elephants into a circus (cf. Pliny, 8, 6, 6, ¶17), and of taking a ship out of the docks (cf. Caesar, *De bello civile,* ii, 3, 2). It was a matter of taking smaller things in or out of larger things. But then the devotees of dialectical reasoning began to use the two words metaphorically (!) to denote moving ideas about in the mind. First, they argued, everybody knows that the only way to reason is to find out which smaller class of object—whether physical or mental does not matter—goes inside which larger class. Classify like with like, and you can make an induction about them all. Having done that, you can make a deduction about the members of the class. Very neat and convincing, *but* how dangerous! Suppose

7

a deaf, dull-witted man with a job in the circus where Pliny's elephants were kept. Since all the elephants he actually knew by experience lived in circuses, the only induction he could make would be that the natural environment for elephants was circuses. Or suppose another dull-wit living in a big shipyard and making the induction that all ships belong to shipyards as their natural habitat, and deducing, when the ship in Caesar's story was taken out of the dock, that it of course ceased to belong to the class "ship." The moral of all this is that (*a*) reason is vastly important, more important probably than the wisest of us actually know; (*b*) even the wisest of us, whether he be a first-class scientist or logician or a first-class poet or artist, is a bit dull-witted and deaf as to the full range of information available to him about the universe; (*c*) even logicians and scientists cannot help using metaphors and analogies unconsciously; (*d*) they always present their case in an argument as persuasively as they know how.

It is necessary to face for a moment these problems of reasoning in relation to poetry, for, as the reader already knows from his preliminary reading of the poem, it is entirely concerned with the art of writing. Also, in both parts of the poem, the author has again and again emphasized that good writing, poetry included, is always both cogent and concise. Cogency and conciseness are near to good reasoning, if not identical with it. Quite clearly Lu Chi thought that this was an essential part of good poetry. He did not say that artistic writing should be such that it ravished the ear and heart of the reader, because "ravishing" was one of his bugbears. But there can be no question that for him the sound was not as important as the meaning, but at the same time important as far as it might legitimately be taken into account. The passage in which he speaks of it—II (*b*)—conveys in its fifth couplet the impression that in the author's view a musical flow of sounds was of direct assistance to a composer in expressing his ideas.

If there be anything in this last suggestion, the author must have been a man of considerable subtlety of mind and have had a highly developed knowledge of literary form, particularly as he was so wide-awake to the dangers of efflorescent writing. From the point of view of the Western student of literature there would seem reason for believing that there is a great deal of practical truth in that suggestion. That being so, the immediate question is: who was this mysterious poet of whom so few of us have heard? When did he live, and how far does history enable us to place him? And since he was a critic as well as a poet, to what level of maturity had come the literary art about which he wrote? And finally, what sort of influence did he manage to exert, particularly in relation to his great thesis that poetry should be understood?

These are questions Western readers of this poem have the right to have answered. Without answers to such questions the translation might almost be suspected of being something of a hoax: as if Lu Chi of A.D. 261–303, in the country of China, and his *ars poetica* were a figment of somebody's imagination. Thus although for a time I felt strongly moved to publish this translation without any frills beyond a minimum number of notes illuminating the references to local institutions and the like, in the end I felt compelled to write this book round the poem, its author and his times, and the stage at which literature had arrived in his day. Further, since the poem reveals a mind which expressed

9

itself in language which was on the one hand simple and direct and on the other highly recondite in its allusions, I found myself driven in the commentary to being far more detailed and critically analytical than I originally set out to be. There were two causes for this, both of them germane to the relevancy of Lu Chi to us today.

One cause is related to the fact that in so much modern English poetry there has appeared a revulsion against conventional poetic language set in conventional prosodic forms. At the same time, and most notably in the most notable poet of today, T. S. Eliot, along with the plain homespun of ordinary speech, most skilfully welded into prosodic form as it is, there are woven highly recondite allusions. It is these allusions which puzzle the ardent appreciator who is not learned enough to track down the ancestors of the poet's images. His native modesty prevents him from criticizing his poet-teacher; and, although there has been in earlier years some quite violent published criticism of Mr. Eliot on this score, those who find him speaking to their condition have not been deterred. There would seem to be an *a priori* case for assuming that the homespunness and the virtuosity must be taken as one indivisible character informing this poet's mind; and the general conclusion to be drawn from it is that if other poets betray the same character, they can only be rightly understood by vigorous efforts to appreciate their obscure as well as their plain passages.

The second cause arises out of the first. To start by way of illustration with Mr. Eliot's *Four Quartets*: if we can judge from the quick succession of published comments on his dark sayings, there is room for considerable difference of opinion as to what his smelted-down adaptations of other poets' images really mean. Indeed, one sees a vision of learned commentators in the future having a wonderful time arguing this way and that over this and that passage. This is precisely what has happened in the case of Lu Chi and his *ars poetica*. Learned scholars in every age have em-ployed their talents in tracing the genealogy of his smelted-down images, and, being scholars, they have not agreed. Although that is unfortunately the case, nevertheless the work which has been done is of indispensable value. Chi-nese scholars today—and how much more the left-handed, ignorant foreigner—cannot understand many of Lu Chi's most important statements without the light which has been shed on them by the scholars of the past. On the other hand, since the doctors differ, the humble appreciator of today has to exercise his own judgment to the best of his ability. Here the expositor found himself in a dilemma: either he should be brief, at the risk of conveying the im-pression that his renderings at all points were unassailably right, or he should show the way in which he had made up his mind, at the risk of being diffuse. He decided that the latter course was the lesser of the two evils. To use Lu Chi's own method of argument, if a coat is too small there is no cloth with which to enlarge it, whilst a coat that is too large can be cut down. In short, those readers who have no interest in the behaviour of words need not read the lengthy comments, whilst if those comments were left out those who realize the fascination of word behaviour could not get what they would be glad to have.

Behind this treatment of the poem lies the assumption that the poem is one of exceptional interest to present-day students of good writing. On this score the expositor has had such expressions of delighted interest from learned literary friends that his earlier qualms are now superseded by the fear lest he prove an unskilled midwife to so wonderful a child. That fear, expressed in that image, raises the question already stated: how is it that this great poem and systematic critique of good writing can have been ignored by the able Chinese exponents of Chinese culture to the West and by those Western sinologists who have produced studies of Chinese poetry? How has it come about that at this late date such a key document in the history of Chinese literature can be described as a babe waiting to be born into the world of Western appreciation? The situation would seem to be fantastic. Yet it is not so fantastic as it appears at first glance. Thus the poem has existed in a Western form since 1926. In that year Georges Margouliès published his *Le "fou" dans le Wen-siuan* in Paris. In that volume, along with translations of four other *"fou"* poems, is a French rendering of the poem under the title *Lou Ki: art littéraire*. That this pioneer work did not excite any interest outside sinological circles can be understood by those who know how easily learned Chinese studies reach the shelves of specialized libraries without being noticed by the literary connoisseurs.

With regard to the Chinese exponents, there seem to be two explanations of their silence. Firstly, although they have been fully aware of the existence of this pearl, they have been fully aware also of the hard oyster shell which conceals it. The task of elucidating the precise meaning is, as has been shown, an onerous one. Further, to get the paired sentences into an English commensurate with the ordered beauty of the meaning is another difficult task. It is hardly to be wondered at that the scholars have been daunted. Secondly, the plain fact is that the literary renaissance in China thirty years ago, which embodied in so many necessary ways the revolt of young China against entrenched authoritarianism, entailed also a violent revulsion against the very style in which Lu Chi's poem was written. Dr. Hu Shih and the other leaders of the literary revolution saw, shrewdly enough, that if the tyranny of the old studied elegancies were not destroyed, the new free living thoughts of their followers might easily be caught back into the traditional moulds. Since the teachers of literature throughout the country had all been through the traditional mill, and a number of influential scholars enjoyed displaying their virtuosity in writing in *p'ien wen* style (double-harness couplets), it is understandable that, in quite a real sense, the baby had to be thrown out with the bath water. This is slowly being recognized today when so many of China's bright young men seem to have so good a knowledge of Western literature, institutions, and natural science and so vague and even slipshod an appreciation of their own past literature. Time will surely rectify this, as it will also rectify the other huge gaps in the world's knowledge of China's significant record—of which, indeed, a half, or even a quarter, has not yet been told.

The expression "*p'ien wen* style" has been used in the last paragraph, and in connection with M. Margouliès' works the term *fou*—in English transliteration, *fu*. These and one or two other terms in literary history require to be understood. The graph for *p'ien* has two parts, one meaning "together" and the other "a horse," and its earliest meaning was "driving two horses abreast." In time it came to be used generally for any two things which could be regarded as making a pair, and it probably carried with it the extra meaning of pulling together or complementing each other functionally. W*en* is a very ancient word, being found on oracle bones of the second millennium B.C. It delineated a pattern of criss-cross lines, and it has maintained its artistic connection all down the ages. In fact, it is the main Chinese term for "art," representational art, literary art, any kind of art including that of government, for it came to be used as an adjective denoting the civil side of administration. Putting *p'ien* and *wen* together, we get the meaning "double-harness style." This was the expression used by scholars in the eighteenth and nineteenth centuries for denoting the particular style of composition in prose and verse which became all the rage in the first and second centuries A.D., and which has, in one form or another, been of continuous influence ever since, until the twentieth-century reformers got to work. For some centuries it was only known as *shih wen* (the contemporary, i.e., fashionable, style) in distinction to *san wen* (discursive writing), which was regarded as being both inartistic and muddled. "Double-harness" is an admirable description of the style, and in this book that is the term used. But *p'ien wen* had a rival, *ssu liu t'i* (four-six style). There the reference is to the two dominant forms of the complementary sentences or clauses (*chü*). A couplet, in both prose and verse, might have two *chü* of anything between three to ten words, but for the most part the pattern was four plus four or six plus six. Chinese being a monosyllabic language (or very nearly so), this amounted to having the same number of sounds to a sentence.

With regard to *fu,* the history of the usage of the term will be found in Chapter III. All that need be said about that history here is that the specialized meaning of *fu* as denoting a special kind of poetry does not occur *for certain* until Han times.[2] By then there was, in the Yangtze area, one romantic school of elegiac verse writers with their distinctive prosody of rough couplets. This was where the Han literary artists found their literary inspiration. The *fu* poetry of the Second Han and Six Dynasties era, developing as it did continuously through those six centuries, broke out of the romanticist's circle of emotional excitements and became the embodiment of the classic mind with its sense of form and of emotion harnessed. The romanticists adopted lyric verse as their medium of expression, and the *fu* became—what sounds so anomalous in our Western ears—a prose poem in which a theme was treated in objective fashion. Lu Chi in his *ars poetica* described it as "the embodiment of an object [of observation]" that had to be "limpidly clear." Add to this the fact that this kind of composition was in double-harness style with the four-plus-four and six-plus-six patterns coming in alternated blocks of couplets from two to a dozen at a time, and some idea of a *fu* begins to emerge. Rhymes in a *fu* tended to follow a paragraphic demarcation, so styled because the progressing of the argument or description being made constituted the division; and here again a paragraph might be anything from three couplets to a dozen or more in length. The prose element, however, was not restricted to these distinctively prose features, so that the Chinese *fu* does strictly stand midway between prose and poetry in the Western sense and combine the essential features of both.

[2] In the *Chou Kuan*, a famous list of six literary modes associated with *shih* (poetry), *fu* stands second, coming after *feng* (song verse), and would appear to designate verses accompanying paired gifts. This has traditionally been taken as early evidence of a specialized literary meaning for *fu*. The question is, what was the date (or dates) of composition of the *Chou Kuan*? To this question historical criticism has not yet found a reliable answer. Cf. also the *Mao Shih Hsü*.

To advance a value judgment which is unpopular today in Chinese literary circles, this discovery of patterned prose and semi-verse-semi-prose is one of the many major discoveries that the world owes to China. One might take this even further and say that wherever there is prose of any degree of controlled clarity and distinction of meaning in present-day Chinese literature, the chances are that the double-harness rhythm will be found lurking in it. And then one might go one step further and advance the hypothesis, not as a value judgment but as a factual one, that a double-harness pattern of thought and language underlies and informs much, if not most, of the famous prose writings and admired examples of poetic descriptive writing in the English language. The authors were unconscious of this—or only dimly conscious of it—but their speech bewrayeth them.

This, to use a poignant American expression, is to stick one's neck out with a vengeance. And yet there are various signs that our literary pundits have begun to suspect something of the sort. This question will be considered more closely in Chapter VI, after the reader has had time to explore the many facets of the double-harness mind in the *Wen Fu* (*fu* poem on the literary art) and to focus Lu Chi, its author, in relation to the literary art. Here it will suffice to quote one grave-minded poet's opinion and another grave-minded poet's actual verse. (By a great act of self-restraint, consideration of Sir Thomas Browne, William Wordsworth, and other notabilities will be postponed to Chapter VI.) The passage is from Gerard Manley Hopkins; it is to be found in his *Notebooks and Papers*. The whole paragraph cannot be split.

But what the character of poetry is will be found best by looking at the structure of verse. The artificial part of poetry, perhaps we shall be right to say all artifice, reduces itself to the principle of parallelism. The structure of poetry is that of continuous parallelism, ranging from the technical so-called parallelisms of Hebrew poetry and the antiphons of Church music up to the intricacy of Greek or Italian or English verse. But parallelism is of two kinds necessarily—where the opposition is clearly marked, and where it is transitional rather or chromatic. Only the first kind, that of marked parallelism, is concerned with the structure of verse—in rhythm, the recurrence of a certain sequence of syllables, in metre, the recurrence of a certain sequence of rhythm, in alliteration, in assonance and in rhyme. Now the force of this recurrence is to beget a recurrence or parallelism answering to it in the words or thought and, speaking roughly and rather for the tendency than the invariable result, the more marked parallelism in structure whether of elaboration or of emphasis begets more marked parallelism in the words and sense. And moreover parallelism in expression tends to beget or passes into parallelism in thought. This point reached we shall be able to see and account for the peculiarities of poetic diction. To the marked or abrupt kind of parallelism belong metaphor, simile, parable, and so on, where the effect is sought in likeness of things, and antithesis, contrast, and so on, where it is sought in unlikeness. To the chromatic parallelism belong gradation, intensity, climax, tone, expression (as the word is used in music), *chiaroscuro,* perhaps emphasis: while the faculties of Fancy and Imagination might range widely over both kinds, Fancy belonging more especially to the abrupt than to the transitional class.[3]

The poet whose poetry calls for quotation is the T. S. Eliot of "East Coker," who, visiting the home of his earlier ancestors in an English village, begins his philosophical meditation with

> In my beginning is my end. In succession
> Houses rise and fall, crumble, are extended.

The whole poem is expressive of absorption in the object of his contemplation, the occasional recurrence of the "I" making this only the more impressive. Much of the poem is in rough double-harness and even has something of the abrupt yet sonorous rhythm of Lu Chi's poem.

> The houses are all gone under the sea.
> The dancers are all gone under the hill.

[3] "Poetic Diction" (an essay written for the Master of Balliol, *c.* 1865).

and so to the climax with its

> We must be still and still moving
> Into another intensity
> For a further union . . .
> . . . .
> . . . In my end is my beginning.

A perfect double-harness ending, the final affirmation complementing the initial one.

It is clear that in this matter we are in touch with something in which time and space assume curiously unexpected dimensions. On the one hand, it not only seems but it is a far cry from one poet in the mid-twentieth century, his lineage and domicile in the Western Hemisphere, heir to the Christian tradition and hugging its religious transcendentalism to his breast, to the other poet born seventeen hundred years back, his lineage and domicile in the Far East, heir to a mainly non-theistic tradition and not attracted by the more clear-cut and positive transcendentalism of Buddhism. And yet in their sense of the high calling of creating words with wings, in their balancing of life against death and death against life, even in the rhythm of their thinking and their accumulated emphases, in their common passion for the plain word alongside of the mind-stretching image, they seem to roll up space and time into an insignificant ball which can be tossed from one to the other with a smile.

And *yet*—to leave rhapsody, to keep feeling from running away with common sense—the two languages, the English and the Chinese, are so vastly different. It stands to reason, does it not, that the minds which think through the one medium cannot be really akin to the minds which think through the other medium. Does it stand to reason?

18

Did the reader experience that when he first read Lu Chi's *Wen Fu,* in spite of the incomprehensible images the poem contains? Have not certain Chinese scholars achieved a rather impressively felicitous English style? Have not Chinese writers during the last thirty years increased the expressiveness of their own language by importing and indigenizing Western terminology into it? And, to come nearer home, have not the French found the English language precisely characteristic of the English quality of mind, and are they not constantly wondering at that mentality so different from their own? Have not the Germans, so differently gifted a people to the British, nevertheless felt that Shakespeare only really comes to life in the German version? And, last of all, have we not reason for priding ourselves on our ability to borrow from so many languages, French and German included, and so enrich our own tongue immeasurably? The problem would appear to be not so simple as our prejudicious "it stands to reason" would lead us to suppose. And *yet,* in spite of anything any one may say to the contrary, the fact remains that there are differences in the categories of thought as between English and Chinese, differences which, apart from questions of national temperament, the French and Germans share with the English-speaking peoples. To that proposition there must be a *prima facie* consent. Not that it matters so much that the Chinese did not have an Aristotle to discover syllogistic reasoning, for, as has been suggested, there are traps for the unwary about that triumph of the human brain; and in any case, the British and Americans believe more in the light of experience than in the light of deductive reasoning. But it surely does make a difference when one race believes that reasoning comes from the head and feeling from the heart and the other race believes that reasoning and feeling both come from the heart.

In his recent book, *The Meeting of East and West*,[4] F. S. C. Northrop marshalled the resources of his capacious mind to demonstrate that the West characteristically uses the scientific method to discover new truth and the East characteristically uses the method of intuition. The Chinese theory of rational thinking as coming from the heart would seem to substantiate Dr. Northrop's judgment. It is surely self-evident that if a man's judgment is dictated by reason it is not dictated by feeling, and vice versa: one cannot get beyond that antithesis. True, one cannot; but there is a little query hidden away in that antithesis, one of which modern psychology has become increasingly aware. It is whether any man at any time in any part of the world ever did take any action which was dictated by reason alone. No one actually knows the answer to that question, but the vastly strong presupposition is that no one ever did act without some mixture of feeling with his reasoning. If that be true, then the Chinese were right in their psychological guess that reasoning and feeling cannot be entirely separated.

It is important to the reader of Lu Chi's poem that he should be aware of this situation, for when the translation gives the meaning of *hsin* as "mind" or "heart-mind" or "mind-heart" or "heart," this is not done out of pedantry or with a desire to show the strange ideas the Chinese have, but because it is a rough indication that reasoning and feeling do get so inextricably mixed. To go a step further, Lu Chi's medium of communication has the word *ch'ing*, which has usually been translated by "feeling," "emotion," or "feelings" or "emotions," or "the feelings" or "the emo-

[4] New York, 1946.

tions." But the odd thing is that when the great Taoist thinker, Chuang Chou, a man with a highly realistic mind, began philosophizing about the universe, he used *ch'ing* to denote the general organization of any phenomenon, or, as we say, the facts about a thing or an event or a situation. That meaning has remained as an alternative one to *ch'ing* ever since and is current today in ordinary Chinese speech. At first sight this seems extraordinarily baffling, for one word to have two such strikingly different meanings. A moment's thought, however, will show that, although *ch'ing* started life as the class word for a number of recog-nized emotions, there was nothing to stop its becoming, as it did, the term for the emotional organization in one's heart-mind. In fact, emotions have such a way of getting entangled in each other that a discerning people would recognize the fact and think in terms of the total emotional organization. Then came Chuang Chou and his followers, and they started using *ch'ing* metaphorically, and this fash-ion caught on. By Lu Chi's time *ch'ing* was also used to denote the mood in which a writer composed a poem or a dialectical discussion. In terms of his *hsin* (mind-heart) that meant its whole organization in relation to what he was starting out to do—to use the old faculty psycholo-gist's terms, both the cognitive elements and conative ele-ments in his particular mood. Lu Chi, in fact, held that a man could not make a good composition unless he had a clearly envisaged mood (*ch'ing*) with great emotional power behind it. (Cf. Plato and Aristotle and all great writers *passim*.) He also held that a trivial subject could not produce a mood of any particular efficacy, and in this connection propounded the theory that a mood (*ch'ing*) was a matter of response to a stimulus. To understand the

force of his *ars poetica* it is obviously necessary that we appreciate this kind of categorical thinking in its creator.

In the light of *hsin* and *ch'ing*, what, then, are we to say
about the meeting of East and West, for example, of
distinctively Chinese and British-American minds? Obviously it would be easy to think, particularly with the
poem's winged words ringing in our ears and heart-minds,
that the two can and do meet. True, but poetry is poetry,
as many lovers of poetry and despisers of it say, and it is an
unquestionable historical fact that the Western peoples did
at a certain time start developing a scientific mind in a sense
which the Chinese did not; and from that has come the
existence of certain special aptitudes of the mind, certain
new powers of critical appraisement in relation to the universe and man. And these are part of our Western *ch'ing*,
our distinctive intellectual and emotional mood or organization in contrast to other cultures, and specially to those
which seem to be poor in science, although rich in artistic
sensibility. Here the devotees of the poetical *hsin* have to
face facts. They are the heirs of Galileo and Isaac Newton,
who made the first physical synthesis of the universe, and
arising out of that historical fact, the very poets to whom
the devotees look for light and guidance can and do fly to
the ends of the earth to fertilize their powers of imagination. If they do not actually do so, they read the books of
the men who have done so. Also the applied sciences of
cheap printing and distribution of books enable them to
strengthen the sinews of their minds by the contemplation
of history, prehistory, geological time, back to the very
beginning of everything. That, then, is the issue, whether
a man with a more limited sense of time-past and a more
limited range of world-vision can really be intellectually

en rapport with the mind of modern man, whether he be cultivated American or cultivated Chinese.

This is the final point for consideration in this introduction, and it demonstrates the value of abandoning windy generalizations like "the Oriental mind" or "the Wisdom of the East" or "the artistic intuitionalism of the Chinese mind." These concepts have some meaning, but on the lips of those who use them the meaning becomes lost in the figments of their escapist imagination. In this book we are concerned, here and now, only with one Lu Chi and his *ars poetica,* a specific document by a specific individual, and the question is as to his concrete apprehension of time and space seventeen centuries back on the Asiatic shores of the Pacific Ocean. The argument on this question is as follows.

With regard to his consciousness of world-space, as Chapter II will show, he knew of the existence of India and its cultural advance under the influence of the Buddha, and he knew of the existence of a Roman Empire in the far west, beyond the intervening kingdoms in central and western Asia. That to him they were hardly on the same level of culture as his own vast civilized area of China is probably the truth, but alongside that we have to place the fact that he was profoundly dissatisfied with the state of that civilization in his day and wished to take part in the task of rectifying it. In that respect his mind was a forward-looking mind.

The problem of time-past is a more complicated one. For us, *anno Domini*—with the Greeks' achievements in cultured feeling and rational thinking a few centuries earlier —spells the beginning of civilization. Anything earlier hardly counts: so runs the conventional idea which we were taught at school. Of course, the Jews, "God's people," had a much longer history, one going back to Abraham, and even Noah and Adam, but that "comes" in the Bible, and "the Bible is religion." In Lu Chi's age the conventional idea of the past was similarly twofold, a secular and a religious one. The religious one also had a prodigious time sweep. When the heavens and the earth split asunder, a mysterious P'an Ku took an active part in starting things on the earth. The "Twelve Celestial Sovereigns" in succession, each holding sway for eighteen hundred years, had control, but man at the end was still sleeping in caves in the winter and roosting in trees in the summer, still wore the skins of beasts and "ate the fruits of trees and plants, crickets and frogs, and rancid uncooked flesh" (see Chapter 49 in Han Fei's book—third century B.C.). Then came "the Sage Monarchs of high antiquity, middle antiquity, and later antiquity." Sui Jen (the fire man), who taught men to cook food, Fu Hsi, Nü Kua (a female demigod), Shen Nung (the godlike husbandman), and others after them, who taught man all the essential crafts of civilized living, including those of writing, interchange of spare products at markets, and above all the sacred secrets of social harmony and permanent peace. Here we see not only the religious imagination at work in myth-clothed theory, but also the exercise of the mathematical imagination, a characteristic of religious beliefs at a certain stage. A millennium is conceived as 1, and $1 + 1 + 1 \ldots$ takes the awe-struck rationalizer back and back in a moment of vision to the beginning of everything.

That brings us curiously near to the geologist's sense of time, which to all intents and purposes is a similar calculation in terms of $1 + 1 + 1 \ldots$, leaving the scientific mind also with a sense of awe at the vast interludes of global time; from which the astronomer's mind leaps off into the blue and with the aid of his mathematical tools gives us neat equations on stellar time and space. A relative of Lu Chi's (cf. Chapter II) had a taste for mathematics, which in those days meant an interest in astronomy, and one Ch'ang Heng (cf. Chapter III), two generations before him, had written a dissertation on astronomy which is still extant. It would be only scientific caution to suspend judgment on this matter until we have mastered that dissertation and can place its cosmological assumptions alongside our own.

The final word lies with the problem whether the exactest of exact sciences, mathematics, is or is not the most imaginative of all the products of the human mind. There is much to be said on either side, and no one is in a position to denounce his opponent as a fool. In fact, the last word comes to lie with Lu Chi, contemplating the uncanny way in which inspiration may come and, on the other hand, may not come, when a man, be he philosopher or artist, puts pen or brush to paper. The author of the *Wen Fu,* having urged his fellow poets that they should at all times do their best to be coherent and cogent, finally creates this winged word: ". . . time and again I stroke my empty bosom in pity for myself: so ignorant am I of what causes the opening and the barring of the door."

CHAPTER II

LU CHI'S LIFE AND TIMES

IN CHAPTER I we asked about Lu Chi's sense of chronological time and geographical space, and we were re-
assured as to his having a quite sensible attitude
towards these concepts which may either narrow or
broaden a man's thinking. To judge by our own traditional
ideas in the matter, the ideas universally accepted a hundred years back in Britain and America, we found that
there is not much to choose, on the score of common-sense
reasoning, between the two sets of part-religious, part-
secular ideas on the rise of civilization and the knowledge a
race has of its early beginnings. Here, at the beginning of
this chapter on Lu Chi's life and times, it will be useful to
elaborate a little on the scholars' outlook in the early years
of the Tsin dynasty. It will help towards an understanding
of Lu Chi's very striking opinions on the lessons of history
and his personal conviction that there was some hope—
not very much, but still some hope—for the future.

With regard to other parts of the world and foreign
cultures, in court circles at any rate it had been common
knowledge from the end of the second century B.C. that
there were organized states and distinctive cultures in
western Asia. In the first century A.D. this knowledge had
been increased and the sense of geographical space enlarged

by sporadic contacts with people who knew what the word "Rome" meant, and the same century had seen the intro-duction of Buddhist missionaries from India and Parthia into Loyang, the capital. These missionaries had a great story to tell of the Buddha's abandonment of royal pomp, of King Asoka's building up of a vast kingdom of peace, and the refining influence their religion had come to exer-cise in the "Western Lands." The official records on these matters were to be seen in the palace library, and if Lu Chi did not trouble to read them himself he knew the men who had read them. Not only so: in his boyhood there was a famous monk, with all the prestige of the title of *po shih* (doctor of learning), at the court of his royal connections at Chien Yeh (Nanking); and later when he was living in Loyang an establishment of foreign and Chinese monks flourished in the city. There can be no question but that India and western Asia were on the map of his mind as an integral part of the wider *t'ien hsia* (all below heaven) of which his *Chung Kuo* (Central Kingdom) was part. On the other hand, it is clear that he was not particularly in-terested in those foreign parts, just as Vergil was not vitally interested in the cultures of Asia Minor and the East, nor for that matter Shakespeare in Sir Walter Raleigh's ex-cited plans or the founding in London in 1600 of the business association for trading with the East.

The three men had enough to occupy their thoughts and feed their souls in other ways. In any case, Lu Chi, for all his longing for inner peace, was not attracted to the Buddhist faith, and perhaps we can hardly wonder at this. There was a pushing, self-advertising side to the Buddhists' activities, and if that half-mystic, half-charlatan, and whole-time wily politician, the monk Fo T'u Teng, can be taken as at all a representative of that side, a man of Lu Chi's noble temper could not but be revolted.[1]

To come to the sense of the past in Lu Chi's age, in A.D. 279 the opening of an ancient tomb brought to light certain manuscripts written in the ancient script on bamboo, among them one which quickly became famous, the *Chu Shu Chi Nien* (Bamboo Annals). The new Tsin emperor called upon his scholars to appraise its genuineness, and it appears that they decided in its favour. This record, according to internal evidence written between 298 and 295 B.C., gave a continuous line of highly sage, less sage, and definitely not-sage monarchs from the time of Huang Ti (Yellow Emperor), whose reign began in 2698 B.C. and lasted a hundred years. The story did not cause any intellectual excitement, for it was only saying, with perhaps a greater show of chronological precision, what everyone believed. Of course, the "Five Emperors" and the "Three Kings," by their heaven-given genius and sacrificial labours, had step by step brought civilization to flower. Was not the great feudal regime which the last of the royal sages, Duke Chou, had organized, with its filial worship of King Wen (the Civilized King) and its code of chivalry, the very pattern of civilization? And had not Confucius, the last of the sages and the only commoner among them, spent his life in recalling men to their allegiance to "the ways of King Wen and Duke Chou"? The tale of it all was there in Ssu-ma Ch'ien's *Record of History* and in a hundred other works of unimpeachable veracity. The only question was whether society in this its hour of danger was more likely to be saved by carrying on with the principle of

[1] Fo T'u Teng by the time of Lu Chi's death must have been living at Tun Huang. In A.D. 307 he arrived at the headquarters of the Hsiung-Nu prince, Liu Yüan, and began his highly influential career.

bureaucratic centralization such as the tyrant First Emperor had tried to use, or by trying a variation of the Han compromise between bureaucracy and feudalism, or by learning from the mistakes of the last thousand years and making a new effort to organize government on the basis of decentralization and permanent fiefs.

A certain number of Taoist idealists approached the problem from a different angle. Let everyone, they said, pay homage to the one and incomprehensible Tao by cutting out all this passion for civilization, by realizing the futility of attempts to organize government. Just keep quiet and let Nature act in and through you; refrain from all foods which arouse lusty desires, and preserve your vital powers by allowing nothing to disturb your interior calm: then the problem of the age will be solved. The Buddhists also had their panacea: believe in the great Lord Buddha and the power of his achieved salvation, and cut the nerve of even the simplest and most human desires by fixing your gaze on a completely transcendent state of existence. To men of a robust temper and active disposition these two ways of thinking did not appeal, even though the murderous ambitions of the great men in the country sometimes brought them to the brink of despair. We shall see in due course what Lu Chi's personal position was and how the divergent appeals of his Chinese traditional culture made him acutely conscious of the chances and changes of this mortal life, and so long "to be away."

Lu Chi, courtesy name Ssu-heng, born in A.D. 261 at Hua T'ing in the Yangtze delta, was the grandson of Lu Sun, the man who by his military genius gained in A.D. 229 the southern throne for the first Wu emperor, and the son of Lu K'ang, who wore out his life on the northern frontier guarding Wu against the forces of the northern empire. Lu Chi's beloved younger brother, Lu Yün, wrote of the family as coming originally from the north and trac' ing its lineage back to the eras of the Three (Sage) Kings and Five (Sage) Emperors, but the tendency of all great families was to do that. The *Three Kingdoms History* speaks of a branch of the Lu family having early gone south; but a hunt through the *Second Han History* reveals one Lu after another as being "men of Wu." This goes as far back as the early years of the first century A.D., when Lu Hung was "pleased to wear Yüeh [i.e., southern] clothes." Two theories are equally probable: one, that sometime in the previous century—i.e., when Emperor Wu's policy included further regulation of the southern tribes—a Lu went south on government service and estab' lished a family there; the other, that this Lu family was an indigenous one.[2]

Whichever way we take it, we can now understand the intense local patriotism which from Lu Sun down charac' terized his family. Lu Chi and Lu Yün had it to a most marked degree, and their biographies show that when they came to live in the north they regarded themselves as in a "foreign country" (*wai kuo*). The summing up of Lu Sun's life was given in the words of the *Three Kingdoms History*: "He devoted his life in sorrow for his country [*kuo*], was the servant of the gods of the soil." That second clause is significant. He was not the tool of any upstart emperor, but a man with his roots deep in Wu soil, his objectives secure

---

[2] If we take the former theory, then here is an early instance of what be' came so great a practice later: namely, aristocratic families moving south, bag and baggage, and there under new conditions reproducing much of the old feudal order. This had far-reaching effects, bringing new cultural and economic factors into play.

borders guarded against all invaders and a prosperous peas-
antry free from excessive taxation and ruthless punish-
ments. He and his son and his grandsons remind one of
the New England and Pennsylvania families at the time of
the Revolution. In both cases a dominant culture from
abroad was recognized and honoured, but men refused to
be slaves to the connection. All along the Yangtze basin
both then and later we can recognize the phenomenon, a
temper of the spirit which accepted all that the north had
to give, but would not sink its identity in the north. Lu Chi
had this southerner's point of view and it helped to make
him the first great literary critic in Chinese history.

Lu Sun apparently was no scholar, but his uncle, Lu Tsi,
was one, having a passion for "astronomical mathematics,"
and a brother, Lu Mao, devoted himself to ethics, practical
as well as theoretical, and developed thereby the most lov-
able traits. Lu Sun's influence on the family was the
stronger, and the profession of arms became the family
career. Lu K'ang became a colonel at nineteen when his
father died, and when he himself died in 274 at least three
of his six sons, Lu Chi among them, followed in his foot-
steps.

Hua T'ing was the name given to the great estate with
which his grateful sovereign rewarded Lu Sun for his long
services in the field and the council chamber. With it went
the high title of *kung* (duke). Situated in the delta of the
Yangtze, Hua T'ing, although originally part of a hunting
preserve of the semi-barbarian kings of Wu, was eminently
suited for rapid development. Lu Sun seems to have set
himself to this work with the same vigour that he brought
to affairs of state. Before he died, the old name for the
countryside was changed to Wo Hsing (Grain Abound-

ing); so that we may infer that some of its present-day smiling appearance must have been there then: rich rice fields, groves of bamboo, mulberry orchards, and in the distance the forested hills round the Hangchow Lake. Here was Lu Chi's home, the home which he and his younger brother, Lu Yün, fellow poet and bosom friend, came to love so deeply. They, too, knew the call of the gods of the soil.

The gazetteers of that region reveal several traces of the family. As will appear, Lu Chi's generation was almost wiped out, but local tradition points out the site of the Lu ancestral temple. A Buddhist temple built in T'ang times outside the gates of K'un Shan (Quinsan) has been recorded as on the site of Lu Chi's house. Near by is a stream on which tradition had it that the family floated in their boats on moonlight nights, doubtless playing and singing to each other. A few miles away, between K'un Shan and Hangchow Lake, is a spring with limpid water and a sandy spit, said to be the place where from time immemorial the Hua T'ing cranes had gathered, and, drinking from the pure water, had gained the sweet, clarion note which distinguished their cry. (We shall meet the Hua T'ing cranes again in a tragic context.) And finally there is near the ancestral temple a mound called "Yellow Ear's Grave." Yellow Ear was Lu Chi's beloved dog, whose story is worth telling in the words of the *Tsin History* (see its biography of Lu Chi, Chapter 54):

Lu Chi, on one occasion being detained in the capital, had had no news from home for some time. Laughingly he said to his dog, "Our family has stopped writing letters. I believe you could help take a letter and get news, couldn't you?" The dog wagged his tail and made a sound. Lu Chi then wrote a letter on a sliver of bamboo and tied it to the dog's neck. It sought out the road south and ran home, obtained the news, and returned. Afterwards it became a practice for it to do this.

We know little about the ladies of the Lu family. Lu Chi's grandmother was the niece of the first Wu emperor and one of his elder brothers had the last emperor's sister to wife. That in due time Lu Chi himself married we know, for among his poems is a charming one addressed to his wife in which he bewails their separation. Where did he spend his childhood? We do not know, but presumably, since his grandfather was dead and his father on military service, his first years were passed at home among the family's retainers and local farmers, and in due time with a tutor to teach him the three R's. When he was fourteen his father died, and, with his two eldest brothers taking higher commands in the frontier army, he had to help in maintaining the loyalty of the troops. He was given the captaincy of his father's personal soldiers, a nominal post perhaps, but entailing some contact with his men and some study of military science. He was exceptionally intelligent and quick, and when we consider that his full-grown stat- ure ran to well over six feet and he had a voice like a bell, it would seem that, youngster though he was, he could hold his own with the old soldiers his father had trained. For five years this curious training of a poet continued. Then came the *débâcle* that changed the life of Lu Chi and his family.

Lu K'ang had warned the Chien Yeh court that re- inforcements were needed and the danger point was the river, but the uxorious, vacillating Emperor Hao could not bring himself to do anything adequate. The result was that a vast army was marshalled by the Tsin generals on the middle Yangtze, a fleet of hundreds of boats was built

33

(some of them double-deckers), and an overwhelming attack was launched down stream. What river defences Wu had collapsed, and Chien Yeh lay at its enemies' mercy. The miserable emperor surrendered. It was the end of the Wu empire, a state, to use Lu Chi's own words, "with a thousand miles of territory and a million suits of armour, its land fertile and its soldiers well trained . . . without equal for its size. If only there had been moderate ability to maintain it aright and good men to use the techniques of government." Lu Chi's two eldest brothers were killed fighting; he and his younger brother escaped. They made their way east, going to earth in Hua T'ing. There they "barred their door and devoted themselves to study." For ten to eleven years they were to be there.

"They barred the door": that is to say, they held no intercourse with the outside world. That was necessary if the Tsin court was to have its suspicions lulled. "Gave themselves to study": that means a library of some sort.[3] We may conjecture that Lu Tsi's and Lu Mao's books and papers were at Hua T'ing. Then the question is what the two brothers studied. The records are silent, but some estimate can be made. For instance, their education had been partially interrupted, so that they might have had some gaps to fill in the great literature of antiquity. In Lu Chi's writings there are few quotations, but in addition to the Confucianist Scriptures he shows himself familiar with, for example, Hsün Ch'ing, the Confucianist philosopher of the

---

[3] The catalogue of the imperial library (c. 25 B.C.) shows a total of "13,269 *chüan* [roughly chapters] by 596 authors, the works being classified in 6 main divisions and 38 sub-divisions." Since then the number had more than doubled, and what with the labours of the scribes (an ill-paid and not unfailingly accurate set of men) and the passing on of new poems and essays from one writer to another, by Lu Chi's time there were stores of manuscripts in scholar families.

34

third century B.C., as also with the Taoist writers. But the brothers were writers rather than bookworms, eager to master later techniques of style, not content to mouth old saws or write a commentary on some old scripture. That is clear from what remains of the "over three hundred" compositions that Lu Chi wrote, and the "three hundred and forty-nine" that Lu Yün wrote. In a word, they were poets, and it must have been during these ten years that they served their apprenticeship, and began to find their own *métiers*.

First of all, however, they had to find where they stood in this world which had gone to pieces before their eyes. To that task they set themselves with all the fiery seriousness of youth. The results are of immense interest to the historian, witness *The Dialectic of Destruction* which they wrote (it is attributed to Lu Chi, but Lu Yün must have had his share in it). It is a long essay in two parts, dealing with the causes of the downfall of Wu. A very revealing document, it is not concerned with the downfall of the Han regime of forty years earlier. That was past history to these young men, and they contented themselves with saying:

Formerly the Han family lost control, evil ministers pilfered the Heavenly Commission. The root of calamity was in the capital and the central district, and the poison spread everywhere. The constitution of the state became enervated and inconsistent, with the result that the imperial house was degraded.

There is no rhapsodizing over the glories of Han, no recognition of its undoubted achievements or sentimental wailing over its decline from its high estate. Lu Chi was not interested, an attitude he was to change when, ten or more years later, he wrote his *Discussion of the Five Grades of*

35

Nobility. What he was concerned with in *The Dialectic of Destruction* was the tragedy of the destruction of Wu, his own home country's tragedy, one so shot through and through with malfeasance and degrading incompetence that it was a mere farce on the stage of history. He is very bitter about it, as well he might be, for he knew how his grandfather had slaved to build up the empire and extend its bounds westward and southward. He knew also how through the long years their father had upheld the Con-fucian honour of the country on its northern border, by reasonableness and fair dealing creating peace with his neighbour commanders across the border. And he knew how completely his father's warnings of a flank attack had been disregarded. The theme, therefore, is so great a coun-try so disastrously betrayed; divided councils producing inaction; the people not even called out to fight for hearth and home.

The generals of the northern and western kingdoms were not hap-hazard choices, whilst our armies were smaller than on previous occasions. The laws of attack and defence still had their tallying conditions: the advantages of defiles and gorges did not suddenly change. So, the age-old logic of victory and defeat, that did not change in the outcome. As is the difference between one revolution and another, so is the difference between the talents of those in charge of affairs.

In this way the two brothers worked the anger and humiliation out of their system. The Greek idea of purga-tion of emotion by dramatic representation never struck the Chinese literary consciousness—as far as I am aware— but the idea of putting turbid evanescent emotion under the harrow of poetic expression, and of a composer's absorb-ing himself in the contemplation of an object and so becom-

ing able to portray it ideationally, this kind of consciousness
did come China's way. In this essay the process is clearly
seen at work. Not only is the bitterness of national disgrace
and personal frustration put into words, but also the event
is objectified, made part of Lu Chi's space-time perspective.
It became a lesson which history had to teach, a series of
causes and effects from which weighty conclusions might
be drawn. The interesting thing is that his conclusions are
more Mohist than Confucianist, utilitarian and not
idealistic.

The former kings envisaged the abiding principle for succeeding
ages, understood the ruling tendency of men's hearts. They knew
that in the composition of human nature there was nothing so strong
as self-regard, in making profit out of Nature nothing equal to
ambition: that the well-being of the upper classes consists in making
the lower classes equally happy, one's personal advantage consists
in profiting other men.

It sounds like an old-fashioned Conservative in England.
Indeed, Lu Chi's political conclusion is that a return to
feudalism is the only hope for society. The First Emperor
had made the initial mistake, and the Han emperors had
failed to rectify that cardinal error, centralization of authority. Since the same mistake had been made in Wu,
decentralization was the only key to successful government. Society must consist of patricians and plebeians; the
men whose learning and trained sense of honour enables
them to rule and the men who can labour with their hands.
Give the former security of tenure, and the latter will learn
what best serves their own interests. About this theory it
can only be said that it was what Confucius himself had
believed, and its psychology had, alas, been disproved by
the later history of Chou society. This Lu Chi knew well

37

enough, but against that he could place the fact that there in Hua T'ing, his family fief, he and his relations were living peacefully in the great house, and no man plotted to put them out.

It is easy to think of the two brothers varying their literary pursuits with hunting: out at dawn to shoot the wild fowl, with the dogs tracking the wild boar and the tiger; and then coming back to the food and wine of the country, with jest and quip springing from the lips of the one to the other, and on summer nights coming out with flute and harp to hymn the moon as their boat floated down their stream. Imagination can hardly err here, for that is what young aristocrats of spirit did in those days. There is ample evidence, too, of both brothers' sense of humour and enjoyment of a joke, Lu Chi's more sarcastic and Lu Yün's light-hearted and irresistible. On one occasion Lu Yün, "clothed in mourning, was getting into a boat, when he caught sight of his reflection in the water. It made him laugh so much that he fell in and had to be pulled out."

Nevertheless, as the years went on, the two men became bored, restless, or the tightening of Tsin control over the Wu country may have made their position untenable. In any case, they decided to go north and seek their fortunes at court. This was in A.D. 290, just after the first Tsin emperor's death. There was much to call them back into public life. The Tsin policy ostensibly supported schemes for decentralization of authority, and that of course fitted in with Lu Chi's own ideas: in actual effect its practice went the other way, court intervention neutralizing provincial powers. But most of all, the capital, Loyang, was the place where there were books and scholars and writers.

There they could meet their contemporaries. There they could hope for appointments, and so employ their talents in public service.

There is no sign that they went hat in hand to the Tsin court, much less of their cringing for pardon. Rather they seem to have been a little arrogant, ready to sniff at the *parvenus* they might meet. The patron they sought was one Chang Hua, a minister of state and a writer of poetry of some note. As the record has it, "He had a great respect for their name, was, as it were, an old acquaintance." When they went to see him, however, Lu Yün disgraced himself. On their being announced, only Lu Chi went in, and Chang Hua asked where his brother was. Lu Chi calmly replied, "Lu Yün has a fit of the giggles [literally, a laughing pain], and so cannot present himself." A moment later Lu Yün arrived. Now, Chang Hua was by disposition careful of his personal appearance, and his whiskers were tied up with silk strings. When Lu Yün saw him, he again had a "laughing pain." Fortunately, their host was not offended, and before the interview ended Lu Yün's power of repartee even made him laugh. He arranged an audience with Prince Ch'i at which Lu Chi acquitted himself with spirit, and both the brothers were given posts. Lu Chi was made a *tsi tsiu,* a supernumerary position awarded to scholars of distinction and involving giving advice in literary matters. Later he was attached to the heir apparent's household as literary secretary. Lu Yün was made magistrate of a town (the people of which came to love him).

But their troubles were not over. People shot ill-natured questions at them. Lu Chi gave as good as he got: rather to his brother's dismay, for we find him warning him,

"Why go on like this in a foreign country where you are not familiar with their outlandish customs?" It was sound advice but not taken. None the less, the two brothers established their reputation in official circles and won the respect of the older statesmen. In 296, we find Lu Chi on the staff of an army in the field headed to attack the Hsiung Nu barbarians who had established themselves some two hundred miles north of Loyang. He wrote a poem, the first we possess of the series in which he showed how from time to time he lost heart. The conduct of the campaign was dilatory, the soldiers were mutinous, and he longed to be back in Hua T'ing.

The seasons revolve in their order, the four forces [*chi*] press on
each other's heels:
the icy breath of winter is the stern killer, my robe is drenched with
autumn dew.

I grieve at the passing of what is completely past; my heart is
stricken by the death of the present:
I have cut off the sound of my voice from the banks of the Long
River, and have entrusted its echo to the shores of the Lo.

That thing in a man, the thought of being away, how unremitting
its pain, how empty of pleasure:
I am sick of feelings which involve me so that I deceive myself, I am
tired of encountering events and so begetting consequences.

By day I turn from my food and burst into fits of anger, in the
leisure of the night my sleep is filled with babbling:
with raised head I envy the wild swans' flight [to the south], I
decant [a measure of] the valley wind, and the scent is of
orchids.

My years fleet past and evening approaches, the anguish of my
heart grows ever keener:
the wind drives the sleet into my room, the ping of the hail fills me
with gloom.

A foreboding of evil is there, and the years proved only too tragically that it was not without cause. The times were evil and destined to get worse, and both the brothers found themselves gradually more and more caught in a net of circumstance over which they had no control. For the time being, however, things went well on the surface. Lu Chi became one of the personal secretaries to the Emperor and was in daily attendance on him.

According to the T'ang era historian, editor and author of the *Tsin Dynasty History,* the evilness of the times was mainly owing to the incessant plottings of the eight *wang* (princes) of the imperial house. This is a late judgment, but it accurately enough represents the facts. With the occupant of the throne practically an idiot, there was only too much inducement to these on the whole incompetent and unscrupulous individuals to scheme, each for himself, to usurp the throne. The effect of this situation was dis-astrous to the economy of the country, for during six years (300–306) there was open warfare among the rivals. To quote the *Tsin History,* "Emphasis was laid on the master hand in control, that of the emperor, but there was a fan-tastic relaxation of administrative authority . . . men of good ability might have no office, men who were blameless might suffer the death penalty." The first Tsin emperor, a man of some rude ability who deposed the weakling fifth emperor of the Wu regime (220–264), had ostensibly made his policy a return to feudalism, and the bulk of the scholar-officials seem to have felt that this was the most hopeful line to take. But the policy was superficial. Al-though the scions of the imperial clan had territorial titles given to them, they had no responsibility for those terri-tories. Yet they had great estates and one way and another could command the services of large numbers of soldiers.

In A.D. 300, Prince Lün, so-called Prince of Chao, with

another of the princes as coadjutor, wiped out the dominant palace clique, had himself appointed chief minister,
and put his supporters in office. Prince Yün attacked him
in the field and was defeated, and the other princes apparently were caught napping, unable to assert themselves
for the moment in the capital. In the first flush of victory
Lün decided that the time had come for him to be emperor.
The record has it that he himself was a man of no learning
and no ability. Be that as it may, he had an extremely adroit
and unscrupulous factotum, Hsün Hsiu, who engineered
the multifarious plots and squarings that were necessary.
The outcome was an imperial fiat of abdication, apparently genuine, in which Prince Lün was designated
Emperor Hui's successor. Since the Hsiung Nu (semi-
barbarians) were entrenching themselves deep within
Chinese territory, there was a case for getting a sovereign
who was really *compos mentis,* but the other princes were
not prepared for Lün to be their master. Prince Ch'iung
took the lead, and after some seesaw fighting Lün's forces
were defeated (301). He was executed, ignominiously crying, "Hsün Hsiu misled me, Hsün Hsiu misled me." The
said Hsün Hsiu and others of the gang were of course
liquidated, whilst Lu Chi and eight others of the palace
officials were thrown into prison. Prince Ch'iung charged
Lu Chi with drafting the bogus fiat of abdication. Whether
or not the accusation was true, he would certainly have
been executed had not Prince Yin and Prince Yen spoken
for him and got him formally "pardoned."[4]

With Prince Ch'iung the dominant figure in the capital
it was impossible for Lu Chi to continue in the Emperor's
service. Here, then, was an opportunity for him to cut

[4] Cf. p. 49, where the truth of the accusation is discussed.

himself loose and go back to Hua T'ing. His friends urged him to do so, for they saw that the state of affairs was bound to get worse: Prince Ch'iung was likely to arouse just as much opposition in the royal clan as Prince Lün had. Lu Chi, however, "had confidence in his own abilities and thought he could relieve the sufferings of his generation." Accordingly, he took office under Prince Yin's patronage, being appointed as *nei shih* (administrator) in the Shantung plain. There he gained a respite for something under two years, during which time his prose poem on literature was completed and sent to Lu Yün for his criticism. He also wrote other poems.

This period of quiet and literary vitality was only too short. In 302, Prince Yin decided to attack Prince Yi, his brother (or half-brother), who had by then got possession of the Emperor. Altogether some two hundred thousand men were put into the field, and Lu Chi was given the command of one flank division. Knowing that he was an object of envy and had a number of enemies in the Prince's following, he declined the post. The Prince insisted, and to excite his ambition promised him that, if the venture succeeded, he would be given a fief and created a duke—the rank held by his grandfather and father under the Wu regime. To this Lu Chi's reply was that the matter was one of public welfare and not of his personal advantage: an answer which enabled one of the staff officers present to insinuate to the Prince that an officer who could thus insult his prince was not worthy of his confidence. The Prince made no answer.

Loathing the whole business, at war within himself, Lu Chi set up his standard and moved his troops into the field. The first thing that happened seemed a small matter, but

43

it was to have grave consequences. One Meng Chao, younger brother to a favourite eunuch of Prince Yin, was in command of ten thousand men and let them go plundering. Lu Chi reported him. Chao in revenge then headed a hundred of his best cavalry, rode into Lu Chi's camp, and started to seize his standard. This was in Lu Chi's very presence, and Chao even turned to him and said, "A barbarian slave a general—I don't think!" Lu Chi's chief of staff urged him to kill Chao, but Lu Chi "was not able to use [this advice]." Chao went on to spread rumours that Lu Chi was going to revolt and wrote to his brother to this effect.

Things went from bad to worse. In the actual words of the record:

Lu Chi gathered the two heads of his army and steadily advanced to engage the enemy. Chao did not take the orders given him, and Lu Chi, acting with great restraint, was thus short of soldiers: he advanced alone and came on disaster.

The disaster was as follows: the objective of the campaign was occupation of the capital, Loyang. About ten miles outside it, troops acting under the Emperor's orders barred the way,[5] and in the battle which ensued Lu Chi was heavily defeated. The corpses of his soldiers were so many that the river was choked with them.

Here was the opportunity for his enemies. They immediately set to work poisoning their master's mind. They swore that Lu Chi was playing traitor to him. The result was that Prince Yin "fell into a great rage and ordered Lu Chi's enemy, Chien Hsiu, to go and secretly deal with him."

[5] One account states that the capital was surrounded by Lu Chi's army and two other divisions of Prince Yin's forces.

That night Lu Chi dreamt he was caught in a carriage with black curtains and could not break his way out. The next morning when Hsiu's soldiers arrived, Lu Chi had put off his armour and was wearing a white cap. When he saw Hsiu his expression did not change from its wont. He said to Hsiu, "From the time the Wu court fell we two brothers have received great favours from the state. We have served in the palace and have done service in the field. Prince Yin ordered me to undertake a heavy responsibility and would not accept my resignation. Today I receive the death penalty. Is not this fate?" He followed this by writing a few lines to Prince Yin in great distress of mind. Then he sighed and said, "The crying of the cranes of Hua T'ing, never shall I hear them again!" Then he was executed there in the camp, being forty-two years old. His two sons, Wei and Hsia, also were executed. His innocence was recognized after his death, and the common soldiers grieved for him: there was not one who did not shed tears. That day a dark fog spread everywhere and a great wind split open a tree. There was a foot of snow on the ground. Public opinion decided that the Lu family was wronged.

In Lu Yün's biography the record is slightly different, although the cause of Lu Chi's fate is similarly ascribed to the favourite eunuch's inveterate hatred of the two brothers. The difference lies in this, that while Lu Yün's fate was hanging in the balance, the most strenuous efforts were made to save him, and the petitions sent in refer to the sentence on Lu Chi as a just one. We need not pay much attention to that, for the petitioners' aim—alas, ineffective —was to save Lu Yün's life. The question, however, has to be faced: was Lu Chi really guilty from Prince Yin's point of view, if not of planning to go over to the other side, at any rate of not doing his best? My own view is that he came rather near to the latter. The account is so circumstantial in an unpremeditated fashion. It shows how completely he was torn two ways: one, by his gratitude to Prince Yin, who had saved his life and given him and his brother real administrative posts; the other way, by the plain wickedness of this struggle among the princes. Lu Chi clearly had not his heart in his commander's job, witness his refusal to soil his fingers by dealing vigorously with that unspeakable fellow, Meng Chao. "I am sick of feelings which involve me so that I deceive myself, I am tired of encountering events and so begetting consequences."

Add to that the question whether Lu Chi was really a good soldier. To this there can be no answer one way or the other. Prince Yin obviously expected brilliant results from one so steeped in the military tradition. That must be why he overrode Lu Chi's reluctance, and why he was silent when Lu Chi struck a blow at his conscience by saying that the matter was one of public welfare. But Prince Yin may have been wrong in his estimate. Poets do not usually make good commanding officers. Lu Chi may have had the training but in the last resort may not have had the quality of decision. Why did he go on when Meng Chao refused to follow his orders? He must have known that he was taking a terrible risk, for his opposing commander was both able and experienced in war. I suspect that he did not care very much which way the battle went. If he won, he was committed to going on with the rascally crew he was mixed up with. If he lost, he might do worse than put his faith in the opposing commander, Prince Yi, who was a villain of a lighter shade than his younger brother, Prince Yin: at times he showed distinct signs of a conscience.

The verdict of Chinese historians has been that Lu Chi as a soldier and a politician was an innocent man in all respects, the victim of a vile intrigue; whilst the verdict of the common people is found in an old rhyme which has lived down to the present day:

> Lu Chi and Lu Yün were very clever men,
> But they could not protect themselves.

Perhaps we can probe a little deeper. As a boy Lu Chi went through a phase in which he tried to obey the traditional ritualist's injunction, *"fei li pu t'ung"* (make no movement contrary to the code). So, during the last poignant moments of his life he was the Confucianist stoic, facing his sorry end with mild dignity, voicing a ritual recognition of the favours he and his brother had received. For the rest, it was fate. So a poet, at the final test absorbed in the drama of his own death, acting as a poet in word and deed!

He said that it was fate. What he meant by that we can hardly tell, although with the Greek tradition still alive in us and with our knowledge of the great Athenian tragedies and their *moira,* we can guess. The Tsin historian goes a step further. He asks the question for the two brothers and the two innocent children (and for us): "The weaving of these pregnant threads began in the south, the gathering together of the calamitous end was in the north. Was this the purpose of Heaven or man's doing?" The question is a familiar one to us, as indeed today is the preliminary to it, the weaving of a pattern in one part of the world and the drawing together of its calamitous ends in another part.

One answer to the question may perhaps be indicated by the manner of Lu Chi's death, its iron composure broken at the final moment. To keep this within its Chinese setting, take this story from the *Second Han History* told in its section on "Remarkable Individuals" and related of an ancestor of Lu Chi's. This Lu Hung, being implicated in a revolt in Ch'u, was thrown into prison and put to the torture to make him confess. "Although his flesh was in ribbons, he did not change his evidence." But when his mother, come post-haste from Wu, contrived to send in a dish of meat to him, he, not knowing that she was in the capital, burst into uncontrollable sobs. The cubes of meat were cut in her fashion, so that he recognized her handi-work. So the man of iron was also a man of feeling. It was the same with his descendant, eight generations later. Death could not discompose him, but his last words were, "The crying of the cranes of Hua T'ing, never shall I hear them again!"

For understanding Lu Chi, the man as well as the poet, and the life he lived from his birth to his teens, from his teens to his twenty-ninth year, and then the thirteen years of his public career, these surface details are illuminating up to a certain point. That he became a man, indeed a gallant gentleman, is, surely, well enough attested. Also it is clear that although his official career and Lu Yün's were moderately successful, they did not raise them into the class to which their grandfather and father belonged. They were never more than "polished instruments," obliged to pay deference to the really powerful at the top. That did not come easy to Lu Chi. Clear also is the fact that the military prestige of their family name clung about them. Lu Chi and Lu Yün were marked men as possible com-manders, particularly Lu Chi; and I think he regarded him-self as one who, if it came to war, could show the rough, semi-illiterate army men how to do their job. In terms of Lu Chi's psychology these were discordant elements which warred within him, and signs of which we can find in his writings. That he was thereby the greater poet is arguable: it depends on our idea of poetry and its relation to life. In any case, he died as a poet. When the last poignant moment came and he made his farewell to life—life which had betrayed him—he "decanted the valley wind, and the scent was of orchids." He was back in Hua T'ing, hugging to his bosom that treasure which no betrayal could wrest from him. Nevertheless, in that life which he lived, was he quite such a gallant gentleman as he appears? Was he *sans peur et sans reproche?* The question must be asked because of one ugly suspicion which attaches to him, and because among his associates there were some curious characters. So along these two lines of inquiry we look for fresh light on our poet-man.

The cause for suspicion comes from Prince Ch'iung, the man who cleaned up the Prince Lün situation in 301. He accused Lu Chi of having drafted the fiat of abdication. What is there to show whether or not he did? Evidence comes in the biography of Prince Lün, where we find the most detailed account of the *coup d'état.* There it is stated that Hsün Hsiu, Prince Lün's rascally factotum, sent Wang Wei, one of the Emperor's eunuchs, to the Emperor's apartments, and that he forged the document and one Tsui Sui brought it with the seal on it. Lu Chi's name does not appear in the account except in the following context: "Emperor Hui drove in his imperial carriage with all due appurtenances and several hundred attendants out of the west gate of the Hwa Lin Garden and went to live in the town of Chen Yung. Keeper of the Records Ho Yin, the eunuch Wang Jui, and Secretary Lu Chi escorted him to the town and then returned, commissioning Chang Heng to guard the Emperor": that is, to keep him out of sight. This suggests that Lu Chi was not mixed up with the Lün-Hsiu gang.

Further, in the *T'ai P'ing Yü Lan* (c. 220) there is an excerpt from an old record, and this states that Lu Chi told the man in charge of him in prison that he not only had not written a word of the document but was out of the imperial apartments at the time, for his daughter had died, and he had gone to his brother to be comforted. Thus, there would seem to be a *prima facie* case in favour of his innocence. The only question which remains concerns the implication of the word "returned" (after he had escorted the Emperor). Did he go back to the palace? Perhaps not, but only to the capital or to Lu Yün's house. Again, there is no evidence pointing to his having joined in the crowd of office-seekers mobbing round Prince Lün on his pretender's throne.

With regard to Lu Chi's associates, his and Lu Yün's biographies are not very revealing, but taking what they say, along with scattered references in the other biographies, it very much seems that, although Lu Chi had many acquaintances, he had but few, if any, close friends: no *chih chi* (knowers of oneself), as the phrase was then and is to this day. There were his patrons, men of power and prestige, older than he was or occupying higher positions: thus, for example, Chang Hua, double Lu Chi's age and a minister of the Crown, the man who helped the two brothers at the start. We find him later discussing with Lu Chi the kinds of men who might be promoted. We may infer confidence between the two, but not close intimacy. With Prince Yin there was not even confidence. Amongst Lu Chi's literary friends there was P'ang Ngo (*ob.* 300), a fellow southerner, a brilliant, if flowery, composer of verse and *fu,* to whom Lu Chi wrote some courteous verses. He came to quite high office at court, but eventually wearied of people's envy and retired to a post in the provinces. A cautious man, fond of his pocket: not much of a friend to our poet. Also there was that extremely wealthy and colourful young spark, Chia Mi, at whose house Lu Chi stayed when he first arrived in the capital. He had distaff influence in the palace, ran a *salon,* and was surrounded by flatterers of his compositions. Nevertheless, a notable set of writers gathered at his table. In a "bread-and-butter" poem to him after his visit, Lu Chi speaks of his own out-landish clothes; so we can picture the young southerners getting Chia Mi's tailor to supply them with more fashion-able attire. One Chih Yi dined at Chia Mi's, and he was worth meeting. He wrote a rather muddled but impressive *fu* on "Thoughts A-wander" in which he showed himself a brooder on time and space. He was very much alive to the processes of reasoning, in discussions with his official chief trying to get at causes and to make proper inferences from them. But he was a Confucianist of the old school, in-curably conservative, and wrote a book of ten chapters in which he traced the old genealogies which had been lost in Han times. So, in spite of his wandering in "the chariot of Earth" and "the broad streets of Heaven," it is doubtful if our poet found him particularly congenial.

On the other hand, why did Lu Chi not get on with Tso Ssu, the man who in one year compassed three tre-mendous *fu* on the Three Capitals, Loyang, Chengtu, and Chien Yeh? He seems to have had a contempt for him, calling him "an old rascal [*ts'an fu*] who wants to do a *fu* on the capitals, which when finished will only do to wrap a wine jug in." However, when he saw the final achieve-ment, he gave it high praise. Perhaps he had reason for his dislike of the author. The story is told that one Ku Yung, a handsome young scholar and a brilliant musician, used to go round the streets of the capital at night playing

his lute. He so entranced people that the women linked
hands and surrounded him. They threw him such generous
offerings of fruit that he went home with a carriageful.
Tso Ssu was a particularly ugly man, but he thought he
could do the same. The result was brick-bats from the boys
in the streets. We can imagine Lu Chi hearing this story
and chuckling over it with Lu Yün, being a little contemptuous of the frustrated egoist.

Then there were the men from the south with whom
he had the tie of "having drunk from the waters of the
Three Rivers." They were a mixed lot. First came Ku
Yung, the handsome scholar-musician. He belonged to one
of the four great families of Wu, his grandfather was a
minister of state; and when the two from Hua T'ing decided to try their fortunes in the north, Ku Yung went with
them, and they came to be known as the "Three Wonders."
Ku's brilliance was undoubted, although his verses have
not survived: but he was a great drinker and money-
grubber. That there was not really much in common
between him and Lu Chi is clear from the fact that in the
year 300 he threw in his lot with Prince Lün—an expen-
sive mistake, for it cost him his life. Yet he was a good-
hearted fellow in his way. On one occasion he was at a
feast and noted the steak-broiler looking hungrily at the
meat he was cooking. Ku cut off a piece of his meat and
gave it to him. Everybody laughed, but Ku said it seemed
hard that the man who did the broiling should not know
the taste of what he cooked.

On the same fateful journey to Loyang, Lu Chi fell in
with Tai Jo-ssu, a man from just north of the Yangtze,
educated and having a passion for adventure. He was then
in company of some bandits, and happening to see that the

two brothers' boat had rich appointments, he arranged to have it looted. Lu Chi saw him dividing the spoils with scrupulous fairness, so he called him and told him that for a man of such parts it was a pity he should be employed in this way. Tai burst into tears, renounced his gang, and joined Lu Chi's party.[6] In Loyang Lu Chi promoted his interests, and before long he was embarked on a military career in which he did well. He repaid Lu Chi in 301 by coming to him and urging him to break away from his ties in the north and go back to Hua T'ing.

In contrast to Ku Yung and Tai Jo-ssu were Chi Chan and Ho Hsün, also of official families in Wu. The former had a modest, diffident character, and we find Lu Chi exhorting him to overcome his shyness and offer his services to the state. The advice was followed, and he had something of a career. On one occasion he showed himself to have a much better understanding of the *Lao Tzu Book* than Ku Yung had. Ho Hsün also was a fine type of Confucian scholar and unable to push himself. So Lu Chi sent in a memorial recommending that he should be given an appointment. The way was opened, and Ho went on quietly serving as an official, filling one post after another. He died in the year 319 at the age of sixty, and the then emperor went and viewed him in his coffin and wept. The record has it that in his youth he enjoyed playing with books and was clever at composition but later "was a stickler for ritual and tradition." We can see the man, honest, loyal, grateful to his friend and benefactor, Lu Chi, but not having much to give him.

And that is the impression we gain of the whole circle of Lu Chi's friends, acquaintances, and associates: they

[6] The record does not say that the property was returned.

53

had not much to give him. So we conclude that there was only one man who knew the real Lu Chi. That man was his brother, Lu Yün, younger than he by one year. It is a heart-warming picture we get of the two together, life-long companions. The younger adored the elder: that is clear from his letters. What Lu Chi thought of Lu Yün we do not know so well, for he was a bad letter-writer, to judge from the few notes which are extant. Fortunately, he could express himself in his poems, two of which are addressed to Lu Yün; in one of them he says:

> Our food and drink, is it not among a foreign people?
> Our kinship, is it not brother and brother?
> Fascinating beauty is the home of other men's thoughts:
> My twisted melancholy goes out to your love.

Both poems were sent to his brother after parting from him on what he calls "a hateful long road." "I am like a westerly flowing stream, you are like a mountain rooted in the east." More need not be said except that from Lu Yün's letters we learn that Lu Chi sent his poems to him for criticism.

Lu Yün, while adoring his brother, yet could recognize his faults: at least what seemed to Lu Yün to be faults—for example, Lu Chi's tetchy arrogance. Further, a letter dated 302 criticizes the *Wen Fu,* recently received, for lacking human feeling and for not paying due honour to the high claims of morality. This is interesting, indeed revealing, for Lu Yün, with his sense of the ridiculous, his helpless giggles over pomposity and foppery, was not the man to ride the moral horse to death. I suggest that this criticism stemmed from his concern for his brother. Knowing that Lu Chi made enemies, Lu Yün did not want his unconventional opinions to be used against him.

54

Not only so: the Wen Fu as it stands now has a very distinctive passage in which the question of whether the artist is warranted in forgetting morals is dealt with. The answer given is definitely not. Licentious art is "in the class vulgar." It is open to surmise, therefore, whether the version of the poem which Lu Yün saw contained this passage. Perhaps it did not, and we owe those singing, highly individual words to Lu Yün's intervention. If so, here is evidence that the masterful, moody Lu Chi, who brooked no interference in his affairs if he could possibly help it, yet listened to one man.

"Three hundred-odd compositions" is the tale of Lu Chi's writings as given by the Tsin historian. Of these some one hundred and fifty have survived (counting his fifty "linked pearls" as one item): two essays of considerable length, eleven fu poems (some with prefaces), fifty-one old-fashioned four-word and new-fashioned five-word lyrics and odes, eleven official writings and state-examination questions, two consolatory odes, one in connection with Ts'ao Ts'ao, the founder of the Wei dynasty (dead two generations back), and one in connection with his son, the Emperor Wen; a eulogy of the first Han emperor, a glorification of Confucius, and a commemoratory ode to the first Wu emperor, and another one to his father, together with five others; and one admonition and one inscription. These with the few scraps of letters make the total.

His fame rests primarily on his fu poems, on his Wen Fu in particular. The last was put into a chüan by itself by Chao Ming T'ai Tzu (ob. 532) in his collection of artistic writings of all ages down to his own time. In the same collection we find a larger selection of Lu Chi's

poetry and prose than of any other writer's.[7] Of his verse
it may be said that some of it was delivered on command
or as an offering to a patron, fellow official, or fellow
writer. This was the practice in those days. If Lu Chi
wrote many such poems, they have not survived, and we
may suppose that he wrote relatively few. What he did
write were in the courtly vein of the time. On the other
hand, the verses to his brother and his poem on the death
of his daughter, his personal lyrics, are direct, unaffected
outpourings of his heart.

It is to his prose poems and dialectical essays that we
must go if we are to learn the stature and quality of the
poet. There he shows how, being the child of his age
politically and socially, he was in his spirit a stranger and
a sojourner. Take his *Wen Fu,* for example; the second
part in the main consists of pungent criticism, culminating
in a paragraph dealing with current literature, the literature of fashion, extravagantly belauded by his contemporaries, but for him "not filling the cup of his two hands."
It is not surprising, then, to find that the subjects of his
prose poems are not capitals and imperial sacrifices, but
music, floating clouds, driving mist, fairies, or, nearer
home, mulberry trees, fruits, turtles. More significant still
are his *fu* on his native land and home, together with
his "Sensing of Time," his "A Sigh over Passing Away,"
and his "Impressions of a Grave Mound." In these his
loneliness of spirit, his sense of time and space as only
relative, strike home to the reader. Behind that stature of
his and that aristocratic air of nonchalance, behind that
bold front in the face of misfortune and that determination

---

[7] For the student the only important item not there is his *fu, A Statement
on Thinking,* which Lu Yün regarded as his greatest achievement, but this
has survived elsewhere. Cf. Chapter III.

to go on, lay a sensitive, melancholy spirit which travelled alone, and saw life and death pass before its eyes as shadows of eternity. It was surely characteristic of him that one day in the palace at Loyang he slipped away from the pomp and circumstance, sought solitude—and found an old grave mound.

In a light boat on the western reaches, at the back of the palace with lightning playing,
I passed the islets on the Lo, following the deeps of the Yellow River.

There I spied an earth-made tomb on the hill ridge, mounded up to make it firm,
I saw the beauty of its well-omened site, standing forth in its piled structure.

Thus pacing to and fro on the bank, in measured stroll by the river's flow,
I stood a-gaze with my mind at attention, on the impulse giving forth a sigh.

I looked down, going back to the furthest days of old, completed the myriad threads in the raveling of time.

The man, born in the age of his abiding, like a water plant in a mountain stream,
he responded to the moulding wrought by time's changes, he obeyed the current—and was gone in a day.

Being born, he made his pitiful imprint on the inevitable; dying, he made his habitation in this solitary mound:
his dead body and bones in the eddies of destruction, his soul whirled up and floating aloft.

He followed the Yin and the Yang into their melting-pot, called to the beginning of the hills to be his companions:
with the fair and the foul all rolled into oneness, who can know what his spirit achieved?

It is a needs-must with the mysterious change into the far-back mirror [of time]:
it is a needs-must with this accord with one set place to be in.

57

You ascended the boat in your turn with the men before, you crossed
the great river [of death], however you grieved;
you were shocked at the suddenness of your completed lot, you
resented the downward pressure of Nature's step-by-step.

Time and again you had confidence and your thoughts were in
accord, yet they could in no way suffice to protect you at this
pass:
Nature's soil for your grave could not be avoided, though better it
were if we men could refuse it.

Wish as we may that our life might delay its uprooting,
I point to this old tomb—that is what it is.

—From the seventh-century *Collection of Compositions*
edited by Ou-yang Hsün (Chapter 40).

Chapter III

A FOCUSING OF THE "WEN FU" IN THE LIGHT OF LITERARY HISTORY

W E TEND in these days to talk lightly about "the historical perspective" to some object of our attention. Since all historical perspectives are relative to the observers' respective standpoints in time, there can be no objection to the term; for if we are to descry the *Wen Fu* not in the flat but in the round, we have to see it as best we can not only as a *that* out there on the sky-line of seventeen centuries back, but also as a *this* which very naturally, if somewhat surprisingly, came into existence when it did. This is a matter of focusing this literary production against the background of the literary history of China down to the time the document was produced. And, since for the Western reader the document was written in a hieroglyphic language foreign to his ways of thinking, there must be an attempt to appreciate the way in which these hieroglyphics came to be for the author of the document the natural, heaven-given means for ordering his thought into intelligible shape.

If we take a deep landscape painting with some object of paramount importance in the foreground, that object can be understood only if the eye of the observer goes first to the dim and misty background and then accustoms

59

itself to the scene by concentration on the details of the
various middle distances. Having thus taught itself to see
these particular things in the round, the eye can then, and
only then, afford to shift its gaze to the objects in the foreground. They then become alive, have meaning. In a
word, they are in some sort of focus. Particularly the
central object of attention takes on significant shape.

This method of approach has been my guiding principle
in this chapter. It will be noticed that when I come to the
Han era I have drawn attention to twenty-two great
names in the literary history of that era. By this device I
hope to make that all-important era alive, something of a
this as well as a far-off impalpable *that*. The trouble about
outline historical studies is that they tend to be blurred,
since there is so little concrete detail on which the reader's
mind can fasten. Too much is left to the vagaries of his
imagination. The over-detailed compilations of history, on
the other hand, tend to stun the mind: we just cannot see
the wood for the trees.

What I have deliberately not done—possibly wrongly—
is to go beyond Lu Chi's day and give vignettes on later
literary history. It seemed to me safer not to do so, for,
after all, the *Wen Fu* was written without the author's
having any idea that there could be a great T'ang literary
age and then a great Sung literary age, and so on down to
the present literary age—which of course may be the consummation of all ages before, but also of course may not.
What I have done is to make cross-references from time
to time to Western literary phenomena. After all, the
student of my picture has some knowledge of Western
language and literary development. My picture cannot

speak to him unless he is encouraged to make comparisons and contrasts.

As with Lu Chi we were happily placed in having a surprisingly good quantity of evidence to help us, so with the very early, if not the nearly earliest, days of Chinese written speech. The An-yang "oracle-bones," dug up on the site of the Yin capital in modern Honan, have brought to the historian riches of which the half has not yet been told. This is strictly true, for the experts are still engaged in fitting together the pieces in the world's greatest jig-saw puzzle. There are tens of thousands of bone and tortoise-shell fragments on which are scratched the very graphs the Yin diviners made thirty-four to thirty-two hundred years ago. Although we still know little of those days, there is one feature in those graphs which stares us in the face, namely, the close conformation of the lines in the graphs to the lines which the firing of the sheep's shoulder-blades and the under-carapaces of tortoise-shells produced in them. That being so, there seems to be one piece of theorizing on which we can safely embark. It is that, as the cracks running in every direction were to animistic minds imbued with mana (since no man could manipulate them), so a diviner in his recording of the oracle patterned his graphs so that they might be imbued with the mana of the spirit-imbued material. That a record had to be made is accounted for, not merely by the im-portance of the question raised (some of the questions were only of temporary importance—e.g., re hunting), but also by the need of the diviner's master to pin his expert down to a decision one way or the other. An oracle facing two ways would suit the unhappy operator, but was worse than useless to the chieftain he served. At the same time, if these mysterious scratches from the operator's hand were taken as imbued with mana, then the man who had created them obviously also had mana; and if the oracle went astray, his angry master would do well to pause before ordering his unlucky servant to be killed. This interpretation would also account for the fact that a number of the graphs vary considerably in the forms used, so that each diviner may be said to have made his own mana.

I stress this because the inscriptions on the bronze ritual implements of that era betray much the same character istics, until we reach mid-Chou times. Thus, although the utilitarian motive was there, the religious motive really determined the forms of the graphs. Certainly these, which were not meant to be legible to the ordinary man, were held to exude power (*tê*) in relation to ghosts and spirits. Then, when the Chou (possibly Yin) annalists got to work, they, being the sons and brothers of the diviners, carried over the calligraphic tradition in a modified way: a very different procedure from that which obtained when the Phoenicians began to use phonetic symbols. If the Phoenicians took the idea from the Egyptian priests and their secret numinous script, they adapted it to their own ends—namely, that of foreign trading. To make contacts with foreign chiefs written records were necessary: to surmount the language barrier a phonetic script was the admirable expedient. Then came the Greeks, also great traders, who established colonies in which Greeks from several localities participated. As is well known, the Aegean sphere of Greek influence was a mass of dialects: the result, a phonetic script with vowels as well as con sonants. (In contrast, witness the Jews, with their highly religious minds, whose priestly recorders resorted at first to consonants without vowels.) Thus, in spite of the influence of the Delphic oracles, literary composition was more for utilitarian than for religious ends.

In northern China the Chou court and the headquarters townships of the great feudatories had divining and recording going on side by side, and thus literature, the actual art of composition, the stringing of sentence to sentence, was born under a religious star. The first efforts at written poetry were the sacrificial odes at An-yang, prototypes of the Yin sacrificial odes which we can read today in the *Odes Scripture*.[1] Imagine them inscribed in the archaic script and intoned by the liturgists, creating mana by their linking of the sacrifices with the potent ancestors. Imagine also the new type of annalist which the Chou court produced, the "recorders of the left" (*tso shih*), who dramatized the words spoken on great state occasions. These we can examine much in their original grammar in the *Ching-wen* books of the *History Scripture*. If the spoken words of monarchs were potent, how much more were those same words when inscribed in the numinous script and read by later generations! Confucius would appear to have made a special journey to the Chou capital to inspect its ritual and its records.

None the less, the business side of writing increased as it was bound to do. We can discern in the scanty evidence from Confucius' day (551–479 B.C.) that a new type of

---

[1] The three Confucianist works which were first recognized as *ching* (sacred, definitive books) were the *Changes*, the *Odes*, and the *History*. The practice has been to refer to these as the *Classic* or *Book of Changes*, etc. Since they were scriptures to the Chinese it is obviously preferable to call them so. The other works which came in time into the Confucianist canon have recognized titles which make them no problem in this respect.

ju (experts in reading and writing) had come to stay: the men who began as government clerks and quickly became administrators in the larger states which had been formed. Their forte was keeping accounts, formulating tax regulations, and issuing government orders and reporting on the observance of them. When, however, this administrative routine was still in its infancy, another development was proceeding on quite a different line— namely, the birth of lyrical poetry, patterns of words set to tunes. Over three hundred of these have survived in the *Odes Scripture* alone, and we find traces of many others not recorded there. These, simple as the peasant ditties among them are, demonstrate a real command of prosodic form, and reveal a questing spirit in that semi-tribal, semi-feudal society. Thus, we are prepared for the next age, the age in which the written language first grew its pinions of dialectical grammar and syntax.

That was a great age indeed, comparable in some ways to the contemporary age in the eastern Mediterranean; each of the two uprushes of conscious intellectual vigour had its own genius. Whether literature in the first age of lyrical songs was more of the numinous or more of the utilitarian type is a problem I leave to wiser heads than mine to solve. As to the prose productions from the fifth to the third century B.C., what we know is that they came from men living in an era of power-politics, when the old-established spiritual *mores* of their fathers seemed doomed to vanish. Some of these minds deplored this; others welcomed it and out of the dominant materialism drew the stark categories of naturalistic logic. What they wrote was in prose, and that prose of a sort which, for all the dark spots and plain imperfections which bother the student today, had already formed the embryonic bones of Chinese written communication. It was not certain whether the womb of time would give birth to triplets or quadruplets, or whether one lusty language child would emerge. There were forces operating in different directions, among the unifying forces the chief being ringing phrases in the *Odes* and the determination of most thinkers to understand each other.

It is worth while trying to clarify what happened. The belief has been widely—indeed, until recent times unanimously—held that Confucius wrote the bald, extremely simply-grammared document, the *Spring and Autumn Annals*. Whether this belief be true or not, it did not occur to Confucius, or to any other incipient thinker of his generation, to put his personal ideas into consecutive literary form. There was, indeed, no class of the private scholar, Confucius was a *ju,* and as such was a government employee. He had his apprentices, aspirants for state service as minor officers or liturgists, and he taught them by word of mouth. In doing so he emphasized the value of the *Odes* and of the lessons of the past as found in the annals and the liturgists' note-books on the rituals. It was his disciples and their disciples after them who prepared the book we know as the *Lun Yü* (*Analects*), in which his pithy remarks appear, for the most part, in homely colloquial form. Their arrangement is on a very rudimentary scale.

I submit that the key to Confucius' mind is to be found in his discovery of the individual to himself. In other words, he found many highly reputable persons of his time acting, as he felt, more like animals than men. This drove him to examine the ancestral traditions of his society, to search for what in our modern tongue are spoken of as divine and human values. It was his discoveries in this direction which inspired his disciples. One or two generations later came Mo Ti, the Mo Tzu (Master Mo) of the book which bears his name (a huge compilation put together during ten to fifteen generations of Mohists). He had a remarkable sense for logic, and although he did not write himself, the imprint of his master mind is unmistakable in the writings of his followers. In his simple but trenchant fashion he used the Socratic *elenchon,* developing arguments on specific subjects by which his opponents were led on to be confounded by the reduction of their opinions to absurdity. After him the tide of intellectual excitement grew stronger and ran yet more freely. Mo Ti's utilitarian logic drove him to believe in the old gods. After him there came men who did not believe in them, and new cosmological theories were worked out along with new theories as to the nature of man and the place of the individual in society.

Whilst the Mohist movement was gaining ground among simple people from east to west, and they were chanting in their regular meetings their Master's teachings, Yang Chu was propounding his Epicurean theory of man. There was also Mencius (about 372–289 B.C.), an avowed follower of Confucius, who denounced both the Mohists and the Yangites and affirmed that man had a natural aptitude for goodness. Mencius, by the way, seems to have been the first man to say *"yu tzu kuan chih"* (arguing from this point of view). That phrase tells its own tale, as does the rise of chain hypotheses: if A then B, if B then C, . . . So far there was, with the possible exception of Confucius' grandson, Tzu Ssu, no solid excursion into metaphysical inquiry, unless some society-fleeing hermits gave utterance to dark sayings on the nature of reality: sayings to be found incorporated in the *Lao Tzu Book*. But then came Chuang Chou, mystic and realist, the apostle of freedom in mind and body, who rolled up the heavens and earth into a bundle of nothingness and with a laugh sat himself down to wait, content to find that this life was really death and the after-life the real thing. He pricked the bubble of all pompous theorists and in the name of common sense and the relative truth of all opinion could beat the *Ming Chia,* the professional logicians of his day, at their own game of exposing the weakness of categorical thinking. And this Chuang Chou was a wizard with words, making them mean what he wanted them to mean, so that later ages, although they denounced his theories, could not cure themselves of reading what he and his followers wrote (see the *Chuang Tzu Book*).

This, then, was what has been with reason called "the Age of the Philosophers." Yet it was only towards its end that we find clear examples of essay-writing. Historians had come into being (see the *Tso Chuan* and *Kuo Yü*), and so had the Ch'u school of romantic elegy-writers. Thinkers had met and collogued in more than one centre established by progressive princes. Yet not before Han Fei Tzu and Hsün Tzu of the third century B.C. did thinkers scratch the title of a subject on a bamboo slip and then, with a store of such slips beside them, work out the implications of that subject. It was an epoch-making day when that happened, particularly as both these composers showed in what they wrote that they knew what the men before them had maintained, and were capable of balancing and appraising one theory against another. Hsün Tzu, the most systematic of the thinkers of that time, did not find prose writing easy: his sentences are often cumbrous, his ideas often difficult to ascertain. But he wrote some clear, didactic verses on man's life and knowledge and ritual, the poetic form being plainly dictated by his teaching purpose. Whether he called these *fu,* we cannot be sure: at any rate, they came in Han times to be known as such.

In the middle of the third century B.C. a semi-barbarous fighter from the borders of central Asia warred down all opposition and installed himself as "the First Emperor" of China. He was a ruthless tyrant, ready to eradicate all learning so that he alone might rule; but he performed one very meritorious act. The written language of the Chou court had been tending, through the centrifugal tendencies of the warring states, to become half a dozen different languages. The forms of the graphs and the grammatical particles varied from one part of the country to another. There was a growing practice of using classifiers appended to the graphs, and there had long been a tendency to make new graphs on a phonetic basis; but there had been no one to regulate these tendencies and standardize the forms of the written word. The First Emperor and his brilliant aide and minister, Li Ssu, were for obvious reasons bent on imposing order on the language. They needed a bureaucracy in which the imperial commands were obeyed to the letter and the evidence filed that they were obeyed. Li Ssu undertook the unification of the language: how he did it is not precisely known, but it was done. Also, a new clerks' script was introduced, one built for economy of strokes and so for speed in making notes. The general assumption is that the use of classifiers was increased. Only relative success attended such efforts as were made to simplify and regularize phonetically based terms, the *hsiang sheng* (sound representations), as some lexicographers and graph-analysts of the first century A.D. called them.

Owing to *ju* opposition to his measures, the First Em-peror decreed a holocaust of the Confucianist works, with the exception of the *Changes Scripture*. Whether the damage done was as bad as the Han Confucianists claimed is doubtful, but the copies that did survive were few, some of them imperfect. When the revulsion came against the First Emperor and all his works, these remnants from the old order—"off-scourings," to use Chuang Chou's term for old books—attained an enhanced value, since they embodied the teachings of the past. This became clear when the first Han emperor found that he could not rule without introducing *ju* ritual and *ju* method into his court and all its administrative departments. In doing this he had good assistance from one Lu Chia, a Yangtze-basin man. Lu wrote verses, of what precise sort we do not know, but Pan Ku classified him in the *Yi Wen Chih* as the initiator of a school of *fu* to which Yang Hsiung belongs. But—be it noted—no one suggested that there should be any inter-ference with the standardized script. It was there to stay, and, further, its efficacy was enhanced by the discovery made about that time that a brush pen plus a piece of silk plus watered soot for ink was a much easier method of writing than scratching on bamboo.[2]

So the modern forms of the graphs came into existence, and, with their coming and an enlarged vocabulary, the men with the power to write in them had better instru-ments for plying their craft. The effect was enormous. As the Han peace brought the national economy to pros-

[2] There is reason to suppose that writing with some sort of hair brush was not unknown earlier. But it did not come into general use until this time.

69

perity again, and the call for government servants grew and their status was elevated, more and more boys were educated. For the first hundred years not much was produced under great scholars' names: it was a period of literary incubation. The gist of the old Chou books was, however, put onto silk in the new script, and the practice of amplifying the old teachings anonymously grew apace. There also came into being a new distinction, one destined to have far-reaching consequences. Whereas in the old days there was only one indivisible body of literature, *wen hsüeh* (literally, written learning), now *wen hsüeh* came to mean scholars' ordinary writings, such as history, commentating, and the like, whilst a new term, *wen chang* (literally, writing ordered or patterned), was coined to designate a new kind of writing, one which, for the sake of a true perspective, must now be carefully explained.

Chang in course of time came to mean prose that was elegant, having elaborately worked-out combinations of sentences. Examination of its use in the *Odes* demonstrates that in those early Chou days the artistic idea was part and parcel of the concept. The device on a banner was *chang*, the pattern in a piece of woven cloth was *chang*. In one of Hsün Tzu's didactic verses we find *"wen li ch'eng chang"* (ordered lines form a design), the sentence referring to the natural order and the way in which ritual expresses this order. Old-time regulations of social behaviour were *chang*. Thus, when in the second century B.C. scholars began to copy the old manuscripts and, in order to make them intelligible, to punctuate the sentences (*chü*) and indicate the paragraphs or small chapters, these last were called *chang*. Those were the earlier meanings of *chang*, in use when the new prose was so designated. In a word, that prose was patterned so as to make it intelligible, coherent, and rational in its appeal. That this was next door to rhetoric is of course obvious to a Western reader with his remembrance of Athens in the days of Demosthenes and of Rome in the days of Cicero; but the essence of the move- ment consisted in making a tighter grammar and syntax so that one sentence after another should convey their mean- ings concisely and clearly. I surmise that when the first Han emperor's old captains sent in their reports, these were very definitely not *chang,* and this was one of the reforms in the court which Kao Tsu found himself obliged to make. Thus arose the idea of prose as a style—indeed, as a number of styles. It came home to the scholar conscious- ness, and there began a careful ordering of sentences and paragraphs. Along with this began the movement which, giving the scornful term *pi* (brush pen) to unstudied, ex- tempore making of notes, reserved the term *wen* for care- fully patterned productions. In Lu Chi's generation that was the situation, and he, the first systematic literary critic, did not whole-heartedly approve of the invidious distinc- tion being made.

With its emancipation from the old numinous associa- tions of the written word, the utilitarian aspect of writing became more and more pronounced. For instance, the first Han emperor (contrary to what was generally supposed by sinologists twenty years ago) took over the First Em- peror's legal code, with some ameliorations of its ruthless severity, and its regulations in the new code had to be understood by the army of officials whose business was to administer it. The written word thus became one of the government's most necessary tools, the tool without which that vast empire, extending from modern Manchuria right down to modern Annam, could not have carried on for a year. The government documents which we can read in the Han histories demonstrate that the first consideration was not literary elegance but clarity and orderly presentation of facts (cf. *Wen Fu,* Part II (*a*) and the Epilogue).

On the other hand, the Han imperial policy was to attach all the religious prestige they could to the throne and to its machinery of government. It is significant, therefore, that sometime during the First Han regime a highly rational, highly mystical, and highly mythical account of the rise of civilization under the beneficent inspiration of the Sage Kings of old was composed. This is found in the *Hsi Tz'u* Part II amplification of the *Changes Scripture:*

> Of old when Pao Hsi kinged it over this world of ours, looking up he observed the signs in the heavens, looking down he observed the distinctive features (*wen*) of birds and beasts together with the appropriateness of the terrain [to these features].
> Some Pao Hsi selected for what was near, namely in his own person, others he selected for what was distant, namely creatures and things [outside him]. In this fashion was the beginning of the Eight Trigrams by means of which he circulated the power of spirit influences [throughout human affairs] and classified the circumstances of all creatures. He invented knotted strings and made snares and fish-nets, the one to trap wild beasts, the other to catch fish. [The idea of] this came by grasping [the significance] of the *Li* hexagram [? trigram].

In other words, as the succeeding passages enumerate, the sages invented stage by stage all the necessary appliances for a civilized community, and did it through the enlightenment they received from particular hexagrams and/or their titles. At the end of this list some redactor seems to have added this gloss:

> In high antiquity cords were knotted, and so there was government. The later sages changed this and used written documents by means of which the officials could do the administration and the people

generally could be investigated. The idea of this came by selection of the *Kuai* hexagram.

That was the prevailing Han mind in the matter: it was also without a doubt part of Lu Chi's mind. The great and potent art of writing had been invented by the sages for the sacred ends of government. From a primitive use of knotted cords—and, as some said, from the sages of old noting the traces of birds' claws and animals' paws on the ground—these semi-divine benefactors of mankind had grasped the idea of a written language and had worked out the different graphs which constituted its component parts. There was also a tendency to confuse the invention of the hexagrams with the invention of writing, or rather to lump the two inventions together (cf. Appendix 2). Thus, the hexagrams inspired awe as symbols which represented not only actual combinations of natural forces producing all the phenomena in the universe but also all possible combinations in the future which might be produced. This awe was transferred to the realm of literature.

All this may seem just animistic mumbo-jumbo to the modern Western mind, for so it seems to educated Chinese youth of today. If, however, we rule it out as mythical moonshine, we shall certainly get our perspective wrong. First, not all myths are the crude production of primitive childish animism. The world's records are rich in most impressive myths, born of men's reasoning attempts to understand the order of the universe. We call them myths when we see, or think we see, that at least one of their basic assumptions is not true. Second, how about the English Protestant's eighteenth- and nineteenth-century myth that the Bible, indeed the King James version of it, was verbally inspired? How about more modern myths—for

73

example, Herbert Spencer's sociological myth built on natural selection in the field of biology, and Karl Marx's myth
that only economic causes count in the making of history?
Third, may it not be laid down as axiomatic in the matter
of impressive myths—particularly the ones such enlightened people as ourselves cherish—that they are the fruit of
very cogent reasoning and at the same time spring from a
sense of awe, awe over the majestic phenomena which we
thus endeavour to explain. Fourth, we have to exert our
pragmatic judgment and decide whether the myth in question has a stultifying or vitalizing effect on the believer;
and if the answer to this question in the case of an alien
myth is an ambiguous one, then let us at least take care
to tread gently where the more mystical part of that dream
is concerned.

This attitude of caution is the more important because
of a certain grave question that agitates the minds of art
historians with regard to the art objects that they date as
Han products or as products of the immediately following
centuries. Our problem of a true perspective necessitates
consideration of this grave question. Put in briefest outline, and restricting our attention to bronze mirrors, the
question is whether the animistic mumbo-jumbo mind carried through those centuries and dominated the different
types of patterning we find. Let the reader compare Plates
I and II, bearing in mind that from the first century B.C.
scholar-connoisseurs were put in charge of the court corps
of craftsmen and that the *fu* writings contain many references to art creations. The design in Plate I is to me plain
evidence of the use of tools for achieving exact measure-
ment and its corollary, precision thinking. It is equally
self-evident that the whole design is based on cosmological

PLATE I.

Bronze mirror back, perhaps first to third century.

abstractions, e.g., roundness denoting the heavens, square-
ness the earth, and so also with the subsidiary motifs.
Now, it is not to be questioned that there are old conventional ideas lurking there, nor that the mirrors were used
as charms. Nor would I suggest that the student should
ignore the category of "myth." The important point is
that it is reconstructed, rationalized myth put into abstract
geometrical formulae. The same applies to the design in
Plate II. Those dragons are conventional symbols of mana.
But note the precision of spacing in those three figures,
note the airy grace of their complementary poses, and note
the contrasting stiff, dead angles of the background design.
I find it difficult to doubt that the designer and/or the
craftsman were not over the threshold of a new world, a
world in which order reigned and in which beauty could
be captured and represented for beauty's sake.

It has been stated that the Han emperors favoured the
exaltation of the sanctity of the written word. This was for
reasons of policy, as is clear to the discerning reader from
Emperor Wu's time (140–87 B.C.) down. The great doctors of Confucianist learning in the colleges he and his
successors supported in the capital were expected to prove
beyond doubt by their redactions and exegeses that the
written word of the sages was behind the written word of
the state. On the other hand, there was much more to the
business than that. In principle, the prime function of the
emperor in governing was to educate. The throne, therefore, was the symbol of enlightenment, and since both old
dogma and new illumination came from *wen tê* (outstanding power with the pen), the imperial court was the supreme arbiter of literary merit. This was not so artistically
demoralizing as it sounds. The high officials had the em-

peror's ear, and they saw to it that he did not make a fool of himself when it came to the question of a supposed new star rising in the literary world. This has happened in monarchic courts in the West as well as in the East; and before printing was invented, it is difficult to see how writers of genius could otherwise have been marked and encouraged and had their works preserved.

With all its weaknesses and hypocrisies, all the tuft-hunting and gross eulogizing of gilded nincompoops and wicked potentates, the system worked. Great literature was produced, and a surprising amount preserved. Taking the Second Han era along with the First, a period about as long as from Caesar and Cicero down to Longinus and his critique of "former writers," the following summary of famous names and specific developments will give some idea of the spirit of the literary world.

CHIA YI (199–168 B.C.) had a meteoric career under that most liberal-minded of all the Han monarchs, Wen Ti; under his encouragement Chia wrote his famous account of the faults of the First Emperor and his regime. This was a literary landmark, being the first appearance of deliberately patterned prose. He dis-covered the Yangtze-valley poet, Ch'ü Yüan (fourth century B.C.), and under the influence of his works produced prose poems (*fu*) of a startlingly new kind.

LIU TE (*ob.* 129 B.C.) was a member of the royal family—a great collector of old books which became the nu-cleus of the imperial library of the first century B.C.

LIU AN (*ob.* 122 B.C.): member of the royal family. He kept open house for Taoist philosophizers: result, a book in twenty-one chapters, an able systematization

76

PLATE II.

Bronze mirror back, not before second century B.C.

of Taoist tenets but with an unconsciously materialistic tendency; as an example of prose writing, the argumentation is often discursive.

SSUMA HSIANGJU (179–117 B.C.): the lighthearted romantic from far west whose amusing marriage and generally bohemian behaviour was then and has been ever since the delight of fellow romantics. Emperor Wu, having read a poem of his, summoned him to court, but he could not bear official life and returned to Szechuan. He had a fine sense of word cadence, with a brilliant gift for satire—the first to fit the *fu* style to this vein. Also, he had that bubbling power in him which waited on no emperor's order to compose—thus, a new landmark a generation after Chia Yi.

TUNG CHUNGSHU (second century B.C.): quite a thinker in his rather muddled, balancing way. He wrote a seventeenchaptered book trying to synthesize religious Confucianism and rationalistic Confucianism; his sentences were well constructed but prosy.

SSUMA CH'IEN (c. 145–86/74 B.C.): his father chief astrologerastronomer. He completed his father's plan of an entire history of the past: result, a work of genius in the scope of its conception; its 130 sections contained an annalistic account of acts of government, monographs on phases of economy and culture, and seventy biographical sketches. Its style laconic and well balanced, it was a model of historical writing for future generations.

TUNGFANG SO (Emperor Wu's time): wit, poseur, ornament of the court. His *Seven Exhortations* were not much as teaching, but brilliant in doubleharnessing freshly conceived ideas. He was a pretty hand at verses.

LIU HSIANG (77–6 B.C.): a great scholar in the academic sense—cataloguer of the imperial library, redactor of texts. He wrote prose fluently as a classicist, not as a romantic; he also wrote well-balanced *fu*.

LIU HSIN (*ob.* A.D. 23): Hsiang's son. He finished his father's task in the library, and has been accused of tampering with the texts for political ends. He made the first division of literature into seven classes, each with sub-divisions.

YANG HSIUNG (53 B.C.–A.D. 18): a Szechuanese. When he came to the capital he was expected to be a second Hsiang-ju: not a romantic, but a mystic with a strong sense of the clouds enfolding the mountains. Famous as a writer of *fu* and a writer of philosophical prose, he was a student of language and a critic of the court.

PAN KU (A.D. 32–92): a scion of a famous family. Witty as well as learned, a Confucian classicist, a historian and the son of a historian, he wrote most of the *History of the First Han Dynasty* in 120 sections, making great improvements on Ssu-ma Ch'ien. This ardent *fu* writer planned the structure of his compositions and made meaning the master—essentially a logical mind, although conventional in his views.

PAN CHAO (first century A.D.): Pan Ku's sister. When he died, Emperor Ho appointed her to finish the history. She wrote graceful prose and verse. (From the modern historian's point of view extraordinary since she was a woman, but not very significant as an exponent of style.)

HSÜ SHEN (*ob.* A.D. 120): composer of an invaluable lexicon in which he linked the modern graphs with the ancient Chou forms, a work as remarkable for its division of the graphs into categories as it is open to criticism for some of its philological explanations. He was a very dogmatic gentleman.

WANG CH'UNG (A.D. 27–c. 100): a Yangtze-valley man of a strongly iconoclastic temper. He wrote a book in thirty-five chapters, exposing the superstitious beliefs and practices of his age and affirming his faith in Confucius as the greatest of the sages. His style is of particular interest, for he wrote colloquially, yet his sentences have a rough and ready pattern, good and clear up to a point.

CHANG HENG (A.D. 78–139): an amazing brain, a combination of scientist and painter. As a composer of *fu* and prose he showed great powers of orderly description, e.g., in three long *fu* on the capitals. He was able also to describe the face of the heavens and to create a profound *fu* on *Thought the Transcender*. A great master of language, but with an ominous tendency to being over-recondite.

MA YUNG (A.D. 79–169): a grandee of the court for many years, he expounded the Confucianist Scriptures to great crowds of young scholars seeking government office; a classicist with a vein of romanticism in him.

CHENG HSÜAN (A.D. 127–200): a pupil of Ma Yung's, he edited and made commentaries on the Confucianist Scriptures with great industry and very little imaginative power.

TS'AI YUNG (A.D. 133–192): a versatile pen, exponent of the short *fu*. He carried the dialogue style into prose and was one of the earliest good composers in the new "five-word" lyrical metre. His epitaphs and inscriptions are much prized. He had something worth saying on the changes in the graphs, and revealed incipient powers of literary criticism—an orderly mind.

WANG TS'AN (A.D. 177–217): scion of a great family, versatile in composition, also having a taste for mathematics, but primarily a polished versifier.

TS'AO CHIH (A.D. 192–232): an unhappy man, his own enemy, and bullied by his jealous brother, the first Wei emperor—a real lyrical poet writing in the new "five-word" genre.

THE SEVEN WORTHIES OF THE BAMBOO GROVE (c. first half of third century A.D.): renounced court life and jeered effectively at all government pretences of moral uplift. Accused by their enemies of being drunk day and night, they nevertheless found time to write every kind of composition, exalting the irrational and yet convinced of the truth of the Taoists' final reality. One of them, Ch'i K'ang, profoundly Taoistic, wrote old-style poetry. His chief medium of expression was patterned prose, which is very good but inordinately long.

WANG PI (A.D. 226–249): died at the age of twenty-three, yet had written a complete and very individual commentary on the *Lao Tzu Book* and most of a commentary on the *Changes Scripture,* thus suggesting a trend towards a new synthesis of Confucianism and Taoism.

Here is detailed material occupying the central part of our historical landscape. These men were the greater lights of the Han world; and it must not be forgotten that there were many lesser lights around them both in the capital and the provincial centres. Most of these writers at one stage or another of their careers held staff posts in the armies, and all of them, apart from the college professors, had to exercise their pens in government business. Thus, to write was their trade as well as the crown of their careers. There were also the great generals, who in the last three generations of the regime came more and more to dominate the political scene: some of them wrote well. The first Han emperor had despised all scholars and thought he could administer his kingdom as he had won it, from the back of a horse. It is a far cry from him to Ts'ao Ts'ao (A.D. 153–220), a ruthless suppressor of peasant rebellions and a cunning destroyer of rivals at court, who yet could write reputable verse and loved his poet son, Ts'ao Chih.

Those four centuries were centuries of colossal political expansion coupled with a continuous solidification of philosophical thought. The literary concomitant to this is the double fact that in that changing era no lyric poets of any force and originality emerged until the very end; what did emerge step by step was prose, both dialectical and descriptive, and the unique Chinese accomplishment, the *fu,* or prose poem. Thus these scholar officials took the loose, confused grammar and syntax of the Chou era and gave hard bones and pliable sinews to it. Also, consecutive writing became coherent and precise, able to move from *a priori* concepts directly to the matter in hand, and, that matter having been dealt with, to clinch the argument with a return to accepted general principles. A study of the state papers still extant demonstrates this without question;

and that this gave release to men's intellectual vigour is evidenced particularly in the writing of history and commentaries. As to the former, the Ssu-ma *Record of History* and the Pan *Book of the Former Han Dynasty* are written history such as no other age in China has ever really equalled.[3] For all the mistakes modern scholars can find (particularly in the *Record*), the mere technique of record-sifting, factual description, specialized information on special subjects, and cautious appraisal can only awake admiration for the acumen of the authors' minds. As to the commentaries, the work of punctuating the ancient texts, of clarifying sentences and paragraphs and chapters, and of expounding innumerable dark sayings, all this was done in Han times, together with learned (if in some ways erroneous) investigations into the history of the language. The commentators' style in communication was laconic, clear, and to the point, even if we have to suspect from time to time that they did not know and only surmised, and that they too easily took for granted that the institutions they saw around them had in essence been there since antiquity. Even Pan Ku offended in this last respect. Take them as a whole, the drafters of imperial fiats, the preparers of reports and memorials to the throne, the authors of histories, and the exegetes of the sacred books of the past constructed a language which was the efficient tool of wide-scale government and the force required for disciplining the vagaries of unstudied thinking.

They did more than this; they made the *fu*: not the *fu* of the early romantic school, nor for that matter the *fu* of

[3] Those of my readers who know these two vast works will be tempted, as I am, to add "or, for that matter, out of China." That would not mean we claimed impeccability for them or the command of modern scientific techniques. Cf. Charles S. Gardner, *Chinese Traditional Historiography* (Cambridge, Mass., 1938).

the fifth to eighth centuries, but the *fu* as it was in Lu Chi's day, a harmonious combination of high poetic imagery and plain pedestrian prose. Many writers in some ten generations did their part in shaping the *fu,* but its virtue came mainly from Ssu-ma Hsiang-ju and Tung-fang So, Yang Hsiung, Pan Ku, Chang Heng, Ts'ai Yung, and—last and not least—Lu Chi himself. The story of their experimenting zeal is of central importance.

First of all, the word *fu* was one of the key words in political language, coming in time to be the standard term for "taxes." During the feudal era it denoted the presents made by one feudatory to another, and it is to be noted that these presents or tribute offerings always consisted of pairs of articles, so that from the beginning the idea of "something doubled" went with the idea of a *fu.* Then in the fourth century B.C. came the advance of the Yangtze power, Ch'u State, into the Yellow River basin (the Middle Kingdom) and the consequent closer mutual acquaintance of the two cultures. Among the Ch'u notables was one Ch'ü Yüan, cousin to King Huai of Ch'u (327–294 B.C.) and his faithful minister, also a poet of extraordinary originality. His master having come to listen to evil councillors, Yüan was exiled to a border region. There he composed the *Li Sao,* the poem for which he has ever since been famous. It is an amazing document because it is so long, so packed with symbolism of one kind and another, so rich in poetic imagery, sometimes so frenzied in its outbursts. It depicts the war in Yüan's soul, of hate against love, of despair against hope. Finally, when the conflict proved incapable of solution, he conceived of his life being laid down as a tribute (*fu*) to his beloved and ungrateful prince. He drowned himself in the river close at hand.

Beginning with this and other poems of Ch'ü Yüan's, there arose in the Yangtze area the highly romantic Ch'u school of elegiac poetry, with Sung Yü, Lu Chia, and other poets in whose writings gods and goddesses, fairies and ogres, appear as the objects of attention. It was by concentration on these strange, unconditioned beings that emotional conflict was expressed and relieved; and it was this which appealed to Chia Yi, Ssu-ma Hsiang-ju, and Tung-fang So when their official duties took them south. Their minds found release by expressing themselves through third-person interlocutors. To judge by the torrents of language which resulted, this seemingly simple device of the imagination was like the release of a spring. By forgetting themselves they found themselves (cf. Chapter VI, p. 222). Also, since they were servants of the emperors, they were in this way able to speak more plainly on policy to their masters than they otherwise would have dared. Finally, in the southern school we find the evidence of a deliberate paralleling of sentences to produce a cumulative effect (such as we find in Hebrew poetry). This mode stirred the northern and western writers of the court, not merely to imitate it but also to imbue it with their own regional genius. With the great flood of new ideas, new institutions, undreamt-of commodities, and strange clothing which that age brought to men's attention, the difficulty was to describe it all in language which was coherent and instructive. Here, then, came the first great step forward in the production of patterned language, namely, communication on the basis of one sentence or clause balancing its mate, and of the mind being thus pushed forward to consider one pair after another of dialectical judgments or descriptive detail. In this fashion a distinctively northern type of *fu* came into being.

Huang-fu Mi (A.D. 215–282) showed this when he said in his *San Tu Fu Hsü,* "The *fu* is that by which an object is followed up and headings are made, by which *li* [reason, principle] is amply embodied, this with the wish that no-body can add anything. Extending the above, it follows that the pattern of writing must be highly beautiful, must break the bounds of (conventional) classification and extend it. Therefore the language must be completely linked together."[4]

Men became intoxicated with language, as in England in Elizabeth's day. For them there was nothing this new ordering of thought could not express, and by the end of the first century B.C. there were in the imperial library over a thousand *fu* compositions arranged in four classes according to the scope of their historical interest. For literary purposes the main lines of distinction lie between the *fu* describing emotions, those elucidating the nature of things, and those trying to express the inexpressible. Yang Hsiung's genius lay in this last direction, and in consequence his sentences became more complicated and the logic of complementality was sometimes stretched to the limit. It is significant that Yang Hsiung began the practice of writing prefaces to his poems, as if he were compelled to clear surface detail out of the way before launching on his poetic arguments.

With the Second Han era things settled down. Pan Ku exercised a restraining influence. It was he who started the fashion for elaborate descriptions of the great capitals. With his orderly mind and his eye for precise detail he did this well, and a succession of descriptive *fu* writers followed, some composing at the emperor's command, others,

[4] See *Wen Hsüan,* chüan 45.

like Tso Ssu of Lu Chi's time, choosing their subjects on their own initiative. The sheer length of these writings necessitated planning and spacing, and with this there came the development, already noticeable in Yang Hsiung, of adding prose connecting clauses to mark the paragraphs. Rhyming patterns marked the paragraphs, and the pat' terning of sounds generally gave a stately air to detailed descriptions which otherwise might well have been intoler' ably dull. Taking into account the continual classical allu' sions, there is a legitimate comparison to be made between these and Milton's longer poems. In both cases poetry was aiming at grand architectonic effects, and the Chinese achieved these partly by using complementality on the large scale of paragraph and section balancing paragraph and section, and partly by alternating lilting prosodic patterns with rougher-sounding prose clauses. Other kinds of com' plementality had become permanent features of the style. In descriptions of modern objects and current events time was added to space by references to history, ancient and recent; and with this went the unfailing concomitant of Confucianist thinking, moral appraisal of the object and its creators—for example, judgments on whether the builders of these great cities or the elaborators of these great state functions were being human-hearted or not.

The interlocutor tradition held to a considerable extent, never achieving the proportions of living dialogue as it did in Greece. Dialectical dialogues were beginning to be writ' ten, but on a small scale, more for purposes of displaying wit than of developing serious discussion.[5] The *fu* writer was content to project himself, at the beginning of his

---

[5] The composition of serious and lengthy dialectical dialogues did not come until a hundred years later, when scholar converts to Buddhism began using this style.

poem, into an impersonal frame of mind by means of in-
terlocution. Once he had obtained objectification of himself, thus stabilizing his mood and disciplining his feelings,
he could work straight along without the extraneous aid
of conversation with one or more imaginery persons. As
time went on, however, a new type of subject for the *fu*
style began to emerge—namely, the mind, the "mind-
heart," as it is in Chinese psychology. Pan Ku made the
statement in a preface that Hsiang-ju and his fellows down
to Liu Hsiang "morning and evening discussed thought."
However that may have been, Pan Ku himself wrote a *fu*
in which dimness and clarity of vision were contrasted.
Then came Chang Heng, a composer of long *fu* poems on
the great capitals, but moving on from preoccupation with
external objects to the internal object, thought. In this
Thought the Transcender[6] he shows extraordinary powers
of self-detachment, the true poet's and the true meditative
philosopher's ability to externalize and so to clarify the
operations of the mind. Yet to him, part scientist though
he was, one of the major achievements of thought is the
creation of beauty: beauty being a discovery resulting from
the relating of one thing or one quality in things with
another. The words I now quote come from the opening
paragraph of his *fu*. Having linked thought with approved
emotion and defined purpose, he said that this combination

reveals the active nature of things by the construction of girdle
    pendants, linking the moonlight [of pearl] with the pink
    [of jade]:
collects the autumn blooms of the shy, retiring orchid and mixes
    them with the *chiang li:*[7]
beautifies the pleated skirt with fiery colours—confident that the
    dust of time will hardly fade them.

[6] M. Margouliès translates as *Méditation originelle.* I must beg to differ.
[7] This seems probably a Chinese variant of the umbelliferous wild parsley.

We must pause a moment and make sure of our perspective in relation to these carefully worded statements. First,
in its context the passage can hardly have been written
without its author, a Confucianist and a gentleman, having
in his mind the association of beauty in symbolic ornament
with beauty in noble conduct. Second, even with that association taken into account, are not the sentiments expressed the trivial conceits of a sophistical imagination?
On the other hand, should they not perhaps startle our
Western minds, as if a new window were opened on the
mind and its powers of thinking? The question must be
pressed home, for at least the traditional tendency in Western philosophizing has been to associate transcendency with
"God" and "eternity" and so rather fail to appreciate the
fact that the association of the particular colour and sheen
of pearls with the colour and sheen of the moon is a
powerful act of thinking, and that thought has a special
function to transcendentalize things by relating them.
So also we have tended to ignore the intellectual urge
which drives men to enhance the beauty of orchids by placing them in juxtaposition to the more feathery plant form
of the wild parsley. We call this artistic intuition and so
remove it from the realm of the intellect and consign it to—
one hardly knows what realm. Chang Heng's idea was
otherwise, and so, roughly speaking, was the mind of all
the double-harness writers of that age. It was part of the
mind which produced the *Wen Fu,* and, when there it
speaks of thought being in control of the document, we
have to realize that "thought" (*ssu*) worked from a cos-
mology in which the universe for man consisted of curves
complementing the rectilinear, light colours complementing dark. On the other hand, Chang Heng did not affirm

88

that thought could not err. His last word in the paragraph was that thought is prone to assume that the vivid colours in a dress are permanent and will not fade.

Chang Heng died in A.D. 139, in the reign of the Emperor Hsün, when ominous signs of political decay were beginning to appear. The bureaucracy was to try feverishly to reinvigorate its energies by calling for civil-service recruits from plebeian families, but the great houses—the Pans, the Changs, the Ts'aos, and others—had by now built up their large estates, and, whether or not they had prestige with the court clique momentarily in power, each could dominate his own part of the provinces. That they could still produce men of character and intelligence, as well as men with literary powers, is evident enough; but as time went on the delicate balance of the whole political machine was thrown more and more out of gear. By the end of the second century force was again in the saddle, and scholars were known "to throw away their brushes." And yet that was the very time when the lyrical muse came to life again with a tide of fashion sweeping in the direction of "five-word" prosody. The versifiers more and more forsook the ancient mode of four words to a line, the mode in which the grammar was fragmentary and the main effects were achieved by ejaculatory doubled words, some of them purely onomatopoeic. The music of those ancient rhythms had been ringing in Chinese ears and in the Chinese soul for hundreds of years, and during most of the Han era "four-word" was in constant use. It had, however, largely lost its vitality, and become the means for a display of archaistic virtuosity. With the extra word to the line, artificial emotionalism was, at any rate, more avoidable. There was room for new colourful adjectives to qualify nouns and for prepositions of all sorts. In other words, grammar and syntax came into their own, and the "five-word" composers could draw on all the language resources that the *fu* writers had so ardently accumulated.

Chao Ming's sixth-century anthology of Han and post-Han literature, having given first place to the *fu*, with these divided into ten main classes, in the second place gives seven classes of *shih* (lyrical verse). Among those classes the largest by far is that of "presentation *shih* and *shih* of formal thanks." That speaks for itself. These lyrics, at first in four-word and then exclusively in five-word measure, were the customary method of complimentary communication between gentlemen. The practice is familiar to us in the history of our Western culture, and we know how it can produce polished trivialities.

There was another side to the third-century vogue. From Wang Ts'an on, we can trace the five-word measure winning its place in men's hearts through its power of expressing emotion. It was, indeed, a subtle medium for self-expression when Lu Chi was born; of the major writers only Ch'i K'ang continued to use only the four-word measure. "Escapist poetry" seems to be the phrase. Sighs and groans figure largely in the very individual and spontaneous outpourings that came, for example, from Ts'ao Chih: sensitive men could not bear their lot, cast as it was in that murderous society of power-politicians. Yet there was something more than emasculating self-pity in these poems: as one generalization on such writing put it, the poet "gained the sympathy of the moon and the winds." There was here a love of nature of a kind which we look for in vain among the Latin poets. These could appreciate the smiling tilth and swelling hills flecked with the white of the fat sheep grazing on them, but when it came to great mountains hidden in the clouds and the majestic force of great rivers, this was *horrendum terrificum* to them. To the Chinese poets they were fascinating, and although at first there were apparently no poems of any merit which embodied the delights of travel, the time soon came when there were. That time was Lu Chi's generation and in Lu Chi's own circle, where Lu Chi and his fellow southerner, P'ang Ngo, stand out as having a sensitive ear for what bird and beast and hill and valley had to say to them. Yet even here a certain mood of melancholy is discernible. Removal to some distant post meant separation from one's friends, and again and again we find that the poems which have survived were occasioned by the sorrow of parting. Amongst these are Lu Chi's odes to Lu Yün at the times of their parting, and Lu Yün's to Lu Chi. They are alive with affection, the love of one man for another in whose integrity of soul he has complete confidence. The five-word measure could compass that kind of expression as well as the polite sentiments of courtly greeting and the outpourings of a passionate feeling of frustration.

Thus we reach at last the foreground with its central object presented for our inspection, that *Art of Letters* written in the Shantung plain in the thirty-sixth year of the Tsin dynasty, eighty years after the fall of the Han dynasty. We know something of its author and his relations and friends, of his enemies also. From the last chapter and this we can see how the author's writings were of his time, comparable with the writings of his friends and yet standing out from among them as a brighter star among lesser ones. The last chapter has also shown how for ten years Lu Chi lived, if not always in the capital, yet in touch with the court and thus was able to see the manuscripts of recent productions. This *Art of Letters* is, therefore, no miraculous freak with-out father and mother and without brother and sister. Yet later ages have acclaimed it as the chief work of that age, and it is studied today as not only a work of high poetic genius but also as the first[8] and one of the greatest pieces of systematic criticism in the history of Chinese literature.

It remains but to add two reflections which I conceive necessary for bringing our object into focus. The first is that recently there have been in Western discussions on literature expressions of doubt about the truth of the long-held belief that prose is one thing and poetry something entirely different. In the one case, the composer, if faithful to his *métier,* should show that he is in this world, with his feet well planted on the mother earth of facts (so called). In the other case, the composer is supposed to live in an-other world, one built up out of his imagination, quite re-moved from humdrum facts. According to such a theory, it is as if Dante and Milton had two selves and had written their prose works with the one and their poetical works with the other. It is as if Blake, that supreme poet, might have worked as an engraver without any realistic percep-tion of what his tools could achieve in relation to the surface of certain types of wood or of what subtle manipu-lations of deepened curves were calculated to give perspec-tive to an etching. It is as if Shakespeare, who knew so shrewdly how to add one gold noble to another and who became a citizen of repute in his native town, was not the same man who in *Hamlet* added one to one in the sombre tale of murders. Unless the reader can overcome this false division of life into prose and poetry, he can never

---

[8] The one previous attempt is given in translation in Appendix 1.

understand the *Wen Fu,* with its intense realism and its insistence that the miraculous word of poetry must also be a word of reason.

The other reflection is that prose and poetry are different in certain respects and that this fact is reflected in the third-century writers' distinctive writings, in the *shih* and the *fu.* In the one, for the very reason that it is the out-letting of an emotional mood, the embroidering of that mood (cf. *Wen Fu,* Part II [a]) must be restrained within the strict limits of prosodic form; for it is the form that has to order the ebullient ego. In the *fu,* the writer is con-centrated on an object, his consciousness of self gone. His mood is one of response to stimulus from without; his very words tend to be in the third person, as, for example, through the words of imagined interlocutors. That being so, the ego is more under control and cannot but be domi-nated by the rationale of the object under observation. It is that rationale which dictates the length of the sentence and the paragraph. If the result be poetry, and double-harness poetry at that, the reason is that to the writers the universe does for the most part contain a beauty of reason. It is by the checking of one judgment with its comple-mentary judgment, by comparing earth with heaven and heaven with earth, that combinations of perceptions lead to understanding, just as combinations of actions lead to realization of values. Of this last, the *Wen Fu* has only one word to say, that all truly artistic writing aims at the encouragement of virtue and the discouragement of vice. In being so succinct, the author of the *Wen Fu* was true to his task. Having embodied his object of attention, he laid down his brush, knowing in his soul that to embark on overt exhortation was to be diffuse, and that to be diffuse was to be in a state of sin.

us, and follow on with a discussion of the
causes of good and bad writing.

8. Some day it may almost come to be said that I
have in a lopsided way explored this mystery:

9. [for] when we writers come to grasping axes
and hewing axe-handles, we do, after all, select
models which are near at hand.

10. As for the variations arising from a writer's idiosyncrasy, this is almost impossible for language
to capture:

11. what I am able to put into words is all stated
here.

The Poem

PART I. Lu Chi's Record of the Superb Artistries of the
Earlier Writers

(a) 1. Taking his stand at the hub of the universe so
that he might objectify his outlook, feeding his
purpose with the sacred writings of the past:

2. he followed through the four seasons with a sigh
at their passing, he surveyed all creation and
mused on its tangled skein.

3. He mourned the fall of the leaves in strong-
handed autumn, he rejoiced over the tender
buds of fragrant spring:

4. his heart was a-shiver with the thought of the
frosts, his mind caught away above the clouds
of summer.

5. He recited the mettlesome virtues of the
[writers] of his day, hymned the clean [lit-
erary] fragrance of the men before him:

95

  6. *he roamed through the crowded treasure-house
of letters, admired the matching of matter and
manner in its exquisitely traceried works.*

  7. *Impulsively he pushed the books away and
grasped the brush, summoned it to [the work
of] this composition.*

(b)   *The beginning was in this fashion:*

  1. *oblivious to all sights, oblivious to all sound, both
sunk in thought and questioning abroad,*

  2. *his spirit was away on a wild gallop to the Eight
Poles, his mind thousands of cubits beneath
the sod.*

  3. *Then he reached this point:*
    *the dawn of his mood grew brighter and
brighter and so more defined, the objects of
his attention lighted up and came jostling
forward:*

  4. *he tested the sap in the words crowding about
him, rinsed his mouth with the sweet dews of
the Scriptures.*

  5. *He was swimming in the pool in the heavens
with its peaceful flow, he had plunged into the
fountain in the deeps and was completely
soused in it.*

(c) 1. *This was the way of it:*
    *he being immersed in phrases painfully con-
senting, it was like darting fish with the hooks
in their gills, dragged from the depths of an
unplumbed pool:*

  2. *he, being shrouded in beautiful language, all*

a-flutter, it was like birds on the wing and the arrow strung to the bow—down they drop headlong from out of the cloud.

3. Gathering the fine diction omitted through a hundred ages, selecting from the assonances neglected over a thousand years:

4. he left on one side the day-old blossoms already full-blown, he unveiled the night-buds as yet unopened.

5. He was seeing the past and the present in a moment of time, he was touching the Four Seas in one blink of an eye.

(d) 1. After this he chose from among the ideas and placed them in order, he scrutinized the expressions and put them where they belonged:

2. some [ideas] with a shadowy quality to them kept on tap-tapping, some [expressions] which were merely echoes ceased twanging.

3. It may be he followed along a branch to shake the leaves, or followed down the ripples [in a pool] and so found the spring.

4. It may be that what was at first obscure by this means became clear, or what he sought as easy became more and more difficult.

5. It may be there was a tiger-change and all the beasts submitted, or a dragon emerged and the birds were caught by the waves.

6. Either he found himself on even ground and advance was easy, or the ground was rock-bestrewn, and he hobbled along in misery.

97

(e) 1. He stilled the waters of his mind to stabilize his
        thinking, he peered into his thoughts and one
        by one put them into words:

     2. he was trapping heaven-and-earth within a visi-
        ble form, forcing all creation onto the tip of
        his brush.

     3. At first he hesitated, with the brush parching
        his lips, but finally the stream flowed forth
        from the well-steeped hairs.

     4. Reason having given stability to the subject-
        matter by setting up a main stem, the artist in
        him reached out to the branches and knotted
        them in their profusion.

     5. He could trust the face of his mood not to fall
        awry, so that at every turn it should be well
        enfeatured:

     6. should the thought be of something delightful,
        there was sure to be a smile, then suddenly
        sorrow was there and straightway there was
        a sigh.

     7. This whether the tablet was grasped with a sense
        of ease and direction or whether the brush
        went to his mouth and he fell into a brown
        study.

(f) 1. What joy there was in all this, the joy which
        sages and worthies have coveted.

     2. He was taxing Non-Being to produce Being,
        calling to the Silence, importunate for an
        answer:

     3. he was engrossing the great spaces within a span
        of silk, belching forth torrents [of language]
        from the inch-space of the heart.

4. Words were expanding the theme, the more as it proceeded: thought was bringing it under his hand, as it became the more profound.

5. He was scattering a fragrance of delicious hang-ing-clusters, putting forth a profusion of green-budding twigs.

6. A laughing wind was flying by and whirling up a solid shape, a mass of shining cloud was aris-ing in the garden of letters.

(g) 1. A body has a myriad differences, [and] nothing can be measured along one line of measure-ment:

2. with convolution on convolution [changing] at the shake of a hand, the [precise] form of the [composition] could hardly achieve an identity. *90 4 4 4*

3. While the massing of the phrases proved the measure of effective skill, it was the meaning in control of the document which made the real workmanship.

4. Whilst it both was and was not he kept on struggling, whilst it was both shallow and deep he could not give way:

5. however much it departed from the square and skulked away from the round, in the end the shape was completed and the portrayal finished.

6. Wherefore, the men whose eyes exaggerated ran to excess, the men who would satisfy their minds prized exactitude:

7. those with a poor command of words had no

99

way through, those who were versed in dia-
lectic alone had a free course.

PART II. A Discussion of the Causes of Good and Bad
Writing

(a) 1. *Lyrical poems are the outcome of emotion and*
should be subtle elaborations: prose poems
[fu] are each the embodiment of an object
and so should be transparently clear.

2. *Inscriptions on monuments should cloak the art*
with simplicity: funeral elegies are tangled
skeins [of grief] and so should be cries of
distress.

3. *Dedications on ritual bronzes are both compre-*
hensive and concise but should be warm [in
tone]; admonitions are to make a break [in
conduct] and so should be forthright.

4. *Panegyrics should be expatiations on admirable*
qualities, with a balanced elegance; dialectical
essays deal with subtle points and should be
clear and comprehensive.

5. *Memorials to the throne should be easily intel-*
ligible along with their polished elegance; ex-
positions of theories are very illuminating—
and deceptive.

6. *The marked-out territories being in this fashion,*
the styles none the less all ban evil and restrain
licence:

7. *[and] since it is essential that the language be*
understandable and reasoning well main-
tained, there is no point in being long-winded.

(b) 1. *Taken as individual objects, [compositions] all have their own special air; taken as recognized styles, they are subject to repeated change:*

2. *as the bringing together of ideas, they put a premium on skill: as words sent on a high mission, they need to be [utterances] of distinction.*

3. *As for the alternation of sounds, and their being like the display in five-coloured [embroidery] where [the colours] light each other up:*

4. *to be sure, there is no certain rule about the movements and pauses, but pot-bellied disproportion is very difficult to put right.*

5. *Should we be versed in ringing the changes and recognize the order of them, it is like the opening of a channel to welcome the flow from a fountain-head:*

6. *if we miss the opportunities and [try] too late to make the combinations, we are constantly grabbing the tail to wrest the head in the right direction.*

7. *With the lights and shades wrongly spaced, the result is a muddied effect, lacking in piquancy.*

(c) 1. *It may be that with a double angle of vision, the second item is embarrassed by the first, the first is in forced relation to the second.*

2. *Perhaps the wording has done the damage, whilst the reasoning is well matched; perhaps the language has obeyed orders, but the judgments are the source of the trouble.*

3. *Keep the two distinct, and both will be to the*

good; deal with them together, and both will
suffer.

4. Inspect your soldiers from the rear rank to the
front down to the minutest detail, decide on
retaining or rejecting by the turn of a hair:

5. let the corrections be assessed with precision, and
they will be as the carpenter's string, of necessity right.

(d) 1. It may be that whilst the style is rich and the
reasoning copious, yet the ideas are beside the
point.

2. [Since] in the last resort there is no going two
ways at once, and whatever you do you must
not add anything,

3. set up a word or two to come at key points, these
to be the warning whip to the whole composition:

4. whichever way the sentences branch one from
the other, they must depend on this [key] if
they are to interweave effectually.

5. There is great merit to this plan, verbosity is
restrained, and the result is that, having selected enough material, one does not make
changes.

(e) 1. It may be the traceried thinking is a woven harmony [in colour], with the clear-cut beauty
of many-tinted foliage:

2. [the composition] glows like gay embroidery,
is heart-searching like the music of many
strings.

3. 'Twas bound to happen—there in my script,

> *word for word, an unconscious tallying with*
> *a previous work.*

4. *True, the shuttle has gone back and forth in my*
   breast: but, alas, that man was before me.

5. *No! 'twould be a stain on my honour, an injus-*
   tice to others; however I grudge it, the passage
   must go.

(f) 1. *It may be a trumpet-flower blossoms forth, a*
      corn-ear rears its head—a dissident and un-
      directed section,

2. *having an undisassociable substance, yet an un-*
   associable ring:

3. *there it stands, a lonely mass, not to be com-*
   passed by conventional speech.

4. *'Tis a cage to the mind, for there is no mate to*
   it; its meanings flit hither and hither, but eject
   them you cannot.

5. *The jade is concealed in the rock, yet the hill is*
   refulgent with it; the pearl is enveloped in the
   waters, but the stream betrays its charm.

6. *The thorn-brake there, so rough and untrimmed,*
   a glory of colour in kingfisher clots:

7. *the rustic ditty woven into the White Snow*
   music for me enhances its grandeur.

(g) 1. *It may be language has been employed in one*
      short strain, one with no traceable sources, a
      foundling production,

2. *which looked close to the Silence but found no*
   friend, looked far to the Void but gained no
   response.

3. *'Tis as if one solitary note were plucked from a*

103

*lute, clean and resounding—but with nothing
to answer it.*

(h) 1. It may be the phrasing finds lodgment in laboured periods, aimlessly gaudy, but not really
beautiful.

2. The body of the composition is a hotchpotch of
the fair and the foul, good material in volume
but irreparably damaged.

3. 'Tis as if the flutes below outran [the lutes
above], answering them, to be sure—but not
making harmony.

(i) 1. It may be reason has been commissioned to up-
hold some bizarre notion, the Void ransacked
in pursuit of something recondite.

2. The language lacks feeling and rarely betrays
love, the sentences drift along and do not
strike home.

3. 'Tis like plangent notes from strings too finely
strung, making harmony, to be sure—but
evoking no feeling.

(j) 1. It may be [a composition] has run away with
itself, outharmonizing harmonies, is a dizzying
drumming [of words] designed to bemuse.

2. It is a vain delight to the eye, in the class vulgar,
indeed a pretentious tune to a sorry theme.

3. It awakens the ruinous licentious songs of the
past; feelings are there, true enough—but the
result is not refinement.

(k) 1. It may be [a composition] by its agreeable restraint is pure and empty, at every turn elim-

inating vexation of spirit and dispersing the
tumultuous waves [of passion];

2. being without [even] the lingering flavour of
the sacred broth of the High Sacrifice, it is
just like the vermilion lute-strings with their
notes so pure and so blurred.

3. Although it contain "one to sing and three to
sigh," indeed be refined—yet it has no charm.

(1) 1. As for the productions fashioned on a scale both
copious and concise, well formed from a double angle of vision,

2. which are both true to principle and adapted to
the occasion, and as themes contain subtle
moods:

3. it may be the phrasing is clumsy but the analogues are skilful, or the reasoning is very
simple but the sentences run lightly.

4. It may be the garb is antique and yet quite new,
or [we see] a muddied stream running itself
clean.

5. Whether at first sight they were sure to be clear
or close scrutiny was required to reveal their
subtlety,

6. compare them we may with dancers matching a
strain by wide-flung sleeves, with singers striking the note in response to the lutes.

7. This, I surmise, is what the Wheelwright could
not wholly put into words, is that essence
which flowery theorizing cannot hope to
explain.

(m) 1. The rules of diction and the musical patterning

in writing, all this I do well in hugging to my breast.

2. And—what vulgar fashion decries, that one should con over and over; what the old mas-ters esteemed, with that one should acquaint oneself.

3. And—to be sure, wisdom issuing from subtle minds may yet be absurd in the eyes of the stupid.

4. Now observe the brilliant effusions and jewelled creations [of today], like to humdrum crops reaped by humdrum toil.

5. [These works] on the level of "the sack-pipes of infinite space," "one with Heaven and Earth in nourishing creation"!

6. The prolific profusion there is in this generation, yet alas! it does not fill the cup of my two hands.

7. The anxiety there is because buckets carried from the well are time and again empty, the anguish there is because one cannot place the singing word.

8. So one hops lamely round diminutive walls, and declines into the commonplace in rounding out a theme.

9. Always dissatisfaction remains when the end is reached—dare we then be complacent and cherish our conceit?

10. The terror is lest with the dust on us from the thudding of jars we turn and are mocked by the chiming of jades.

(n) 1. As to the interaction of stimulus and response,
       the intermingling of the flow with the block-
       ing of the flow:

     2. their coming cannot be prevented, their going
        cannot be stopped:

     3. underground things go like shadows vanishing,
        back to life they come like echoes awakening.

     4. Comes the lightning release of Nature's spring—
        where, then, is disorder and unreason?

     5. The wind of thought comes forth from the
        breast, a fountain of words is in the teeth and
        the lips:

     6. a riot of tender shoots thrusting up into bloom—
        which brush and silk alone can adjudicate:

     7. a pattern emblazoned to fill the eye, a music re-
        mote yet flooding the ear.

(o) 1. Then comes the blocking of every kind of feeling,
        the will [to create] gone, the spirit held
        bound.

     2. It is like being the stock of a sapless tree, being
        empty as a dried-up river.

     3. Lay hold of the mutinous soul by sounding its
        secret depths, pay homage to its vital fierce-
        ness as you search for the very self:

     4. reason screened and obscured begins to creep
        forth, thought comes screaming, forced out
        from the womb.

     5. These are the reasons why either there is much
        to repent when [we write] with our mood
        exhausted, or with our purpose in command
        we seldom err.

6. *This thing which is in me but which no efforts of mine can slay!*
7. *Wherefore time and again I stroke my empty bosom in pity for myself: so ignorant am I of what causes the opening and the barring of the door.*

Epilogue

1. *Behold now the utility of letters, a utility endorsed by every kind of principle.*
2. *It extends over a thousand miles and nothing can stop its course; it penetrates a million years, the ferry from one to the other.*
3. *Looking one way, it hands down the laws to the ages to come; looking the other way, it examines the symbols made by the men of old.*
4. *It gives aid to governors and generals when ruin is impending, proclaiming good custom [the cause of] survival.*
5. *No road is so distant it cannot be brought near, no principle so abstruse it cannot be ordered and related.*
6. *It is mate to the fattening dews of cloud and rain, the image of spirit influences, those authors of change and revolution.*
7. *It covers metal and stone [with inscriptions] so that virtue is published abroad, it flows through the music of flute and harp—and daily it [should be] new.*

It is an arresting piece of work, this prose explanation, with its tribute of whole-hearted admiration coupled with cool discrimination of "the fair and the foul." We can feel Lu Chi objectifying his personal experience by means of their acts of word release, their commissioning of language, and the vicissitudes they encountered in the art of composing. Having done that, he is ready to say, "*Therefore* I compose this *fu*"—in two parts. The objectified mood is to be brought out into the open and nailed down for inspection, and he sees that mood as having two strains to it, an experiential and a dogmatic. Note his order of treatment: Part I, the experiential; Part II, the dogmatic. I am reminded of a mariner's compass-card with its dead north delineated, and the man at the helm calculating the magnetic variation. In Lu Chi's case, allowance is made for emotional variation, as is clear from the story told in Part I. Thus, his readers are enabled to approach more scientifically the appraisals given in Part II.

N.B. 1. As to the length of the paired sentences, in the text the first pair consists of seven words plus seven words with one introductory word, whilst the seventh pair consists of ten words plus nine words, again with one introductory word. All the other pairs in the foreword are on a four-plus-four basis, although some have five words in one *chü*. (For the meaning of *chü,* sentence or clause, cf. Chapter I, p. 14.) This use of seven plus seven words and then at a particular later point of ten plus nine not only varies the monotony of the four-plus-four pattern; it also shows a transition of thought—in other words, a paragraph. The transition of thought, very clearly marked here, must be recognized if Lu Chi's mind is to be appreciated.

N.B. 2. As to the double-harness texture of Lu Chi's

mind, two examples may be given here. In couplet 1 he starts off with *Yü mei kuan* (I every-time look-at). Couplet 4 starts with *mei tzŭ shu* (every-time the-self is-put-into); the *mei* is repeated, but in the first case it is in connection with the personal "I," in the second case with the impersonal "the-self." The second example is in connection with the "vicissitude" in couplet 2 and "I am constantly anxious" in couplet 5. The one expression regards the situation from the angle of an unavoidable process of Nature: vicissitudes are, so to speak, acts of God. Couplet 5 presents the same situation, but from the subjective angle of the writer able in some measure to overcome this disability.

Couplet 1. "Minds": the mind here is, of course, "mind-heart"; cf. Chapter I, p. 20.

Couplet 5. "Meaning": *yi,* an extremely difficult term for which to find a precise equivalent in English. In some contexts it is plainly equivalent to "purpose," in other contexts more like "idea," but sometimes plainly neither. Here is a case in point. *The Meaning of Meaning* (Ogden and Richards) demonstrates, I think, how our modern level of consciousness in this connection gives us a new nuance of expression, viz., "meaning."

"Artistic form": *wen,* cf. Chapter I, p. 14. This phrase hardly renders the full scope of *wen,* which denotes the "ordered lines of," query "the symmetrical structure of," i.e., the composition as a whole with the various meanings in right relation and proportion communicating one whole meaning.

Couplet 7. "Superb artistries": *sheng tsao. Sheng* is a more general kind of adjective, expressing admiration for any abundantly fine object of attention. *Tsao* is more difficult. As K'ung An-kuo (second century B.C.) pointed out, *tsao*'s original meaning was "those aquatic grasses" (i.e., plants and rushes) which have pronounced aesthetic form (*wen*). In Han times it came to be used for an artistically conceived literary production, one to be admired for its successful achievement of aesthetic and ordered value. But is that all? How came the connection between the two phenomena to be made? I suggest that the idea of "tracery" was in the mind of the men who started the practice: the sharp, almost stabbing, effect of the pattern of rushes against the undifferentiated blur of, e.g., the Yellow River, or the Huai River or the Yangtze, if southerners started the practice. A successful composition was something cut out of the blue, a tracery of patterned language. Remember the tracery of the new brush-written characters, each one conveying distinctive meaning. Picture painting with the brush did not really begin until Ku K'ai-chih (*ob.* A.D. 332) (cf. Plate III), but its studied, even ordered, patterns are all part of what good Six Dynasties scholars had in mind when they thought of *wen* and *tsao*. For *tsao*, cf. Part I (*a*), 4, and *tsao ssu* (traceried thinking), Part II (*e*), 1.

Couplet 8. "Lopsided": this, of course, represents modesty. Convention required some such self-disparagement. I have no reason to suppose that Lu Chi did not mean it, although quite clearly he is feeling that he has got something pretty good to communicate. "Explored" is surely a little arrogant, for *tsin* means doing the job thoroughly.

Couplet 9. "Grasping axes . . .": a very good example of a "smelted and trimmed" quotation from a classical work, in this case *Odes*, I, xv, 5:

In hewing an axe-handle, how do you proceed?
Without an axe it cannot be done.
In taking a wife, how do you proceed?
Without a go-between it cannot be done.

In having an axe-handle, in having an axe-handle,
The pattern is not far-off.
I see the lady,
And forthwith the vessels are arranged in rows.[1]

The pattern, of course, is in the hewer's own hand, the vessels those used in the marriage ceremonies. Lu Chi's readers would have the two images in mind, so there was no need for him to be explicit. Since marriage go-betweens were older women, not comely like marriageable young women, the presumption about the axe-handle is that it need not be a perfect model, but just a handy one to hew by. So, proud as Lu Chi is of the job in hand, his pride is in control, enough for a pretty wit to come through. The words in the *Odes* (st. 2, 1. 2) are *ch'i tse pu yüan* (the model for it is not distant). Lu Chi says *sui ch'ü pu yüan*. The *sui* (after all) is good: it seems to point to Lu Chi's saying to his fellow writers, "You know well that, however good the ancient models are in theory, actually when you start writing you turn to modern patterns." Such a remark would be perfectly in keeping with third-century double-harness writers' practice.

Couplet 10. "A writer's idiosyncrasy": *sui shou* literally is "the following along of the hand." The image, of course, comes from visual art, but presumably more from the art of calligraphy than from that of carving. Painting had not reached the stage in Lu Chi's day when it could create a term for "idiosyncrasy." In this connection the flourishing art of casting highly decorated bronze mirrors might

[1] James Legge, *The Chinese Classics* (Oxford, 1892), Vol. IV, Pt. I, p. 240.

be taken into account. The methods of production gave scope to a craftsman's individual genius. (Cf. Plate II.)

The Poem

Part I

Paragraph (a). I have hesitated as to whether to use "stanza," but Lu Chi seems to me to have taken such pains to make a consecutive, rational story that we owe it to him to stress that aspect. *Fu* writers were skilled hands at making clear-cut paragraphs. Are Mr. Eliot's divisions in *Four Quartets* stanzas or paragraphs?

Couplet 1. "His . . . he": actually, there is no word in the couplet which denotes the subject of the clauses. This is not an unpardonable omission on the part of Lu Chi, but a characteristic feature of Chinese classical style, although pronouns are put in where they are really needed. There is, of course, no question but that Lu Chi is here referring to the former writers, and therefore "they" is the right word. But "they" with the past tense is rather heavy in a number of passages in this Part I. Further, I challenge any one to read the author's statements and not come to the conclusion that they embodied his own experiences. So I translate "he." "One," with its mellifluous sound and engaging anonymity, would have done, but it has been used to death by certain personages who, lacking the moral courage to say "I believe," take cover under "one tends to believe."

"Taking his stand": a favourite expression of Lu Chi's. It comes in his other writings. In general usage it appears quite often to be associated with the idea of waiting ex-

pectantly. In a poem to his brother he writes, "standing
a-gaze I . . . ," indicating what he longs to see.

"Sacred writings of the past": *tien fen,* of which *tien*
denotes "accepted standards" and *fen* "rich soil (?)."
By Lu Chi's time it was a conventional synonym for sacred
writings. On his lips the term's scope of reference included
Taoist authoritative works as well as Confucianist.

Couplet 5. "Mettlesome virtues": literally, the *tsün*
(mettlesome), *lieh* (fiery) quality of the *të* (outstanding
spiritual power in a person) of his day. The root meaning
of *tsün* is the quality found in a fleet and mettlesome
horse, the root meaning of *lieh* is "burning fiercely"; but,
speaking semantically, the metaphorical use of the two
words together entailed a diminution in their separate significance. Hence "mettlesome" may stand for the two
words. "Virtue" is not used in the narrow moralistic
sense: cf. Latin *virtus* and "by virtue of."

Couplet 6. "The matching of matter and manner":
pin-pin being one graph written twice. Phrases of this kind
are a great problem, since so many of them seem to have
no connection between the meaning of the single graph
and that of the two-word concept. Most of these binoms
are phonetic loan words from the spoken language. Fortunately, the first extant usage of *pin-pin* occurs in
Analects, VI, 16, where the context gives clear indication
of the meaning. Couvreur's *La Dictionnaire chinoise,* following the definition given by Pao Hsien in the first
century A.D. and generally accepted ever since, gives the
most admirable description: "dit de deux choses qui sont
de qualité ou de quantité égale, et se trouvent réunis
ensemble" (the italics are mine). By Lu Chi's day the
phrase was being used in contexts of various kinds: hence
I venture to give such a precise interpretation.

"Exquisitely traceried works": *li tsao, tsao* being the same word as in Foreword, couplet 7.

Couplet 7. A dramatic *dénouement.* Lu Chi is partial to such, and sometimes an innocent-looking sentence has a satirical twist to its tail.

"Summoned": often has the connotation of abruptness. That is required here, for the text contains *liao* (abruptly or any-old-how). In a trial version I wrote, "and scribbled away at this composition." That is too free, of course, but it has its merits. *Hsüan* (summon, proclaim, etc.) is also found used in the sense of letting something—for example, water—out from a restricted area. Lu Chi can hardly have meant that actual composing was done at this point, but he did mean that the pen got busy scribbling.

Paragraph (b). The first paragraph consists of seven six-plus-six couplets. There are no opening or closing words standing outside the *chü* rhythm. Thus, Lu Chi swings straightway into prosodic form. In (b) we come on a striking change in form. First, there are two introductory clauses standing outside the couplet rhythm. These are both three-word phrases: "The beginning was . . ." and "then he reached. . . ." There is also an extra initial word to couplet 1: *chieh* (in all cases). Second, the *chü* rhythm changes from six plus six to four plus four for two couplets, after which it goes to six plus six again. When we realize that there is marked difference between these two kinds of *chü,* the longer one having a definite swing to it and the shorter punching out the meaning in short steps, we begin to appreciate one element in the genius of *fu* writing. Cf. Chapter III, pp. 84 f. It is a highly deliberate form of art, the more so because meaning must in the last resort dictate the rhythm of the grammar. We can see how a composer, having got started with a certain rhythm, might easily let it run on, while a sensitive thinker—yes, thinker—would realize that the tempo of his thought required a different grammatical rhythm. I suggest that this is something of the experience of some modern poets, particularly Mr. Eliot. To be able to do this requires extraordinary alertness of consciousness, extraordinary sensitiveness of the ear to rhythm, and *also* extraordinary fidelity to the objectified mood. Cf. also my comment on II (*a*), 4.

Couplet 1. "Oblivious . . .": the language of the text consists of Taoist technical terms used in connection with mystic trance, or yoga—*shou shih* (to put away seeing) and *fan t'ing* (to turn hearing back). There is no need to suppose that Lu Chi is doing more than borrowing the terms for a more general meaning. "Questioning abroad": at first sight a little odd, since Lu Chi was sunk in thought, but Li Shan suggests this meaning. After all, at this stage a composer, however sunk in thought, could hardly avoid having questing feelers out.

Couplet 2. "The Eight Poles": amounts to all directions plus reaching a great distance away.

"Beneath the sod": some commentators suggest "aloft," but there is nothing in the Chinese to show whether the image is one of up in the air or down under the earth. But in Chang Heng's *fu* on *Thought the Transcender* (*Ssu Hsüan*), we find *chiu huang hu yü ti ti* (pursuing the murk below the earth). Cf. also couplet 5, sentence 2.

Couplet 5. "The pool in the heavens": again we find the clue in the *Ssu Hsüan Fu*. In his imagined journey round and under and above his world Chang Heng de-

117

scribed his flight into the heavens, first to the stars, then to the sun, then to the Milky Way—and then, with most admirable logic, into undifferentiated space. *T'ien huang* is the term he used for the Milky Way. Lu Chi's expression is *t'ien yüan, yüan* perhaps denoting a deeper kind of pool than *huang*. The use of this image along with that of "fountain," coming as they do after the sweet dews of the Scriptures, suggests that this couplet 5 should be taken as having metaphorical import.

Paragraph (c). As a paragraph, extremely interesting from the point of view of the poem structure. As his two-word opening phrase shows, the subject-matter of (c) is pretty much that of (b), the difference merely being that Lu Chi starts a good step later in the process of word-search and carries it a triumphant step further in that magnificent leap of his imagination in the last couplet. But there is more to it than that. In the first attempt to "embody," the archetypal "he" is not presented as having much of a struggle: in fact, he swims in a pool with a peaceful flow. In the second presentation, he is the sportsman out for game and having to use every bit of his strength and skill to make his bag. The right phrases only reluctantly consent, they are all a-flutter. In fact, the poor fellow has the devil of a time getting them into his bag, for there are hundreds of them out there in the beyond (cf. couplet 3), and those he does manage to grab hold of are half of them *clichés* (cf. couplet 4). So, whilst (b) was a good enough job of poetic craftsmanship, giving an idealization of the process, (c) is intensely realistic. The two pictures complement each other. The question is: how did Lu Chi come to do it like this, with the two paragraphs the same length? Did he see from the outset that there were the two aspects and calmly allot so much space to each of them? He must have been more than human if he could do that; and yet with his double-harness mind he was clearly able—with how much labour, we can never know—to get the flitting images into shape and pin them down where they belonged. Again there is the question: how much was there which passed through his mind and which he ruled out? I ask these questions thus early in the commentary, for not only in (*b*) and (*c*), but also throughout the poem, Lu Chi has plainly given such rigorous attention to spacing. I submit that to the Western critic there is a problem here: the live question in our generation of whether submission to requirements of strict form puts a poet's genius into a strait-jacket. Perhaps Lu Chi went too far with his passion for order and conciseness.

Couplets 1 and 2. There is an unusual *chü* rhythm here, one of four plus five plus six. Also, the strict parallelism of the two couplets makes one wonder whether the complementality in double-harness thinking did not really become effective on a two-couplet basis rather than on a two-*chü* basis. The fact is that it depended on the writer and the relative simplicity and complication of the picture he wanted to paint or the argument he wanted to pursue. With regard to the unusual rhythm here, there are a number of instances of four plus six, generally followed by another four plus six, but not always, and in some cases the four-word *chü* and the six-word *chü* are complementary in meaning. That being so, it seemed advisable to write the four-plus-five-plus-six combination as I have done. The commentators have followed this practice.

"Down they drop . . . cloud": the image seems to me to entail Lu Chi's standing on a hill-side with the mist all about him. Suddenly the birds emerge to view, and he just catches one before it disappears into the mist. There are plenty of pheasants and other wild fowl to be found in the Hua T'ing region today.

Couplet 5. I thought at first that I had caught Lu Chi napping, and he ought really to have had his "blink of an eye" in the statement about seeing, and the "moment of time" in the other sentence. But, of course, he meant it as it is, and it makes sense. I am reminded of early as-tronomers looking at the setting sun and the rising moon in the blink of an eye, and then, if one may put it so, the fingers of their minds reaching out and linking the two objects of attention between thumb and little finger. Fur-ther, if anyone thinks Lu Chi is talking "pure hyperbole" here, in fact "nonsense words," I should like to ask him whether that combination of visual and mental finger-spanning by watchers of the heavens was not in fact the beginning of the science of astronomy. In any case, some words written in the hubbub of these last years have the same instantaneous time-span, with the implication pressed out in a way with which Lu Chi's mind would, I suggest, have been able to cope.

> In my beginning is my end. In succession
>
> .   .   .   .
>
> The time of the seasons and the constellations
> The time of milking and the time of harvest
> The time of the coupling of man and woman
> And that of beasts. Feet rising and falling.
> Eating and drinking. Dung and death. . . .

120

        . . . Out at sea the dawn wind
        Wrinkles and slides. I am here
        Or there, or elsewhere. In my beginning.[2]

Paragraph (d). Couplet 1. Having reached out to the stars in six-plus-six rhythm in (c), our poet comes down to mother earth here with a solid pedestrian four-word grammar to these two sentences. Clearly, he is convinced that unless composers undertake the humdrum work he describes, they will fail in their purpose. I cannot recall anything quite of this kind in the writings of Western critics. Possibly it has escaped their attention. Some poets now and again drop a word, disclosing this workshop secret: witness T. S. Eliot's "leaving one still with the intolerable wrestle With words and meanings."[3]

Couplet 2. There is textual trouble here. The first question is in connection with the two *chieh,* pronouns requiring antecedents. It does not follow that they both have the same antecedent, but in both cases the word may refer to "ideas" and "expressions." I favour this conjecture, and so translate as "some [ideas] . . . some [expressions]." The second question is in regard to the second graph. In Hu K'e-chia's mid-nineteenth-century textual apparatus (cf. Appendix 3), we find the statement, "the text is wrong." He and his fine scholar adviser do not say in what respect it is wrong, and the nearest clue we have to what they had in mind is the fact that the Five Ch'en question Li Shan's text and suggested emendations. The Li Shan text reads as follows:

pao	shu	chieh	hsien	k'ou
huai	hsiang	chieh	pi	t'an

[2] T. S. Eliot, "East Coker," I.
[3] Ibid., II.

In a first attempt at translation this reads:

embracing	heat	ones	all	strike (*or* tap)
cherishing	echoes	ones	cease	twanging

The five Ch'en proposed that *shu* should be emended to *ying* (shadows). This seems an admirable suggestion, for shadows were related to echoes for composers of that era, and I can find no trace of the idea of heat being comparable or contrastable with shadows. On the other hand, shadows do not tap or strike, and although the fecund imagination of the double-harness composers made them liable to mix their metaphors, they do not do so so inartistically as making shadows become audible. Fortunately, there is an instance of *k'ou* being used in a strongly metaphorical sense. In *Analects* IX, 7, Confucius is reported as saying: "When a common fellow asks me a question, he being in an empty state [of mind], I *k'ou* the two ends of the subject and deal with it exhaustively." *K'ou* is rather cryptic here, and Ho Yen (a leader in the Ching-Chou school of thinkers and commentators, a group to which Lu Tsi, Lu Chi's grand-uncle, belonged) expounded it as follows: "What Confucius meant was that he set forth the beginning and the end of the matter so as to state it exhaustively, giving all he knew without grudging." The idea eases our state of perplexity. The associating of sound with *k'ou* is removed and in its place we get a concept approaching very nearly to "strike home" in its metaphorical, non-physical sense. The Five Ch'en commentary also suggests emending the graph *pi* in Li Shan's text to the quite differently formed graph, *pi,* which means "of necessity," "sure to," and urges that *t'an* means "gets played over." I see no adequate reason for accepting this suggestion.

Couplet 3. "It may be": *huo* is an ambiguous term. It can mean "either . . . or," or it can introduce a series of alternatives. The Chinese by Lu Chi's time had long been conscious of what logicians call "the disjunctive antith-esis," but they seem to have developed a constitutional antipathy to a stark "either . . . or" and avoided thinking about that kind of situation as much as possible. They had such terms as *kuai* (directly in contradiction to), but what they liked was a "both . . . and" kind of logic, a middle way. This comes out in their use of *huo,* which for the most part is better rendered by "it may be."

"Followed along a branch . . . followed down the rip-ples": it is hardly fair for poets to intrude their reflections into the philosopher's realm, but some of them cannot refrain themselves; compare the Western "metaphysical poets." Perhaps it is good for the philosophers to have their sometimes cumbrous generalizations put in poetic imagery. So, here, Lu Chi envisages the composer working on the one hand from the general to the particular, on the other hand from the particular to the general—deductive and inductive reasoning put in terms of branches and leaves and ripples and fountain-heads. At the same time we have to remember that no Chinese thinker invented the formal syllogism, and the deducting and inducting that dialectically minded and empirically minded thinkers did was more or less by the light of nature, as we should say. Trained Western philosophers may doubt the legitimacy of using the two terms, deduction and induction, but Mil-ton's words (in a somewhat different connection) may well apply here: "that out of many moderat varieties and brotherly dissimilitudes that are not vastly disproportionall arises the goodly and gracefull symmetry that commends the whole pile and structure"[4] of reason. Lu Chi was an adept at making what his era called "linked pearls," i.e., three—in some cases four—linked propositions, among which the last was a conclusion deriving by inference from the preceding ones. Apparently it was a form of court amusement, for the conclusion is often plain to view as true in theory and not true in fact. (So a Chinese mind playing with our sacred syllogism!)[5]

Couplet 4. It looks to me that Lu Chi is taking the experience of the actual writing a step further here. He has represented the ordering of ideas and expressions and shown two main methods of treatment. Now he urges that although you may think you have got your selected material in order, yet when you come to the actual weaving of it into the growing body of the composition, what you took to be difficult turns out to be easy, or vice versa. Any comments from would-be composers?

Couplet 5. The composition is taking very definite shape when suddenly a new idea intrudes itself. The two images used here have far-back ancestors. A "tiger-change" is found in that (to Lu Chi) well of wisdom, the *Changes Scripture:* there it refers to the coming of an awe-inspiring great man like a tiger emerging from its seasonal moult with burning stripes to take its place as king of the forest. A "dragon emerging" also refers to a great man making himself felt: this meaning is found in the *Chuang Tzu Book*. In the *Changes Scripture* there is no mention of the beasts and their submission, and in the *Chuang Tzu Book* there is no mention of birds being caught in the waves

[4] *Areopagitica* (Oxford ed., 1878), p. 47.
[5] A preliminary study of these linked pearls will appear in the proceedings of the East-West Philosophers' Conference, held at Honolulu in 1949. I understand that this volume will be published shortly.

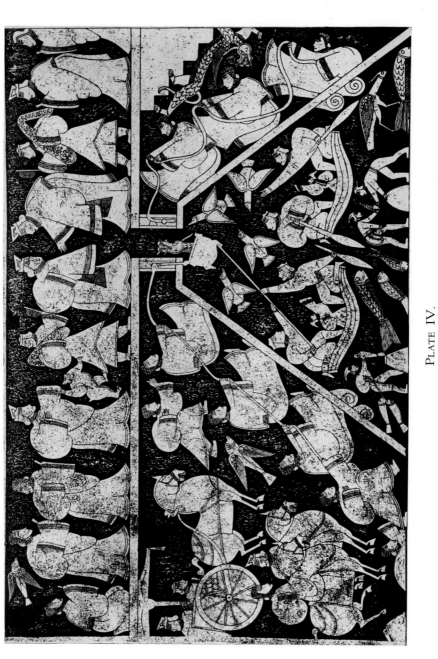

PLATE IV.

Dragon emerging, birds scattering, as the First Emperor attempts to raise a Chou sacred cauldron.
Rubbing from a stone relief picture, c. A.D. 151.

caused by the emergence of the dragon. These are Lu Chi's own vital additions to the images. With regard to the second image, Hua T'ing was quite close to the river where the great Hangchow tidal bore was and is to be seen, but I have found no specific reference to it in the Lu Chi or Lu Yün *collectanea*. There is, however, another line of inquiry which is more productive of tangible results. Near a Han grave of a certain family Wu in Shantung there are stone pictures, one of them depicting the First Emperor (*c.* 246 B.C.) trying to raise the "Nine Sacred Tripods" which the late Chou court officials had thrown into the Lo River. In this picture—a very spirited treatment of the theme—the Emperor's discomfiture is portrayed when, one tripod having been raised with ropes near to the surface, a dragon suddenly emerged from the tripod and bit the rope in two, so that the tripod sank to the bottom. One detail of the picture represents waves with birds scattering in every direction.[6] The story was a favourite one. See Plate IV.

Couplet 6. "In misery": *pu an* (literally, not at peace or not comfortable). The expression in itself is very, very simple, but the overtones of *pu an,* in both the ancient and modern language, are very strong. A sick man who was *pu an* in Lu Chi's day was really sick and feeling so.

Paragraph (e). Couplet 1. After his gruelling experiences the poor composer has to regain his composure.

"Stilled the waters": *teng* is to make water completely still and transparent, with the sediment all gone to the bottom. To say "empty the mind" is very near to Lu Chi's

[6] Wilma Fairbank, "A Structural Key to Han Mural Art," *Harvard Journal of Asiatic Studies,* VII (April, 1942): fig. 6.

idea, for the Taoist practice of contemplative abstraction entailed a turning away of the mind from perturbing thoughts. But the water image with sediment settling is a more profound description.

"Stabilize": *ning* (original meaning, to freeze).

"Peered into his thoughts": the T'ang commentators seem to agree that *miao* (with the "eye" classifier) must mean deepen, and they give evidence for their opinion, but I am not entirely convinced. The basic meaning of *miao* is "to screw up the eyes" and so "to see small," i.e., to get into perspective. That would make admirable sense here, and Ku K'ai-chih the painter, with his new consciousness of perspective, was barely two generations after Lu Chi.

"Put them into words": literally, "made words." As dry and laconic as that? Yes, that is one side to Lu Chi. But note the contrast this makes with the next couplet.

Couplet 2. The pedant says, "But this kind of talk can only apply to writings of high poetic import or of deep philosophical thinking." True. I presume Lu Chi had such writings mainly in his mind. But a surprisingly large number of Chinese pedestrian compositions, e.g., state papers, do contrive to put their business in a setting of heaven and earth and man-in-nature.

"Trapping heaven-and-earth": there is often some element of doubt as to whether a Chinese thinker means the heavens and the earth, or heaven-and-earth denoting the whole physical universe, or Heaven and Earth denoting dual transcendent powers behind the universe, or Heaven-and-Earth, one single transcendent power. With Lu Chi, a man of the third century, impregnated with Taoist thought but not reckoning himself a Taoist, the alternative seems to lie between "heaven-and-earth" and Heaven-and-

Earth." Putting this statement alongside (*f*), 2 and its "taxing Non-Being to produce Being, calling to the Silence, importunate for an answer," I favour the physical "heaven-and-earth": as long as the Western reader makes allowance for the overtone to the concept. To the typical scholar's mind "heaven-and-earth" was something intrinsically worshipable.

Couplet 3. "Parching his lips": sucking the brush till the ink was dried out. Ssu-ma Hsiang-ju, the great *fu* writer and romantic of the third century B.C., was known to do this (cf. *Wen Hsin Tiao Lung,* Chapter 26: "Hsiang-ju held his brush in his mouth and ruined the hairs"). It sounds rather a disgusting habit, but I suppose many book-of-the-month authors, when in the throes of composition, do not preserve the elegant appearance they present to their reviewers.

Couplet 4. If Lu Chi had been a good Confucian dogmatist, *li* would perhaps be more accurately translated by "truth" or "right principle"; but being Lu Chi he must mean what is here translated as "reason," as, indeed, I submit, did the *hsüan hsüeh chia* (transcendental logicians) of his generation. There is no need to assume that he had a very profound meaning to *li* here. Cf. II (*e*) and the slogan to be set up as a "warning whip" to the composition as a whole. *Li,* therefore, is a rational statable proposition which *fu chih* (gives stability) to the subject-matter, doing that by setting up a "main stem." The distinction between what *li* in a man can do and should be expected to do and what *wen* (artistry) in a man can and should do is highly interesting and will come up for consideration in Chapter VI. Meanwhile cf. (*g*), 1, (*h*), 1, Part II (*d*).

"The artist in him": this is my rendering for the one

word *wen.* Margouliès' translation is *"le style,"* and I wonder what he really means. The technical sense of "style" as one of a number of recognized forms of composition hardly appears in Lu Chi's writings, and where it does he uses *t'i* (body with limbs). Cf. II (*b*), 1. If Margouliès is thinking of it in the sense of the *"le style est l'homme même,"* then I submit that *wen* must mean something less idiosyncratic—in fact, artistic impulse as distinct from reasoning *li.*

"Branches": *tiao,* both big and little branches down to the twigs.

Couplet 5. "Enfeatured": what face? In the light of the following couplet there can be only one answer, the face of the mood. Yet this is surprising in view of Part II (*a*), 1, where a *fu* is "an embodiment of an object." It looks rather as if Lu Chi had here unconsciously slipped into thinking only of high lyrical and elegiac poetry, but it is not necessarily so.

Couplet 6. This couplet seems to me somewhat *de trop* inside this paragraph, and it makes an excellent beginning to the following paragraph. However, the rhyme prevents us from putting it there, unless some wizard in ancient rhymes can make the *jan* sound at the end of the couplet fit in with the rhyme class of the succeeding paragraph.

Paragraph (f). Couplet 1. "Joy": *lo* could quite legitimately be rendered as "pleasurable." The same word does duty for both meanings. James Legge has a very discerning translation of the passage in the *Chi T'ang* (Book 22 of the *Record of Rites*): "The ruler led on all his officers to give pleasure [*lo*] to the august impersonator of the dead. Hence the Son of Heaven in his sacrifices [gave expression

128

to] the joy [*lo*] of all in the kingdom." There can be no question that the Han philosopher of ritual there means in the second case a solemn religious joy. So Lu Chi here, conscious of that sublime joy which great composers know amid the agonies of their labours.

Couplet 2. "Taxing Non-Being": *k'o hsü wu.* K'o is used to denote both taxing and divining. Li Chou-han says it means here *shuai* (to lead on), but *shuai* seems to me a little insipid for so sublime a context. I would suggest, therefore, that at the time Lu Chi was writing he was en-gaged in administration and had to deal with the taxing of the peasants. However good an administrator might be in those days, a good deal of wringing had to be done to get the taxes in. *Hsü wu:* "empty," "nothingness," one of the Taoist synonyms for their final metaphysical absolute. *Hsü wu* or just *wu* cosmologically expressed that state of "non-being" with which Chuang Chou (fourth century B.C.) had familiarized the scholars. Lu Yün is recorded as having had a vision of Wang Pi (the most famous ex-positor of the *Lao Tzu Book*), and so to have become spe-cially interested in Taoism. One way and another, we may assume that Lu Chi had a quick and lively appreciation of this austere image. Cf. Part II (*g*) and (*i*). I pray the reader, therefore, to do justice to it, and recall how in our Western tradition "inspiration" has generally been taken as coming from God. Cf. Part II (*n*). To what god or gods do modern poets cry when they call to the Silence? . . . The capital letters are, I think, more likely right than wrong, but I feel equally confident that Lu Chi thought of "an answer," not "the Answer."

Couplet 3. "Span of silk": in Lu Chi's time all writing was done on silk.

"Belching forth": that is the vulgar word Lu Chi uses. Chinese poets have no compunction over using the word.

"Inch-space of the heart": common in poets of that era. I suspect it had a connotation of emptiness, as a passage in the *Lieh Tzu Book* (probably a third-century product) shows.

Couplet 6. "A mass of shining cloud": there is no word for "shining" here, but *yü yün* means cumuli piling up in the sky, and cumuli are often shining white, whilst just "clouds" in English conveys a different meaning.

Paragraph (g). This kind of switch-over from rhapsody to pedestrian detail is to be found in some *fu* writers—not all, by any means. It is extremely characteristic of Lu Chi. This is the final paragraph before he comes to a general conclusion. In the previous paragraph he was portraying one aspect of the final stages, the aspect which gives joy to the composer. Here he gives the other side, the stern discipline which true craftsmanship entails, the everlasting dichotomy between language and meaning, here subtly described under the form of skill and workmanlike accomplishment.

Couplet 4. "Both was . . .": the poem has few phrases which have come directly from an ancient source. Here we have one—cf. *Odes,* I, III, 3: "Whether there was anything or whether there was not, I exerted myself to find it." By leaving out two words in the original Lu Chi gives his deeper meaning to *yu wu* (was and was not). The phrase for struggling is *ming mien, ming* being a pictograph for "toad," with man added as a classifier, thus a fat toad hopping laboriously along gives the idea.

Couplets 6 and 7. In couplets 5 and 6 of (*f*) Lu Chi gave

what Western critics, I presume, would call the poet's
conclusion. Here he gives a cool critical appraisal in general terms: four categorical judgments introduced by *ku fu*
(wherefore, speaking in general), the two words being outside the section rhythm of five plus five. For another five-
plus-five rhythm, see (*e*), 2. Thus he moves out of his
poet's seat on to the bench of the critics. Impressive, I
think, by virtue of the patent fact that he had to struggle
with intractable and inchoate material in order to "finish
the portrayal." Impressive also because it demonstrates
how well he objectified his personal experiences in his
Composer X of the past. The theme of Part I has been
subjective experience that ends on an objective note. Compare Part II, which is objective appraisal that ends on a
subjective note: "Wherefore I time and again stroke my
empty bosom . . . so ignorant am I. . . ."

"Whose eyes exaggerated": a completely literal translation. The T'ang commentators give no ancestor to this
expression, and the dictionaries (including the *Shuo Wen*
and *P'ei Wen Yün Fu*) take one no further. Did Lu Chi
then create the concept? In one way it does not matter
whether he or some recent writer did. The point is, of
course, that there was the kind of appraising mind which
the phrase reveals, particularly in this connection here.
Li Shan appreciated this, for he commented: "The business
[*ch'i shih*] they—i.e., the two classes of men—had in hand
being very different, their compositions [*wen*] were also
unlike." As our modern highly trained intelligence would
react, it stands to reason, but it is useful to know that by
A.D. 302 there were Chinese who appreciated the fact.
Further, Liu Liang (T'ang era) said that the phrase included the concept of *hsüan* (deluding). Clearly Lu Chi

had the idea of self-deluding in mind. So, one kind of man with his visual-mental quirks sees an illusory world, portrays things in exaggeration, out of proportion, and presumably is uneasy about his final effects, for it is the other kind of man who, prizing exactitude, gets mental satisfaction. It goes without saying that Phidias could not have sculptured as he did unless he had prized exactitude. Was his success part of the Greek genius for mathematics? I ask, not knowing the answer to the question, because Ku K'ai-chih, the father of Chinese landscape painting, has a series of paintings under his name (in the British Museum), in which scrupulous attention to exactitude is a marked feature. Yet the Chinese people had not the same genius for mathematics that the Greeks had.

"Versed in dialectic": *lün* (dialectic). Cf. Part II (*a*), 4, where *lün* stands for "dialectical essays." The word seems to have had an earlier meaning connected with conversation, but by Lu Chi's time, indeed earlier, its central meaning was precisely that—"dialectic."

Part II

Paragraph (a). Now we come to a complete survey of literature as classified in Lu Chi's day. Liu Hsieh, the masterly critic of the sixth century, criticized this classification as incomplete, but it is a better one than the Wei Emperor Wen (*ob*. 226) had given in his *Discussion about Literature*.[7] It is complete enough to satisfy anyone but so meticulous a critic as Liu Hsieh.

Couplet 1. "Lyrical poems": there were at the time lyrics written according to the ancient form and lyrics

[7] See the translation of this in Appendix 1.

trying out new forms. Lu Chi makes no distinction: both are expressions of an emotion (*ch'ing*) or mood. Here, obviously, he has emotion more in mind (cf. Chapter I, pp. 21 f.).

"Outcome": *yüan* was being used at the time by Chinese Buddhists for "is caused by." I am not sure whether Confucianists and Taoists were using the word in the full scientific sense of mechanical cause and effect, and Lu Chi apparently had rather a contempt for Buddhist claims (cf. II, 1).

"Subtle elaborations": for *ch'i mi* the commentators are content to suggest "subtle" (*ching miao*). I should have thought *ch'i mi* must be a little more than that, including the idea of being elaborately woven. *Ch'i* might mean "pretty," "charming," in which case the meaning would be a "charming elaboration." In any case the commentators must be right in representing Lu Chi as contrasting the genius of the *shih* (lyric) and the genius of the *fu* (prose poem).

"The embodiment of an object": object (*wu*) must be taken as having a very wide range of meaning, including events and even such intrinsically emotional situations as home-sickness. Thus, the dividing line between a *shih* subject and a *fu* subject was likely to get a little blurred (cf. Chapter III). There can, however, be little doubt that in Lu Chi's mind a *shih* contained a subjective treatment and a *fu* an objective treatment. The distinction seems to me a superlatively important one for literary criticism.

"Transparently clear": *liu liang*. The image is taken from a stream with a clear flow. Presumably "turgid waters" are in keeping with the *shih* style, but not with the best kind of northern *fu*. As Li Chou-han said, "A *fu*

133

portrays facts, therefore it is an embodiment of an object."
Is it permitted to wonder whether some Western poets—
e.g., the French Symbolists and their disciples—might not
have done well to appreciate this distinction, at least other
than they did?[8]

Couplet 2. "Should cloak": the grammar of this dictum
is different from that of the previous couplet. Instead of
erh (and, or, and so) there is *yi* (by means of). Cf. couplets
4 and 5, which also have this construction. It is here that
one begins to suspect that there is a caustic edge to some,
at any rate, of Lu Chi's dicta. There were inscriptions
which did not stick to the facts, and funeral elegies which
showed in what elegant fashion the authors could express
the sentiment of grief. Cf. the indictment of some contemporary literature in II (*m*).

Couplet 3. "Admonitions": references to verbal admonitions (*chien*) from inferiors to superiors—e.g., sons
to fathers—appear in late Chou literature, but formal
written admonitions (*chen,* as here) are not found until
Han times. There started then the practice of admonishing
the emperor in writing.

"Make a break": *tun ts'o* is a musical term for a pause
with a fresh start to follow, so the analogue is clear enough.
There was need to urge that the admonition should be
"forthright," for a graceless emperor was only too ready
to take violent umbrage over too pointed an admonition.
The result was that the "honest servant," torn between
duty and danger, was wont to express his meaning very

[8] In Chapter VI, p. 207, there is a further reference to the French Symbolists.
My attitude to them as there expressed reveals my lack of sympathy with
what are to me their highly tortuous minds. My cautious question above is,
I believe, warranted, and I let it stand in its baldness, avoiding strictures on
composers who in any case were, like Chuang Chou, wizards with language.

PLATE V.

Bronze mirror back, probably sixth to ninth century.

gingerly and indirectly. This cautiousness respected the psychological fact that if a warning was to be effective, the party warned must be led to think that he had himself had the idea of reforming.

Couplet 4. "Balanced elegance": *pin wei.* Cf. I (a), 6, the matching of matter and manner. *Pin pin* is clearly the earlier term, so that the creation of a new expression, with *wei* added to *pin,* points to a new refinement in meaning. *Wei*'s stock meaning is "elegance." In a panegyric the adulationary vein might well run to excess. Good bronze mirrors of this period were *pin wei,* and it was about this time that their patterns began to be somewhat rococo. (See Plate V.)

Couplet 5. "Memorials . . . should." Cf. the grammar of couplets 2 and 4. The commentators are all convinced that *hsien ya* means something like "polish that is unstrained," and I bow to their combined authority. It is, however, tempting to take *hsien* in its alternative sense of "barring out," particularly as Lu Chi's only surviving state paper is distinguished by its even bluntness of factual statement and complete absence of obvious polish (*Tsin History,* Chapter 68, "Ho Shao's Biography").

"Deceptive": one of Lu Chi's masterly *bouleversements.* Cf. II (g), 4, (n), 4, Epilogue, 7, and on a grand scale, II (o), 3, the final statement in his critique. There were several people whom he might have had in mind. For example, Wang Pi wrote a commentary on the *Lao Tzu Book* and the *Changes Scripture,* and his work, though brilliant and illuminating, is not distinguished by its fidelity to the meaning of the original text. The same applies to Hsiang Hsiu, of the generation before Lu Chi, whose exposition of the *Chuang Tzu Book* brought out its wonderful flavour (and incidentally helped create a fashion for free meta-physical speculation) (*Tsin History,* Chapter 49).

Couplets 6 and 7. I have played with the idea that the rough draft which Lu Chi sent to Lu Yün did not contain the sentiments of these two couplets. As we know (cf. Lu Yün's Letter 8, discussed in Chapter III), Lu Yün was dissatisfied over there being no "singing of the praises of virtue." Did Lu Chi then make this concession? We do not know, the evidence not being sufficiently tangible. In any case, the sentiments are very revealing. He is not a disciple of the art-for-art's-sake school, but he insists that writing has its own code of honour, namely, intelligibility and rationality, and, that being so, "there is no point in being long-winded." In characteristic fashion, at the end, he hits out at the moralizers who just go on and on. Possibly he had in mind that dignified bore of the Wu court in his boyhood, Wei Chao, the historiographer and commentator: there is in Wei Chao's biography the record of an exhortation he gave to his prince which reminds me forcibly of an English boy who said to his mother, "How *can* I be good if you keep on talking." The young prince years later, having become emperor, had Wei Chao de-graded, to his surprise. The frivolous spirit of comedy suggests an obvious reason.

"Long-winded": *jung* (*j* pronounced like French *r*) *chang,* in Lu Chi's day probably pronounced *rum-ch'am,* with a rolling lilt on the sounds. The English language is full of binoms like "long-winded" (which has its own onomatopoeic force), and a younger sinologist training himself in the sound of language would do fine work in compiling comparative lists of such Anglo-Saxon and Chinese felicities.

Paragraph (b). Couplets 1 and 2. The new paragraph is marked not only by a change in rhyme but also by a change in rhythm. The first paragraph had the ordinary six-plus-six combination, each sentence having its middle stress on the fourth word. Here we get a stress on the fifth word (in fact, something like four stresses to a sentence— viz., on the first, third, fifth, and sixth words). There is also a repetition, *ch'i,* which gives the effect of hammer- strokes:

> *ch'i wei wú yeh to tzu, ch'i wei t'i yeh lü ch'ien:*
> *ch'i hui yi yeh shang ch'iao, ch'i ch'ien yen yeh k'uei yen.*

In the ordinary six-word sentence there is a slight pause on the third word, the grammar and sense as well as the rhythm calling for it; but the grammar and the rhythm here call for a pause at the *yeh.* *Yeh* is a particle used in the middle of a sentence to stress a meaning; it is often at the end of a complicated subject of a sentence. The pidgin- English rendering would run as follows:

> They taken as things *yeh* (having) many deportments
> They taken as styles *yeh* (showing) repeated changes
> They [as] combinations of ideas *yeh* put a premium
>   on skill
> They [as] commissioned words *yeh* make-important
>   being-distinguished.

Here is the authentic critic, surveying his field, making cross-generalizations after classifying by recognized style groups. To me a goodish achievement for a man who had no comparable predecessor to stimulate his mind. Students might do well to compare Lu Chi with Horace in his *Ars poetica*.

"They": there is no antecedent to this pronoun, but he is doubtless referring to compositions of all kinds. Without wasting a word, the author plunges into what he has to say. I suggest that this plunging is a sign of that unself-consciousness which comes with objectification of the mind (cf. Chapters II and III).

"Air": *tzu* was and is constantly used of distinctive feminine beauty as shown in the individual deportment. Compare our phrase, "she has an air about her."

"[Utterances] of distinction": *yen* usually translated by the vague word "beautiful," but *yen* was constantly paired with *chih* as its opposite, and *chih* is more "rustic," unpolished," than just ugly. In this context, therefore, "distinguished" would seem to be the word.

Couplet 3. For all his anxiety that the meaning should be in command, Lu Chi none the less deals thus early with the music of poetry *and* prose.

There is some question whether the two words *yin sheng* rendered as "sounds" should be taken to mean (1) "sounds" (*yin*) and (2) "vocal inflections" (*sheng*). I do not pretend to know whether there was such a phrase as *yin sheng* used by Lu Chi's time to distinguish between the phonetic of a character and the inflection which went along with it: the Han key-passages seem to me to contradict one another on the relation of the character *yin* to the character *sheng*. On the other hand, although the "four tones" were not classified, named, and accepted until after the Buddhist Conference in A.D. 489, yet the tonal cadences in the language did exist before that date, and good writers had a sensitive ear for them; witness the passage under discussion. I suppose Plato in his time and Cicero in his both had a highly developed taste in sound-variation, but the teachers of rhetoric had not classified these cadences in strict fashion. With the Chinese language tending to be entirely monosyllabic, it became necessary to have strict demarcation between homophones by means of tonal inflections.

"Five-coloured": I say "embroidery" out of deference to the commentators and the reference in II (*e*), but it seems to me that Lu Chi might just as much have been thinking of lovely five-coloured designs such as can be seen today on painted earthenware vases in the Boston Museum of Fine Arts or on the painted bronze mirror in the Fogg Museum. Both these examples are demonstrations of contrasted colours—green, yellow, red, black, and white "lighting each other up." Perhaps, however, the main point of interest here is Lu Chi's comparison of art in sound and art in sight. It is not a haphazard comparison (see II (*g*) and (*k*), the final couplets in each paragraph).

Couplet 4. "Movements and pauses": sounds are one thing, pauses another. As every composer knows, the happy rhythm of a sentence is indissolubly connected with the combination of word-sounds plus a judicious admixture of pauses.

"Pot-bellied disproportion": *ch'i ch'i* (two different characters). It is worth noting that the phrase was used by an early Ch'u poet in a description of an isolated mountain peak as both too high and too squat (cf. II (*f*)). The second *ch'i* normally means a metal pot, and, as the archaeologists have shown us, some of the early bronze pots had thin necks and big bellies.

Paragraph (c). Couplet 1. Out of his eighteen envisaged subjects for criticism Lu Chi selects this one for first place, so presumably he thought it of high importance. It certainly is so for Western readers, for this double-harness way of thinking and writing is not our deliberate way of thinking and writing consecutively. At least, it is not part of our *conscious* literary tradition (cf. Chapter VI). In regard to double-harness, it looks admirable to project your mind deliberately, to get two complementary points of view about what you are thinking. But, of course, as a method it is no panacea to bad thinking. Lu Chi sees at once that the composer may well find on examination of what he has written that Sentence A and Sentence B do not really complement each other. Their relationship is forced —a fault both literary and logical, and one we are familiar with in English prose and verse. The fact that the text has the vague *t'iao* (item) in the first sentence and *chang* (section) in the second sentence points conclusively to the meaning being in reference not only to complementary sentences but also to complementary paragraphs. Complementality on the larger scale has been so much taken for granted by Chinese scholars and so little discovered by sinologists that I must pray the reader to keep it in mind. In this connection I turn to an instance of it on the grand scale in the *Wen Fu* itself, the subjective treatment of literature in Part I complemented by the objective treatment in Part II. To me this combination is superb. I should be glad to know whether it strikes any literary expert as forced.

Couplet 2. "Perhaps . . . perhaps": *huo . . . huo.* Presumably not a disjunctive antithesis, since the source of trouble might lie in both language and meaning. I render *yi* (graph quite different from the *yi* of the Foreword, 5) as "judgments." The two words are more or less synonymous, but I find this *yi* here containing the notion of a mental decision.

Couplet 3. Doubtless all would-be poets and philosophical writers are alive to the wisdom of this course. Presumably this passage reflects Lu Chi's own experience. In this passage we have evidence (supplemented by evidence in other parts of the poem) of this ancient composer presupposing the need for self-consciousness in craftsmanship. I would commend to the student of literature the collection of the evidence in Lu Chi on this matter, and then the collection of the complementary evidence arising from his conviction about objectification of mood.

"Be to the good": *mei* generally means "beautiful," but it is also used in a vague sense of "good." Here it has to tally with *shang* (suffer, i.e., suffer injury) in the second sentence.

Couplet 4. "Inspect your soldiers": so the poet who had been trained in the profession of arms.

"Minutest detail": *tzu chu. Tzu* and *chu* are the names of two ancient fine weights. Six *chu* made a *tzu,* and four *tzu* made an ounce. The expression was in common use to denote minute detail, and that is of course Lu Chi's meaning here.

"The turn of a hair": "turn" is our English idiom, the Chinese being *hao mang: hao* (down on a plant), *mang* (a point). Again, a common expression for a minute distinction.

Couplet 5. "The corrections": an overfree translation of *so tsai,* literally, whatever is fashioned.

"The carpenter's string": a length of string steeped in lamp-black and tightly held at both ends was flicked on to a board which was to be cut in a straight line. In west Chou times, possibly earlier, just a piece of string was used to get a straight line in the building of houses (see *Odes,* III, 1, 3, a short epic which looks as if it has a very ancient origin). The combination of string and lamp-black occurs first in the *Li Sao* (*c.* 343 B.C.). There is no room in this commentary for enthusiasm over Lu Chi's use of this image, but "the inked string" was a term in common use among thinkers as well as carpenters and had been so for a long time. The use of these everyday expressions to denote highly intellectual concepts is a very important study. For example, *mao tun* (lance and shield) was used to express logical inconsistency. Cf. the comment on I (*d*), 3: "followed along a branch."

Paragraph (d). Couplet 1. It is a little difficult at first to envisage what Lu Chi has in mind. If the form of the expression is abundant, i.e., fully adequate and the reasoning copious, one would think that the ideas must necessarily be *chih shih* (pointed in the right direction). First, bear in mind that Lu Chi can only have been thinking of writings of essay or article length. Then, I think, we are familiar with the feeling, in relation both to our own writings and to those of famous writers, that good though the style may be, the meaning is off the point. That, I suggest, is what Lu Chi has in mind, and I acknowledge my debt to Liu Liang for his masterly exegesis. He, however, suggests that Lu Chi was criticizing the style as too rich and the reasoning as too copious. Perhaps so, but I am afraid I am not so sure as he was.

Couplet 2. "In the last resort": *chi* (limit) used as a strengthener of emphasis.

Couplet 3. "A word or two": *p'ien yen* (literally, a splintering of words). There is a famous passage in the *Analects,* XII, 12, in which Confucius says of one of his disciples: "Yu is the man who with *p'ien yen* [Legge: "half a word"] is able to decide a lawsuit."

"Warning whip": *ching ts'e.* It is characteristic of Lu Chi to use in this different kind of context a phrase to which good moralizing Confucianists were partial. He does not actually say so, but it is obvious that the whole composition has to be gone over, and sentence by sentence shoved into line. Does not our expression "tightened up" relate to this kind of situation?

Couplet 4. "Interweave": *tsi,* root meaning "to weave," also "success." I vote for "weave." Lu Chi had just been using the image of dark and light shade, in the last couplet of (*b*), and then in the last couplet of (*c*) he had written *so tsai:* "corrections," literally "whatever is fashioned." Both these ideas come in the farmers' calendar poem of the *Odes Scripture:*[9] "they [the women] begin their spinning (*tsai tsi*), making the dark, making the light (*tsai hsüan tsai huang*)." Considering that Lu Chi had such a strong consciousness of composition as real hard work, and considering the tricks which memory-visualization plays, I suggest that we have reason for interpreting *tsi* as "weaving" and "interweaving." It produces a mixed metaphor in the couplet, but that in *fu* writing was not regarded as a vice.

[9] Cf. Legge, *The Chinese Classics,* Vol. IV, Pt. I, p. 229.

Paragraph (e). My experience with this paragraph may be of use to translators of double-harness. Interpreting *t'a jen chih wo hsien* as "others being more important than me," and *shang lien erh yen yi* as "an injury to modesty and a transgression of public morality" (both of them quite legitimate renderings), I started by assuming that Lu Chi was dealing with pornographic passages. I rejected Lü Ting-chi's suggestion that the subject of the paragraph was plagiarism, for Li Shan especially pointed out that *nang p'ien* referred to ancient works. It seemed absurd to think that Lu Chi was objecting to stealing from such works, for trimmed versions of ancient sayings were extremely common in Han and subsequent literature. However, there is no question but that my first impression is wrong and Lü Ting-chi is right. *Nang* is by no means restricted in meaning to the past of long ago: it might equally refer to the recent past. And with regard to unacknowledged quotations from ancient classics, either the passages were so well known that no one would suspect plagiarism, or, the more common practice, the ancestral expression was so trimmed in language and smelted in idea (to use Liu Hsieh's admirable figure of speech in this matter) that the words did in fact become the later writer's own creation. Quite clearly Lu Chi was not thinking of that kind of plagiarism, but of an unconscious reproduction, or re-creation of some wingéd word which another poet—alas, before him in time (*t'a jen wo hsien*)—had already created.

With regard to this kind of plagiarism, the literary conscience of ancient China and the modern West seems to be the same, but I should like to ask the literary pundits in the West about the smelting and trimming kind. Is there any reason to suppose that poets in particular and writers in general in the West have been less given to what we might call semi-plagiarism than the poets and writers in China? We know well that in China they have been much given to it—on this point, cf. I (a), 6, (b), 4, and (c), 3 and 4—but are not latter-day creative writers in the West so saturated in earlier literature that they do, as a matter of fact, smelt and trim to a large degree? It is not suggested for a moment that they set out to deceive their readers. On the contrary, they rightly and necessarily build from and on to what has been built before, and that they do sometimes consciously, sometimes uncon-sciously. My impression is that if there is a distinction between Chinese and Western practice, it is that the Chinese writers have done it rather more often con-sciously, rather less often unconsciously; whilst the West-ern writers have done the reverse.[10] The distinctive practice in the West may have come from the fact that our writers learnt Greek and Latin in their youth, languages with very different sentence rhythms in prose and poetry. But then we must also take into account what has been so well ap-preciated in critical studies, the effect of the King James version of the Bible on English style.

Couplet 3. " 'Twas bound to happen": the Chinese is just one word, *pi,* which, standing at the head of the sen-tence, had tremendous emphasis, particularly with the sharp change-over from enthusiastic description. The *pi* turns up again in the last words of the paragraph: *pi chüan* (must go out). Cf. comment on (f), 2 and 5.

Couplet 4. "My . . . me": seldom do we find the char-

[10] It may be that the practice is changing, but surely it is open to doubt whether it can change to any radical degree.

acters for "I," "me," "my" figuring so prominently in a Chinese sentence. Usually they are left out altogether. Yet here *yü* and *wo* (the self-centred "me") appear, *yü* as the penultimate word of the first sentence, *wo* in the same place in the second sentence. The nuance of emphasis is therefore quite clear.

Paragraph (f). This paragraph also deals with an embar-rassing subject—or rather, we should say, a subject which, by its highly controversial nature, is calculated to create nervous tension. That subject is whether a writer under strong internal compulsion is warranted in breaking the even flow of his composition and flouting the conventions of compositional discourse. Lu Chi maintains that a man is warranted, and that the result, rough and untutored as it may be, enhances the literary value of the composition. One almost wonders whether the thought of a stain on a man's honour in the preceding paragraph had not sug-gested to him the greater, more intimate question of his poet's honour to speak the truth, whatever the loss in literary elegance. The paragraph certainly is one of the most pungent in the whole *Wen Fu.*

To come to details, the first two couplets are like (*e*), having a four-plus-four sentence rhythm, with the same double-stress quickened rhythm in the second couplet. Then comes six plus six, continuing to the end of the paragraph, but with a striking irregularity in couplet 4, the second sentence of which is seven words long. The subject of discourse is anomalous, and the rhythm cor-responds (see comment on couplet 4).

There is a problem here about the size of the matter

146

considered. The text does not explicitly indicate whether Lu Chi was thinking of just one dissident, uncorrelatable sentence, or whether he was thinking of something on a larger scale, say a paragraph. Li Shan seems to have thought—I am not entirely persuaded that he actually did think so—that Lu Chi meant "one *chü.*" The Five Ch'en accept that suggestion, and Lü Hsiang enlarges on a composer's finding a wonderfully subtle meaning, un-related to the rest of the composition, etc. I suppose Lu Chi might be thinking of that situation, but I am not really convinced. For one thing, do we ever find a solitary sentence of that sort in double-harness writing? As far as my reading takes me, no. Even in Yang Hsiung's *Kan Ch'üan Fu,* with its underlying withering sarcasm, I cannot find a sentence that upholds this interpretation. So also in Ssu-ma Hsiang-ju's *Satire on Hunting.* There are plenty of *tan chü* (solitary sentences) in the dialec-tical essays, but in good double-harness these are generally conclusions to a piece of arguing and are complemented by the conclusion to a complementary line of argument. That kind of sentence does not fit the description Lu Chi gives. This being so, then what actually was it that moved him so deeply that he called on his best powers to describe it? I am entirely at a loss, unless we assume that he was thinking of a whole paragraph. Then it seems to me that we have an exact corresponding object (*tui hsiang*) in (*m*), where he deals with great boldness and consummate command of satire with certain extravagantly praised com-positions of his day.

Couplet 1. "A trumpet-flower": *shuo.* The plant is a climber of luxuriant growth which throws out striking clusters of red-gold trumpet-shaped flowers. It is common in east China, and we may conjecture that Lu Chi had seen it growing in Hua T'ing.

"Dissident": *li chung,* uncorrelated with anything else. *Li* was used by the logician Kung-sun Lung (fourth century B.C.) to denote uncorrelatability. In Lu Chi's generation there were some of the men who came to be known as the *hsüan hsüeh chia* (transcendental logicians), and they were reading the *Kung-sun Lung Book.*

Couplet 2. "Substance": *hsing,* literally, "form," "shape," "body," here in its context of contrast with "ring," i.e., the sound, I submit that substance in its non-technical sense is correct.

"Undisassociable . . . unassociable": in the book under the Taoist Ho Kuan Tzu's name occurs the following: "With regard to the shadow attached to a certain body, and the echo answering a certain sound, the meaning here is that in dealing with the shadow there cannot be any disconnection [*chu*] between it and the body, and in comparing this with an echo [coming from a sound], it would seem impossible that the two should be linked [*hsi*] [without an interval of time]." Now, Lu Chi's statement here in literal translation is "the body cannot be disconnected [*chu*], the echo seems impossible to be connected [*hsi*]"; and one surely is warranted in adding in brackets to the first sentence "from the shadow," and to the second sentence, "with the sound." That is the way smelted-down passages so often act in relation to the respective meanings of their originals. It does not, however, always happen, although clearly it does happen here. The paradoxical behaviour of shadows and echoes exactly illustrates the nerve-racking dilemma which Lu Chi has in mind. On the one hand, the assertive idea is such that the composer dare not eject it, rough and untrimmed though it be. Its sheer outstanding quality brings the writer's conscience under conviction to it. On the other hand, it does not fit and will offend the critics.

To give a wider sweep to Lu Chi's contention, there is our modern controversy between the classicists and the neo-realists, the sticklers for form charging that the latter perpetrate passages which are aesthetically indefensible. The neo-realist's reply is that the universe is like that and the poet's essential task is discriminating portrayal (mimesis). It would appear that the controversy is not merely a modern one, nor one to come up for discussion only in the West.

Couplet 3. "Compassed": *wei* (literally, to interweave as in weaving woof threads onto warp threads). In late Han times there was a prodigal production of *Wei Shu* (Woof Books), characterized by their superstitious tendencies. In Lu Chi's day intelligent people were coming more and more to despise these as intellectually disreputable. Lu Chi may easily have thought of them here; but what he much more clearly had in mind were the polite verses and formal letters interchanged between scholars, compositions in which they embroidered their sentiments —and were never offensively rude. Surely he pleads here for the literary art, that on occasion its conventions may be broken to allow a great-hearted composer, a *megalo-psuchos,* to speak his unvarnished mind.

Couplet 4. " 'Tis a cage to the mind": *lao lo* (basic meaning, to put in a pen, to corral).

"Eject": there is a textual question here. I follow the Five Ch'ens' suggestion of *chih* (eject), but the alternative *ti* (pin down) might do equally well. As often in Chinese, there is a double ambiguity which appears to make direct opposites equally possible. It may be that Lu Chi was already feeling the compulsion in his mind of the "lonely mass" which became (*m*) and which he could not bring himself to "eject."

The irregularity of rhythm mentioned above comes in the second half of the second sentence. The two sentences run as follows:

> *Hsin lao-lo erh wu ou*
> Mind cage-located and so no mate

> *Yi p'ai-hui erh pu neng chih*
> Meaning flitting-hither-and-thither but not can eject

Seven words where normally there are six. The opening stresses obviously come on *hsin* and *yi,* so that in both cases the first three words give a dactylic effect (— ᴜ ᴜ). This is very common in six-plus-six couplets, but the same effect is not so often found with the remaining three words. Some sort of connective coming in the fourth place makes that impossible. Thus the stress in the second half of the sentence tends to be on the fifth word. That fits here in the first sentence, and Lu Chi could quite well have conveyed his meaning with *pu chih,* for that would be understood as meaning "cannot eject." But no, he must make it *pu neng chih,* with the stress on the *chih,* so that from the point of view of rhythm there is a dactyl in reverse (ᴜ ᴜ —). Irregular, to be sure, but how very effective! I say that this is irregular. Prosodically, quite obviously it is so, but it should not be inferred that this kind of irregularity does not occur in good double-harness composition. On the contrary, it does, for instance, in *fu* poems of Lu Chi's generation. Where it does, it is obviously done purposely, to convey a certain emphasis or refinement of meaning, so that here we have evidence of that resilience of rhythm and indeed competence in grammar which is characteristic of double-harness. One wonders whether Lu Chi was so absorbed as he worked out his idea here that when he came to the point he quite unconsciously wrote *pu neng chih*— or perhaps he wrote *pu chih* and then, on looking over what he had written, changed it. It would be good to know, for, I suppose, what the really great master does is to carry concentration to a point where his diction faithfully repro- duces the very pulse of his thought. In this connection remember Lu Chi's advice (II (*d*), 5) about selecting sufficient material and then not making changes. On the other hand, the experiences described in I (*d*) indicate quite clearly his consciousness of trial and error being un- avoidable preliminary to achieving *le mot juste*. As Liu Hsieh noted, some composers do it in a flash, others suffer agonies in trying this way and that. Nevertheless, distrac- tion of attention, for example, weakness for strutting, act- ing to one's self or one's public, that cannot but disastrously affect the requisite co-ordination of poetic powers. Words- worth in certain moods failed just there (cf. Chapter VI, p. 219).

I would urge that this couplet be taken as a *locus classi- cus* for students of double-harness thinking and writing. It shows (without meaning to) that for Lu Chi, with his double-harness mind, an uncomplemented line of argument —or an uncomplemented proposition—obstructs the mind instead of liberating it. Compare the argument in Chapter VI on Descartes and his *cogito ergo sum*.

Couplet 5. Crude jade is found embedded in ordinary

stone. Jade enthusiasts maintained that there was a sort of mystic light to be descried on the hill-side where fine specimens of this mystically purifying and entrancing precious stone were to be found. The same applied to pearls at the bottom of a pool or stream. The reference Li Shan gives is Hsün Ch'ing (third century B.C.). It is worth noting that Hsün says the presence of the jade *yün* "fattens," "gives a sleek shine to," the trees on the hill. Lu Chi says the hill is *hui,* "made brilliant." Hsün says the banks of the pool do not become dry. It might be argued that Lu Chi is taking pains to avoid a plagiarism. If so, how about couplet 2 and its word-for-word correspondence with the Ho Kuan Tzu passage? A delicate point! But it must be borne in mind that in the centuries between Ho Kuan Tzu and Hsün Ch'ing and Lu Chi the two ancient writers' words may have become common property among poets.

Couplet 6. "The thorn-brake there": in pidgin English, "the untrimmedness of that thorn-brake."

"Kingfisher clots": *chi ts'ui. Chi* means "a clot"; *tsui* (basic meaning, kingfisher's feathers). Ch'ang Hsien favours *ts'ui* in its derivative sense of "bluey-green." The image is "massed shades of bluey-green foliage," but a translator has no right to deprive his reader of such pleasures as "kingfisher clots."

Couplet 7. "The rustic ditty": *hsia li* (literally, down in the village). The words were the name of a certain song in the *Ch'u Tzu,* but obviously the term had come to be used generally for any rustic ditty. Here the reference is to the tradition that Kuang, the legendary music-master of the Chou court, had interwoven a rustic song into his famous White Snow music. His orchestra was said to consist of "fifty harps," and probably there were other instruments, wind, string, metal, and stone. Alas! only the fame and the powerful effect of it have come down to us: one legend was that "fairy birds flew down to listen to it."

On the issue of the relation between beauty and ugliness, Li Shan says that "although we know that ugliness and beauty are not akin, nevertheless the one brings out the grandeur of the other." I quote this prosy remark because the *Lao Tzu Book* had made Chinese scholardom very conscious of this element of relativity in judgments of value.

Paragraph (g). The first of a series of five thumb-nail critiques, each of them three couplets in length. Each delineates a brand of composition which misses the mark. In these critiques Lu Chi seems to have poetry particularly in mind. Each of the five small divisions has a different rhyme, in contrast to Part I (*a*), (*b*), (*c*), where seventeen couplets have the same rhyme-scheme.

Couplet 1. "One short strain": charming little poems about a fan or a lady's hairpin and the like, what the Romans used to call *nugae*.

"A foundling production": *ku hsing*. The commonest meaning of *ku* was "orphan." It also used to mean "lonely," but I suspect Lu Chi's sarcastic vein at work. These trifles come from no deep well of emotion or noteworthy response to noteworthy stimulus.

Couplet 2. Rather grandiose and euphuistic? On the whole, perhaps not. The seeming extravagance of the image in this context helps to remind us that for their author *wen* meant "words sent on a high mission." He also spoke of great composers "taxing Non-Being, calling to the Silence, importunate for an answer." Apparently that remark must be taken as applying quite widely in Lu Chi's various fields of *wen*.

Couplet 3. "But": *erh*. In each final clause of each final couplet in these five short critiques there is, as the translation shows, a "but" clause to end with. Here in (*g*) there is no indication of special adversative emphasis, but in (*h*), (*i*), (*j*), and (*k*) the adversative strength of the statement is reinforced by words introduced into the preceding clause, *ku sui* in (*h*) and (*i*), *yu sui* in (*j*), and *ku chi* in (*k*). Thus, in every conclusion to these critiques except the first there is strong adversative emphasis laid on the final remark made. Since one feature of Lu Chi's style is a way he has of getting a quirk of sarcasm across in the second half of the sentence, it would seem clear that the "but" in this couplet 3 of (*g*) should also be underlined. I take this opportunity of drawing attention to the important part which *erh* and another particle, *yi*, play in double-harness thinking. Their correlative use in a six-plus-six-word combination is extremely common. Again and again we find *erh* in the first *chü* tallied by *yi* in the second *chü*, or vice versa. Since the rhythm of the six-word *chü* lays an emphasis on its fourth word and the *erh* and *yi* as a rule occur there, these two connections are plainly of strategic importance in the ascertainment of meaning. I suspect some writers of being careless in their changing from *erh* to *yi* (and vice versa), but the more trenchant ones, Lu Chi among them, I am persuaded, are not so. I take this use of *erh* and *yi* to be one item in the list of proofs that after the unification and standardization of the written language there came to be a steady tightening up of grammar and syntax. Most patently *erh* and *yi* have logical significance.

Paragraph (h). As Chapter III has shown, there was throughout the era of the Six Dynasties a tendency to very florid euphuism—to which a revulsion came in T'ang times. As to such writers in Lu Chi's day or just before, I do not feel qualified to pass judgment as to whether or not their imagery goes beyond what good taste allows. I can only say that after saturating myself in Lu Chi's writings, I find P'ang Ngo (cf. Chapter II, p. 50) rather rococo. I doubt whether Lu Chi would have liked Swinburne's verse, and I suspect that he would have actively disliked the more florid of Swinburne's prose productions.

Couplet 2. "The fair and the foul": that, of course, is what Lu Chi thought about it, not what the author thought he had accomplished.

"Damaged": *hsia.* The primary meaning of *hsia* is "a flaw in a piece of jade." Such flaws are irremovable.

Couplet 3. "The flutes below": I am indebted to M. Margouliès for revealing the significance of this phrase. His erudition has discovered that the flutes were placed below the steps up to the hall of audience, whilst the rest of the orchestra was in the hall and so separated from the flutes by an appreciable distance.

"To be sure—*but*": *sui* (cf. comment on (g) 3) is so often rendered in dictionaries and translations as "although" that a word of warning is necessary to avoid losing a quite common nuance of meaning to the word. In English "although" represents a concession that there is something to be said on the other side. On the other hand, if one party in an argument says, "I of course grant you that ... *but,*" he is not conceding an inch. That represents the extra nuance to *sui* in certain contexts. The *ku* that goes with *sui* here has the meaning of "in fact" or, I would venture to say, "according to the logic of the situation."

Paragraph (i). Concerning compositions that have no drive of conviction behind them, where the author is just trying to be clever. There were many of these in Lu Chi's day, just as there were many before and after him. The practice for an emperor and high dignitaries of his court to call for "command" poems, and even for witty dialogues with conundrums in them, could not but produce this kind of writing. Besides, amongst the many aspirants for posts the most honourable way of attracting attention was by a brilliant bit of writing. Very like, in some ways, London in the eighteenth century, with the new race of needy writers who had to attract a great man's patronage. For the scholars whom Lu Chi knew, the groundlings whose ears were waiting to be split were in high places.

Couplet 2. "Love": *ai* expresses the emotion of loving or "being dear" and is in a very different category from *jen*, the great Confucianist virtue of actual man-to-man-ness. The *ai* in this couplet startled me when I first saw it. What made him say that? I looked at it more carefully, and it opened a window or two on the nature of real writing. It is enough to quote Li Chou-han's comments: "In employing thought on objects, it is necessary that there be the fact of having an emotional loving pleasure in it before it can take shape in words."

"Drift along": *fou piao*, not *p'ai hui* as in (f), 6, the situation being somewhat different. Lu Chi's imagery is exquisitely exact.

Couplet 3. "Evoking no feeling": *pu pei. Pei* is usually

quite rightly translated as "grieved," "sorry," or, alter-
natively, "to sympathize." But it sometimes has a wider
range than that, denoting a tender or, as the case may be,
poignant emotion. Here *pei* must be compared with *pei*
in (*j*), 3, where it relates to feelings aroused by licentious
music. Therefore, my rendering here is "feeling," in (*j*),
3, "feelings."

Paragraph (j). A favourite subject for discussion with
Han Confucianists was the decline of morals, amongst them
sex morality, in the epoch of the Warring States and the
end of Chou. The question is: how far did sex morality
decline, and to what extent did a higher consciousness of
sex hygiene come into existence with its concomitant sporadic outbreaks of profligacy in certain places, i.e., courts?
Here, in Lu Chi's condemnation of licentious writing, we
have a piece of evidence. Clearly, certain scholars were
guilty of prostituting their literary talents in depicting the
lilies and languors of eroticism. I say that without hedging,
because my first impression of this passage was that our
critic might be describing nothing more than slightly *risqué*
elaborations of the amatory theme. After testing each
phrase this way and the other, I have come to the conclusion that this interpretation will not work. Lu Chi's sense
of moral-*cum*-literary refinement was offended by something worse.

Couplet 1. "Run away with itself . . . harmonies": here
the meaning presents a small problem. *Hsieh* and *ho* appear in the dictionaries and glossaries as synonyms for
harmony in regard to music, but I can find no instance of
the two being used together to mean just "harmony." I

take it, therefore, that the phrase *hsieh ho* means making over-elaborate word harmonies producing luxuriant rococo effects.

"A dizzying drumming": *ts'ao ts'o.* I have added to the light conveyed by the T'ang commentators the light of a passage in Chang Heng (*ob.* A.D. 139), the famous *fu* writer, quoted in the *Chung Hua Ta Tzu Tien,* where *ts'ao ts'o* is used in conjunction with the sound of drums. The words are, of course, onomatopoeic. It would appear that the phenomena of jazz and swing were not unknown in third-century China.

Couplet 2. "In the class vulgar": what does "vulgar," *su,* mean here? Quite clearly, I think, an act which not only goes counter to polite manners but is also repulsive by its coarse-grained assertiveness. With that as his meaning, Lu Chi is being pretty damning in his criticism, the more so as these compositions must have been polished literary efforts.

Couplet 3. "Ruinous licentious songs": Lu Chi gives the actual names of two such songs, so I would maintain in spite of some commentators' hesitation. There can be no reasonable doubt about the first, the *Fang Lu,* which, by the way, was made in Ch'u State. The second one, the *Sang Chien,* is less easily traced, but available evidence points to there having been a song of this name, which was that of a place in Shantung where some ruinous defeat took place in late Chou times.

"Refinement": *ya,* not as easy a word as it looks, but the late Victorian "refinement" is good enough, for here it may have overtones of moral refinement to it, although Lu Chi is mainly thinking of literary refinement. Cf. (*r*).

Paragraph (k). Lu Chi's mind swings over to exactly the opposite kind of situation. In dealing with the preceding four paragraphs, the T'ang commentators do not give the slightest indication of their being interested in the very natural question of what authors and works Lu Chi had in mind. The same applies here, and it is rather annoying, since we should like to know for certain whether he is referring to Taoist or Buddhist literature. Probably he had both in mind. The earliest impact of Indian and West Asian Buddhism on the Chinese mind was to induce syncretic efforts, and this syncretizing mind was fully awake in Lu Chi's day. Also, there had been the fine Taoist writer, Ch'i K'ang, poet, mystic, and mental and physical hygienist, who died the year after Lu Chi was born. His writings were much esteemed. I hardly think Lu Chi would refer to them as insipid. As to Buddhist writings, the evidence of their existence is all that the historian needs. There was a well-established Buddhist monastery in Loyang, the White Horse Temple (founded A.D. 69), which in Lu Chi's day was producing a flow of translations of Buddhist sutras and also metrical hymns for service purposes. Lu Chi's father must have known Chih Ch'ien, the Buddhist monk of central Asian stock, trained in Chinese by Han court scholars. Chih Ch'ien was received at the Wu court, given high status as a scholar, and encouraged to translate the scriptures. This he did, putting them into really good Chinese in a way that previous writers had not done. In the same generation Buddhistic composition proper began, a man writing out of his own heart and mood (*ch'ing*). There was, therefore, ample material for Lu Chi to choose from, and to give my own impression of some of it, I can appreciate his reaction—appreciate also the faint touch of wistfulness which I find in him.

Couplet 1. "Agreeable": *wan.* The intrusion of this concept here strikes me as curious. Hence my suspicion that there is a touch of wistfulness in the description. Cf. also "at every turn": *mei*—the emphasis is so very marked. Cf. the poem quoted in Chapter II on his being tired of doing things with consequences. Possibly he is being sarcastic, but I doubt it. In the original comment to a translation of Chih Ch'ien's, we find: "The Bodhisattva mind treads the Great Road [*Tao*], it seeks to embody the Tao, to be engrossed in it, without form and therefore in speech empty [*k'ung hsü*]." Lu Chi could easily have seen such words. Also, he was in the very place where Ts'ao Chih (191– 232) had lived at one time. Ts'ao Chih, the sensitive poet who made a mess of his life and was bored to death by his brother, the first Wei emperor. He had leanings towards Buddhism.

Couplet 2. "Sacred broth": *ta tang*—literally, "great broth." Every so many years there was a particularly solemn sacrifice in the imperial ancestral temple, the Great Sacrifice. The ritual of this was of a peculiarly austere kind, and the broth in the sacrifice seems to have been water only, possibly with just a *soupçon* of flavouring.[11] So, the insipid quality of this kind of writing is flicked into view with an exactly appropriate image.

"Vermilion lutestrings . . . blurred": this was another ritual refinement of the Great Sacrifice. These specially coloured lutestrings were strung loose so as to produce a blurred sound, obviously to have a numinous effect on the

[11] Cf. James Legge, trans., *The Sacred Books of China* (*The Texts of Confucianism*) ("Sacred Books of the East," Vol. XXVIII), p. 96.

worshippers. To Lu Chi, with his sense of music, it was just *not* music. Remember that his second post at court was *chi ts'ui,* an official with duties in the imperial ances-tral temple. Whether this brilliant gibe is compatible with that touch of wistfulness which I suspect, I do not know. I think it is compatible in a poet in whose temperament both romantic and critical qualities lived side by side. The chanting in the White Horse Temple may well have struck him as a little bogus, as also the pompous solemnity of the Great Sacrifice; the more so if his soul was longing for he hardly knew what. There was something irrational about these shows, as about this kind of composition, an irra-tionality brought out by the fact that the music was sup-posed to be so *ch'ing* (clear and pure), and yet the notes were, as Cheng Hsüan, the great Han commentator on ritual, said, *cho* (muddied).

Couplet 3. "Although . . .": the *sui* (cf. (*h*), (*i*), and (*j*)) comes at the beginning of the first sentence. Then the second sentence starts with *ku chi* (certainly, very). So *sui* here means plain "although."

"One to sing . . . sigh": a current practice in religious music, one man chanting and three to act as chorus with ejaculations at suitable points. Whether this was done at the chanting of the Buddhist offices, I do not know.

Paragraph (l). The argument moves on, four-plus-four sentences for two couplets marking the new departure. Having disposed of the lesser species of compositions, Lu Chi turns to those which embody the essential features of good writing. There is surely no need to restrict the pur-view of this paragraph to poetical composition. The in-teresting thing is that he is quite realistic about these

highly commendable writings; they are not perfectly perfect. I suggest that we can have confidence in such a critic.
His sense of the ideal is under control.

Couplet 1. "As for": *jo fu* lies outside the four-plus-four
rhythm.

"Copious and concise": *feng yo.* Chang Hsien seems to
think that the *feng* is adverbial to *yo.* I submit that
"aboundingly precise" is too artificial.

"A double angle of vision": Chang Hsien says that it
means "looking at the earlier half and the later half of the
composition." I suggest, with a full sense of my audacity,
that he does not quite do justice to the grammar here: *fu
yang chih hsing* (literally, a looking-down, looking-up
body). His lack of perspicacity may be attributed to the
fact that double-harness thinking was so much second
nature to him that it did not occur to him that Lu Chi
might be just stating that fact. *Fu yang* was one of the chief
scaffolding expressions in double-harness thinking.

Couplet 2. "True to principle . . . occasion": *yi* (the
right and proper) and *shih* (adapted to the occasion). This
idea figured very much in the Han works on ritual, particularly those concerned with the problems in casuistry
which arose in late Chou times owing to social and economic upheavals. Confucius is represented—I think with
essential historical accuracy, though the stories are doubtless dressed up somewhat—as having insisted that where
the circumstances made the strict ritual with regard to the
burial of parents impossible or inhumanly burdensome, the
rite must be adapted to the occasion. In other words, "The
Sabbath was made for man. . . ."[12]

[12] Cf. *Analects,* III, 3, 4, and *passim* (Legge, *The Chinese Classics,* Vol. I,
pp. 155-56), also *Record of Rites, T'an Kung,* I, 3 ("Sacred Books of the
East," Vol. XXVII, p. 154).

"Analogues": *yü*. I want to press home this rendering of *yü*. *The Oxford English Dictionary* derives "analogue" from the Greek (via the French) and defines (1) an analogous word or thing, (2) a part of an animal or plant representative of a different part in another, (3) a representative in a different class or group. Taking up the search from the Greek end, Liddell and Scott give for *analogon,* "analogous, proportionate, conformable" (cf. Plato and Aristotle). In the *Timaeus, analogia* occurs as "equality of ratios, proportion: as $a:b::c:d$ or $a/b=c/d$. Comparing *The Oxford English Dictionary* and Liddell and Scott, "analogue" would seem to have retained much, at any rate, of its Platonic meaning of precise comparability. We turn to the *Tz'u Hai* (the best of the modern Chinese dictionaries). There we find *yü* defined as (1) *kao hsiao,* "to give to understand"; (2) *ming hsiao,* "to clearly understand—" e.g., *Analects,* "Confucius said, 'The man of honour is *yü* about *jen* [human-heartedness], the man without a sense of honour is *yü* about profit' "; (3) *p'i,* "a comparison or simile." For "simile," see *The Oxford English Dictionary,* "a comparison of one thing with another, especially as an ornament in poetry or rhetoric." Now— refraining from writing a monograph on this matter—I submit that *yü,* being associated with the concept of "giving clearly to understand" or "clearly understanding," is more rightly translated by "analogue" and its associations than by "simile" and its associations. Further, I put it to my semantic mentors that Lu Chi, the poet-critic, in using his *yü* in (*k*) about the very pure writings and saying that they are like the "sacred broth," etc., is, in the strict sense of a Platonic *analogia,* making a proportionate comparison of $a/b=c/d$. I submit to my readers, English and Chinese, that this is reasonably self-evident and I submit to the literary critics that poets can, and do, do that kind of thing. The exceptional imaginative intelligence required if the poet is to hit the bull's-eye is another matter. It may be that the image he uses exactly corresponds to the idea that he is trying to define. On the other hand, it may not. But perhaps he has such skill with words that he may deceive the reader into thinking that it does. And the moral rider is: let us stop calling names when we refer to romantic poetry and rhetoric. I do not mean that I think *The Oxford English Dictionary* does, but there are a good many people who do, thinking of poetry's analogues as whimsical conceits— as if experts in logical analysis were never known to perpetrate analogical atrocities.

Couplet 4. Note that in this and the next couplet the first sentence in each refers to language, the second to content.

"Garb . . . new": this seems nonsense at first sight. The key word, *hsi,* has two main meanings—one, "the lining of a lined garment"; the other, as a verb, "to repeat" and "to carry on with." The meaning here obviously is "to reproduce an ancient style of writing"—for example, the prosodic form of the *Odes Scripture.* A study of the *Wen Hsüan* shows that this practice still was used in Lu Chi's day in spite of the great popularity of the new prosodic form (cf. Chapter III). Thus, Lu Chi means that with the antique garb it was nevertheless possible to achieve something fresh and new.

"A muddied stream": *cho* (muddy) in its root meaning is the antithesis to *ch'ing* (limpid), and from late Chou times down *ch'ing* and *cho* had been used for describing streams, or states of affairs (as, for example, an age being *cho*) and psychological states (cf. *Lao Tzu Book,* Chapter 15). Since couplets 1-3 cover both matter and form, presumably the image here refers to compositions which are blurred in the beginning but become limpidly clear as they go on. "Runs itself" is my embellishment, the Chinese word being *keng* (changes).

Couplet 5. On first examination this couplet appears to contain a third item of critical appraisement of the same kind as those in couplets 3 and 4. Then I noted that the Hu K'e-chia text printed this couplet along with couplet 6. This strictly is the arrangement demanded by the sense. That being so, couplet 5 is in the nature of a subordinate clause to the main clause given in couplet 6. The paragraph as a whole thus makes a very pretty example of succinct movement in the mind: first, three stages of analysis, each two couplets in length, these followed by the conclusion in one couplet. Considering the magnitude of the theme and the complexity, it is a superbly clear piece of literary analysis.

Couplet 6. The sentence rhythm here is seven plus seven.

"Compare them we may": *pi yu.* I need the teaching of the learned here. According to my experience, *pi ju* was in that era more common than *pi yu,* and my impression is that *yu* generally meant what in English is expressed by "as if," whilst *ju* generally corresponded to "like." If this impression is right—and I have no conclusive evidence— why did Lu Chi use the less common *pi yu?* This raises the question of "analogues" as compared with "similes" and again "conceits": the last given in *The Oxford English Dictionary* as "a fanciful, ingenious, or witty notion or expression." So then, did Lu Chi by any chance regard his comparison with dancers and singers as somewhat fanciful?

165

To judge by general practice in regard to images through the Second Han era and after, I should say, no. To judge by the aptness of the two images here, again, no. And yet with his passion for precision, he may well have thought that timing and hitting the key by dancers and singers were similar only up to a point, that there was something in literary artistry which went beyond that point: this in spite of the fact that in none of the types he describes is there faultless perfection.

"Dancers . . . sleeves": they had mittens as well as sleeves, and the clay tomb-figures in so many American museums show the dramatic poses they struck.[13] Note how Lu Chi makes the dancer hit the tune and the singer hit the note.

Couplet 7. The sentence rhythm here is different from that of couplet 6, and again we find introductory words, this time in both sentences. This is very unusual in *fu*. The couplet starts off with *shih kai* ("this, I surmise," or "roughly speaking"). The second sentence starts with *fei*, emphatic negative, the more emphatic for being outside the sentence rhythm of six plus six.

"The Wheelwright": I give him a capital letter, for he was very famous. He comes in Chapter 13 of the *Chuang Tzu Book*, entitled the *Tao of Nature*. The author (certainly not Chuang Chou, but a Han Taoist thinker) decries his fellow men's unthinking way of accepting what they sense about an object as representing the facts about that *that*. He applies the same criticism to books, so unthinkingly prized as representing the full intention and meaning

---

[13] The most graceful of these figures I have seen is in the Honolulu Academy of Arts. The pair in the University Museum at Philadelphia has special interest because it shows the detailed complementality of gesture which two dancers would display. Cf. Plate VI.

PLATE VI.

Dancing girls: clay tomb-figurines. Han dynasty or later.

of the author. His position is that there is an incommunicable essence in a wise man's mind, so that what is written is
only the dregs of that mind and soul. He gives an anecdote
to illustrate this: Duke Huan of Ch'i State was reading
one day in the hall with a wheelwright working down
below. This latter, on learning that his master was reading
"words of the sage," asked him why he wasted his time
reading dregs. The Duke rather naturally was incensed and
replied that he would cut off the wheelwright's head if he
could not justify his words. The wheelwright then explained what an intricate combination of hand and mind
was needed for the shaping of a good wheel. He found that
he could not *yü* (in the *kao hsiao* sense of "give to understand") this subtle skill to his son, it was what the mouth
could not express *(pu neng yen)*, so that when he died this
genius would die with him. That being so, and the sages
being dead this long time, "What you, sir, are reading is
just the dregs and nothing more." Lu Chi might be sure
that his readers would know the context of this allusion
when they came to this passage. That being so, and he
being convinced that good books were not just dregs but
the precious life-blood of a master spirit, it is well to notice
two nuances. He starts off by saying *k'ai* (roughly) and
then turns *pu neng yen* to *pu tê yen,* a stronger expression,
the *tê* meaning "wholly capture." Again we should like to
know whether he just did this in his stride or achieved it
after fussing over it. Whichever way the final form of the
statement came, there it stands, a masterly analogue (or an
ingenious, witty notion) and a comparison characteristic
of his age, in which art was associated with good craftsmanship.

  "Flowery theorizing": *hua shuo.* Li Shan quotes a passage from Wang Ch'ung which clearly makes *hua* have the sense of our "flowery." *Shuo* is the word used in II (*a*), there translated "expositions of theories," which, we remember, were dubbed as "deceptive."

Paragraph (m). This is the longest paragraph in the whole of the *Wen Fu*. Reckoning by the rhyme, it is ten couplets long. At first sight one wonders whether it does constitute a paragraph, since it divides naturally into three sections, couplets 1-3, 4-6, and 7-10, and the connection between them is not immediately obvious. Lu Chi has so far demonstrated not only that he believed in keeping to the subject, but also that he himself had an admirable power of doing so. Even Part II (*a*) and (*b*), which are a little discursive, are nothing like so discursive as (*m*) would seem to be. Actually, it is not discursive at all in the sense of making a hotchpotch of irrelevant material, although couplets 1, 2, and 3 jump from one generalization to another without any visible connection. The cause for this emerges in couplets 4-6, where he bursts out in a slashing condemnation of contemporary literature, or, at any rate, of the rococo productions which were so much admired by the polite society of his day. I say that quite definitely, although Li Shan is completely silent on the point, and the Five Ch'en seem to me to try to bowdlerize the meaning. In II (*f*), Li Shan's comment contains the expression "making a composition which is *li hai*" (violent, ruthless, bound to be offensive). That, I submit, should be taken into account here. In cases like this I am slow to feel positive, but here I do. There can be no question, in the light of couplet 6, that Lu Chi was denouncing, and determined to do so without fear or favour. Luther at Worms ("So help me God!") for the honour of religion, Lu Chi here for the honour of *wen*. Once that is under stood, the psychology of couplets 1-3 and 7-10 becomes clear. In the former he was making a cautious approach; in the latter he was placing himself in the same boat with the writers he had to scourge. However, the translator needs to beware lest his interpretation be more offensive than Lu Chi actually meant it to be.

Couplet 1. About this and the next couplet there is the feel of copy-book maxims being handed out. Lu Chi is desperately in earnest, and he knows he is going to be offensive, so he does his best to make the matter one of principle. This is not to say that he is being gingerly in his approach, for he grasps the nettle firmly enough; but his very caution would warn his readers that something was coming, particularly when they got to couplet 3.

"I . . . hugging to my breast": *ying chih so fu*. The words would recall to the readers the noble passage in the *Chung Yung* of the *Record of Rites* where Confucius said of his beloved disciple, Yen Hui: "If he succeeded in one element of good he grasped it firmly and hugged it to his breast and never let it go."[14] The "I" here is marked by a *yü* in the text, so it is one hundred per cent certain that Lu Chi wanted to emphasize his personal adhesion to the sentiment expressed.

Couplet 2. I have introduced this couplet with an "And," simply because its subject-matter has no ostensible connection with the one before. To avoid a too-personal rendering and since no "I" comes into the text, I here use the sometimes convenient "one."

[14] Cf. Legge, *The Chinese Classics*, Vol. I, *Doctrine of the Mean*, Chapter 8.

Couplet 3. There is even less connection between the subject-matter and that of couplet 3. So again "And."

"To be sure": *sui. Sui,* as has been noted before, usually plain "although," but found in passages which give it an extra nuance. Lu Chi has a hidden meaning here. There are two alternatives: he is covertly referring to himself, or he is covertly referring to the people he is going to offend. My own theory is that the former is certain, the latter uncertain. I would not like to swear to it that there is not a touch of "if the cap fits . . ."

Couplet 4. "Now observe": one word *pei* (literally, that, those) (cf. (*f*) 6, "the thorn-brake *there*"). The *Odes* has it constantly for drawing attention to an object, as if to say, "observe that." In double-harness writing it turns up quite frequently. I suggest that by his use of *pei* as the first word in the sentence Lu Chi's readers would know that now he *had* reached his point.

"Brilliant effusions" and "jewelled creations": not sarcastic, but because Lu Chi piles on the meaning with two highly laudatory expressions, and *ch'ung fu,* the first of them, has a rococo significance, therefore I conjecture that the two should be in inverted commas: what people spoke of them as. Chinese grammar at that time did not have the device of inverted commas, and to indicate such a nuance Lu Chi would have had to spare a word—*yüeh*—to make this clear.

"Like to humdrum crops . . . toil": the text actually has "the beans there in the Middle Plain," *chung yüan chih yiu shu.* In the *Odes*[15] we find, "In the Middle Plain there are beans in the field, the common people gather them." I submit that the second sentence has to be taken into ac-

[15] Ibid., Vol. IV, Part II, Book V, Ode 2.

170

count for discovering the real significance of this startling but very Lu Chi-an quirk, *volte-face,* or whatever we should call it. The jerk is even clearer in the Chinese, for *ch'ung fu yü tsao* (brilliant effusions, etc.) are complicated graphs, whilst the next group are very simple ones. I also would point out that Lu Chi, at the time he was writing the *Wen Fu,* was in civil charge of the Middle Plain and could actually see the peasants sweating, their backs bent, harvesting their crop of beans (cf. "taxing" in I (*f*), 2). The bite about this remark is that in high society poetasters are apt to convey the impression—I include the present as well as the ancient past—that their "jewelled creations" have been tossed off in the mood of a *jeu d'esprit.* Lu Chi seems to say to such, "Now, gentlemen, let's be honest—you and I know only too well what midnight oil has been consumed!" Hence, "humdrum crops reaped by humdrum toil." In this connection remember that Lu Chi had been a member of Chia Mi's circle (cf. Chapter II) and at the dinner-parties in his house would have heard many such "brilliant effusions" read and perhaps may have recited his own. So also, as a member of the heir apparent's household and as secretary to Emperor Hui, he would see all the newest "immortal productions"—until finally he tired of them.

Couplet 5. "On the level of": *t'ung* (the same as, of the same class, equal to), a stronger word than *jo* (like to) in the previous sentence. The combination of *ch'ung fu* and *yü tsao* in the previous couplet may not be sufficient evidence for the inverted commas there, but when Lu Chi says *t'ung* here, surely we can sense an echo of the contemporary laudation of those same works.

"The sack-pipes": there is a high ancestor to this, namely

the *Lao Tzu Book*, Chapter 5. The passage describes heaven and earth as *pu jen,* having no partiality for things in Nature. So also the true sage has no partiality for men as men. Then come these words: "In the space between heaven and earth they are, as it were, a tube-sacked set of pipes. Empty them and they do not collapse, in action they give out all the more (sound)."[16] Transcendental pipes these, their music like the skirl of the winds from the four airs of infinite space (cf. Chuang Tzu, chuan 2): of the winds which were part of the nourishing forces which fructified the soil. The Taoist mind deliberately indulged in paradox and hyperbole in order to set people exploring beneath the surface of things. The attraction of the image here lay in the wind's being invisible and yet so potent: empty, nothing, yet omnipresent like the Tao. As an impressionist picture of the ideal Taoist saint and his impalpable power among men, the passage has its rugged force, but it is of course pure hyperbole—as indeed that unknown Taoist poet surely knew it was. Lu Chi knew it also, for the fantastically exaggerated note it strikes is the very *raison d'être* for his smelted use of it here. With regard to our Western "music of the spheres" which Pythagoras thought he had discovered, and the idea of which has cropped up in so many compositions since Shakespeare's day, it seems to me to be in a different category. But perhaps I am wrong. The odd thing is that the physicists are now telling us how further discoveries in radiography may add to both the "sack-pipe of infinite space" and the "music of the spheres."

[16] "They are": the Chinese pronoun may mean "he" or "they." Which meaning is right here I do not know, but the sage must be included. "Sound" is not in the text, but *jo* (flute or pipe) makes my interpretation likely. Ho Shang Kung's commentary (second century B.C.) supports me.

"One with Heaven and Earth": the ancestor to this is in that arch-representative of Confucianism, the same *Chung Yung Book* which Lu Chi used in couplet 1. In its Chapter 22 we find:

It is only the man who is entirely real in this world of experience who has the power to give full development to his own nature. If he has that power, it follows that he has the power to give full development to other men's nature. If he has that power, it follows that he has the power to give full development to the natures of all creatures. Thus it is possible for him to be assisting the transforming, nourishing work of heaven and earth. That being so, it is possible for him to be part of a trinity of power (Heaven, Earth, and Man as sage).

Although Lu Chi in his smelted use of this passage omits the idea of the trinity which is in the original, it is obviously to be understood as part of his meaning. I say this because the idea of a trinity of Heaven, Earth, and Man (the *San Ts'an,* the three Potencies) was a basic one in Confucianism, indeed in all Chinese naturalistic mysticism.[17] That being so, we have various alternatives here. Either Lu Chi himself thought these effusions were of that rank (which would be absurd) or he made the comparison sarcastically, which would make his statement highly offensive, or he is quoting what the admirers said. I prefer the last.

I have searched for a contemporary *fu* which fulfilled the specific conditions of Lu Chi's appraisal. I find an excellent illustration in P'ang Ngo's *Hsi T'ien,* a *fu* on the ploughing of the sacred field by the first Tsin emperor fifteen years before Lu Chi wrote his critique. In P'ang Ngo's description of the imperial procession to the field

[17] Legge's translation of *ts'an* is a "ternion." I must protest: "trinity" is the only word possible. *Ts'an* is a picto-ideograph—the picture is three stars in triangular combination with a tail of lesser stars, i.e., the Great Wain; and if there be a Confucianist mystic in God's Heaven, he surely sings to the Holy Trinity as *ts'an.*

one can positively feel him rolling the luscious sounds on his tongue, revelling in the jewels of the imperial carriage, the rich embroidery of the umbrella, etc. It is a miracle of descriptive poetizing, but definitely lush. Further, P'ang Ngo does not use the *Chung Yung* statement as Lu Chi does, but he has so much to say about Emperor Wu as being in the same class as the Sage Kings of old and as making the earth bring forth abundantly that his words would suggest that idea to his readers. Indeed, a flattering admirer might well have described the *fu* as being itself of that same fructifying order. Further, my eye catches *ch'iung* (glowing red) (cf. couplet 4) and *ai* (profusion) in one couplet in this *Hsi T'ien Fu*, and I recall that it was written fifteen years before Lu Chi wrote the *Wen Fu*. Finally, couplet 8 talks of declining "into the commonplace in rounding out a theme," and that, for all its pompous flattery, is just what that *fu* of P'ang Ngo's does. I do not suggest that Lu Chi was pillorying his old acquaintance in particular, but in his concentration on his general denunciation P'ang Ngo's writings would easily flash into his mind, and unconsciously he might get nearer to delineating him than he deliberately meant.

Couplet 6. "The prolific profusion there is": *fen ai* (profuse growth of trees and plants). There were the imperial hunting parks, with their belvederes and sunk fences, etc., and I am tempted to translate "so many lordly pleasances." But, if Lu Chi was thinking of such, he would hardly have said *fen ai,* so it seems to me.

"Alas": *chüeh* stands first in the sentence. I am inclined to think this is a genuine sigh. Yet what he says is completely withering.

Couplets 7-10. To get the psychology determining these emollient remarks, the reader might run through pp. 20-22 in my *Chinese Philosophy in Classical Times* (Everyman's Library). He will find there a picture in terms of Confucius' personal statements about the *chun tzu* (the man of good breeding and a sense of honour). Lu Chi's writings display very little actual reference to *chun tzu*, even less to himself as striving to be one. Yet in him, I think, we find one: a wayfaring one, not a saint.

Couplet 7. "The singing word": *ch'ang yen.* The phrase has distinguished ancestry. Legge translated it by "admirable words," and I have no doubt that he is correct. None the less, the graph means "to sing," and "the singing word" for the word that hits the mark at the right time in the right place is hard to beat.

Couplet 8. "Walls": the Li Shan text is *yün* (sound, rhythm), so by juggling the sentence might be made to mean "boggle over a simple phrase." I prefer the Five Ch'en emendation to *yüan* (walls) (cf. Hu K'e-chia's *Textual Apparatus*).

Couplet 10. The image is that of peasants making a tom-tom sort of music and being quite pleased with it. Then they turn and see a group of court nobles with their jade pendants all a-chime. That in Chinese ears was the *ne plus ultra* of pure musical sound. In P'ang Ngo's *Hsi T'ien Fu* he gives an onomatopoeic representation of the sound the pronunciation of which Li Shan gave as *ch'eng ch'ang* (in the modern tongue).[18] Since the modern pronunciation in this case corresponds with the ancient and

[18] The rhyming dictionaries seem to favour *keng k'eng*, but Li Shan's variant has its attraction.

both words are and were on the high-level tone, we can reproduce the very sound of the chime as the scholars heard it sixteen centuries back.

Paragraph (n). This paragraph deals with the psycho-logical accompaniments to what in our Western ideology is known as "inspiration." *The Oxford English Dictionary* definition is as follows: "Figurative senses. 1. The action of inspiring; the fact or condition of being inspired; *a* A breathing or infusion into the mind or soul, *specifically* (in Theology) . . . [the Old Testament prophets are cited as instances]. *b* . . . the suggestion, awakening, or crea-tion of some feeling or impulse, esp. of an exalted kind [Shakespeare cited]. *c* The . . . prompting (from some influential quarter) of the utterance . . . on some public matter."

Lu Chi's approach to this matter is on the surface a very different one, but whether in reality it is so in the last resort is by no means so obvious or certain. Remember that he had his sacred scriptures, and that, at any rate, the dominant idea about the Sage Kings of high antiquity was that they were directly inspired from *T'ien* (Heaven) in their inventions for the benefit of the people—ploughs, boats, carriages, etc., but also writing. With that fact in mind, we are the more able to appreciate the force of his particular treatment of the subject.

Couplets 1-3. The sentence pattern for the first three couplets is four plus four, and *jo fu* (as for) are the intro-ductory words outside the pattern. Couplet 1 is a sub-ordinate clause, couplet 2 being its main clause. Its two sentences have a rather uncommon ripple:

176

lai pu k'o o, ch'u pu k'o chih

Then crash comes

Ts'ang jo ying mieh, hsing yu hsiang ch'i.

Then with couplet 4 the paragraph swings into the six-plus-six measure.

Couplet 1. The mechanical feel about this is unmistakable. A factual mind is at work, noting the existence of action and reaction—to use Isaac Newton's formula with its associations. Actually, Lu Chi's statement takes us beyond the range of that formula, since an association with time is introduced by the word *chi* (a smooth skein of silk), also used constantly to denote an uninterrupted period of time. Thus, there is revealed an appreciation of time as bringing an inevitable reverse process into action, just as by the very nature of the universe the Yang gives way to the Yin and the Yin to the Yang, till time shall be no more. This is one Chinese ontological category, and it is here applied to the psychological world. Lu Chi takes it that this dualistic process functions as substantially in the one as it does in the other. A flow, whether of water or of mind-release, cannot but in course of time bring about a blockage, and a blockage in due course a release. This flowing and damming is normally outside man's control.

Couplet 3. "Shadows vanishing . . . awakening": I presume he is thinking of a shadow vanishing with the mechanical approach of night. So also with an echo mechanically following from a sound.

Couplet 4. "Nature's spring": *t'ien chi*. The phrase comes in the Taoist *Chuang Tzu Book*, Chapter 6, where it says that if a man's passions are deep, his *T'ien* (or *t'ien*) *chi* (Nature's periodic release of a catch) does not work effectively. Whether this refers to the body or the mind I do not know, but I surmise that it refers to both. In the *Huai Nan Tzu Book* (mainly Taoist, second century, B.C.) the effective action of the *T'ien chi* is associated with a man's having joy in himself. Being in that state, he is able to lock himself into this release of the catch, and it is expressly stated that the man's social status—poverty or wealth—neither helps nor hinders a man in this matter (unless he allows it to do so). What was a *T'ien chi?* First of all, as to a *chi,* there is an excellent passage in the *T'ai Chia* chapter of the *History Scripture.* A young king is exhorted to "be like the forester who, when he has adjusted the spring [or catch (*chi*)] of his bow, turns and examines the quarrel to see whether it is right, and then lets go." Thus a *chi* is the *nu ya,* "simple mechanism," of a crossbow. Hence, Nature not only has its mechanical action and reaction as a reciprocal process acting in time: it has also special moments when it marvellously "lets go." Bishop Heber would seem to be not far from Lu Chi when he says that "spring[19] unlocks the flowers to paint the laughing soil," and we may legitimately imagine Lu Chi responding and saying that indeed the swift coming of spring is like the writing-man's soul being released from the winter of its frustration.[20] (Cf. Plate VII.)

"Unreason": *pu li* (literally, not reason). It is an uncommon expression. I have found only one other instance

---

[19] "Spring" in the sense of the season spring.
[20] *Chi* is the last word in the sentences inscribed on the Ku K'ai-chih landscape (see Plate III) with its archer and his cross-bow, its sun and moon, its hills and valleys, its birds and beasts. These sentences point out how everything in Nature is in continual change, "heaps of dust like a swiftly acting *chi.*"

PLATE VII.

A design of coiled springs. Lid of a lacquered box, second to first
century B.C.

of its use before Lu Chi, namely in Chang Heng's *fu*, *Thought the Transcender*. Here for once the learned commentators have no passage to cite. The free movement and the damming (*t'ung sê*) image that Lu Chi is using is one that has had a peculiar significance in Chinese political philosophy. China's agriculture depended to so great a degree on irrigation that the derangement of the free flowing and damming meant the collapse of the social order. So a period of bad government and its accompaniment of anarchy was often described as a state of affairs in which the *t'ung sê* did not function. To the Chinese mind that state of affairs was emphatically "unreason."

Couplet 6. "A riot of tender shoots": the literal Chinese is "a disorderly mingling of tender sprouts in their rushing up in mixed abundance." The image speaks for itself, but the pundit may question the addition of "into bloom." In interpreting double-harness writers one is forced at times to venture on such additions. As an analogue describing thoughts emerging from the underground of consciousness, the "conceit" would seem to have some virtue of accuracy.

"Thrusting up": *sa t'a* was sometimes used of horses rushing together into a disorderly pack.

"Brush and silk": as we should say in English, "pen and paper." This sentiment may sound distinctly rhetorical to some readers, but surely it is the high office and prerogative of the written word to make order out of the disorder of extempore speech. With all due deference to the *élan* of spontaneous eloquence on the one hand, and all due recognition for the faults of laboured writing on the other, the fact remains that without pen and paper, or its alias, brush and silk, few people could rise to the clarity and coherence of sustained argument and discriminate exposition.

"Adjudicate": I am sorry to jar the reader with the juxtaposition of tender shoots and the official weighing up of a case and giving a decision, but *ni* was in common use in Tsin government circles as the term for making such decisions. *Ni* was also used as "to compare exactly" or "to discriminate," and that, of course, would do very well here; but I want to bring home to the reader that the minds of those days which produced poems were also official minds. It would be very profitable to know what experts in mediaeval Latin had to say on this matter.

Couplet 7. "A pattern emblazoned": *wen hui hui. Wen* is the word the reader knows so well by now, "a pattern of lines," "an artistic work," "a literary composition." *Hui hui* was used in connection with the ordered design on a banner.

"A music remote": *yin leng-leng. Leng-leng* means either "cold" or "remote" or "solitary." The idea here would seem to be something the opposite to warm and snug and "matey." The choice lies between "austere" and "remote," or "austerely remote." Lu Chi, a government official in the Great Plain, with his horrible patron just over the horizon, could yet conceive of patterned words (literature) as a far-away music which flooded his ears. Yes. The pipes of Pan. And yet Lu Chi's pipes gave an austere music which —here, at any rate—did not ravish his soul. Nor for him did it cause *panikos phobos*. I suppose that our nearest approach to his idea is to be found in the quieter, more austere treatment of the theme "music of the spheres": a theme which Milton treated with great poetic power, but also rather thunderously, in his "Ode on the Morning of Christ's Nativity."

Paragraph (o). Couplet 3. "Lay hold ... soul": the text, alas, has alternative readings. Li Shan favours *lan* (lay hold of), whilst Lü Ting-chi supports *chien* (to look closely at). The doctors disagreeing, I suggest the following solution. First, apart from the textual variation, *ying,* the adjective to *hun* (soul), presents a problem. Its basic meaning is "a camp," which might do here as "entrenched," particularly if we use *chien* as equivalent to "to look at." But the sense of that seems to me to lack force in a particularly forceful passage. So I turn to the *Lao Tzu Book* (Chapter 10), where *ying* is the adjective to *po* (animal soul): "Can you control your animal soul?" *Ying* also occurs in a poem of Lu Chi's addressed to his uncle, Lu Shih-kuang. There he bemoans his lot as a government official, running hither and thither, and says his *ying po* is longing for his native soil. "Entrenched" does not work in these two contexts. But there is an alternative meaning which Couvreur's *Dictionnaire* expresses very well as *"avide, gourmand."* Compare also *Ta Tai Li Chi* (the "Wen Wang Kuan Li Chapter") and *Huai Nan Tzu* (Chapter 1). In all four passages, "mutinous" is obviously the meaning, and, since a camp in those days was a place in which mutinies did occur with considerable frequency, the connection with "a place of mutiny" and "a mutinous temper" seems at any rate plausible, not to say reasonable. Finally, let the reader turn back to Chapter II and Lu Chi in the field with an army sent to deal with the encroaching barbarians. He then had experience of a mutinous camp.

A striking image! A regiment of illiterate soldiers in miserable, defeated mood, ready to turn tail and scatter, mum-
bling and grumbling, avid for the comforts of home or the
capital. So the composer's *hun,* his "spirit soul," in the
time of its disgruntled frustration, becomes no more than
a sulky animal soul with its ungovernable appetite for
sluttish ease!

"Vital fierceness": *tsing shuang.* "High spirits" or *élan
vital* were and are common meanings for this combination,
but *shuang* was also used to denote fierceness of appetite,
and the two words occur together in the *Tso Chuan*
(under the seventh year of Duke Chao), as also in the
Lao Tzu Book (Chapter 10). Thus, when a lusty babe
was born, his *hun* and *po* being in tremendous fettle, he
was *tsing shuang.*[21] Nothing less than "vital fierceness" will
fill the bill. Moreover, Lu Chi scorned the danger of carp-
ing criticism which could so easily point out that "laying
hold" and "paying homage" in the same breath is to perpetrate a lunatic paradox. None the less, this is both high
poetry and, perhaps, the only rational way to deal with
such an irrational situation. To a double-harness thinker
the two forms of action were not antithetical, the one
cancelling the effect of the other, but complementary. In
the second half of the nineteenth century good parish
clergymen, admirers of Charles Kingsley's "muscular
Christianity," claimed that the way to treat the village
sinner was to knock him down with one hand and pick
him up with the other.

Couplet 4. "Screaming": again there is a textual variation. The Five Ch'en text's reading is the one I adopt,

[21] Cf. Plate VIII, a photograph of a fresco in a monastery near the Tunhwang
caves. It seems to represent a Ch'an (Zen) Buddhist devotee at the moment
of his mystic illumination, when his soul (his *hun,* not his *po*) is born anew.

182

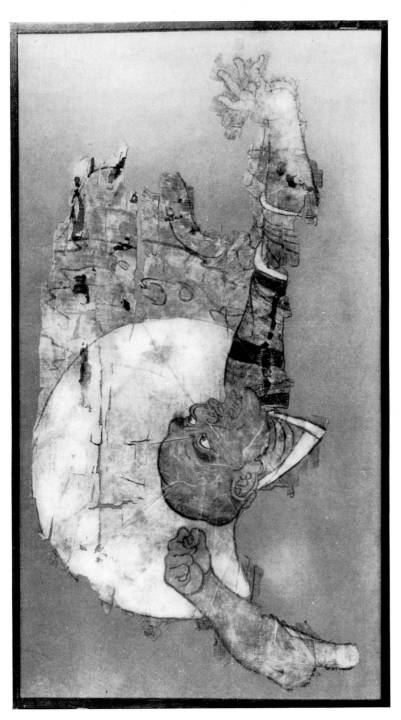

PLATE VIII.

A Ch'an (Zen) Buddhist devotee at the moment of his mystic illumination. Fresco, fifth to eighth century.

the Li Shan one meaning no more than "writhing." As a matter of fact, both readings give us onomatopoeic expressions, Li Shan's being *yi yi,* the other *cha cha,* so that, considering the level of our knowledge of pronunciation and meaning in Lu Chi's time, we may conjecture that the two sets of doubled characters had much the same meaning: writhing and screaming. There is some doubt about the sound *cha cha.* The *Tz'u Hai* gives *ya ya,* but with *ch'i jo ch'ou* (it like being-forced-out) immediately following, there seems a likelihood that *cha cha* is the right pronunciation.

Couplet 5. "These are the reasons": *shih ku.* This construction was constantly used at the end of an argument or a massing of evidence, where it introduced the final conclusion. The simple words of this couplet would have associations for Lu Chi's readers, calling up memories of their childhood, when their tutors solemnly explained how "the Master once said: 'If in speech you rarely err, in action you will rarely repent.' " Lu Chi clearly had no compunction in using the sacred words for the making of a maxim dealing with composition.

It would be illuminating to have a symposium of Western writers discussing the truth of this dictum. How about Immanuel Kant—having his *Critique of Pure Reason* on the stocks for years and years, finally forcing himself to finish it, and then, as soon as it was published, wanting to recall it?

Couplet 6. "This thing": the strictly literal rendering of the Chinese is "the in-me-ness of this thing." In fact, to be even more meticulous, one should say, "the this thing's in-me-ness." The trained student of language will appreciate the abstractness of meaning thus effectively attained. I submit that the movement of the mind—perhaps on a different level—is comparable to what happens to a student of philosophy when he goes beyond acceptance of the traditions of logic and begins considering the logicality of logic. This movement of the mind becomes progressively clear as the double-harness writers attain greater mastery of their genre. I make no further reference to it here or elsewhere in this book, for it is a matter which can only be dealt with by furnishing examples from many sources. And then it would be mainly of interest to specialists in the comparative study of language.

Epilogue

There is no sign in the text of this section of the poem's being on a different footing from the rest of it, but it is to my mind so clearly what in English literature is called an epilogue—that is to say, a rhetorical peroration—that I venture to call it such. Many *fu* have specified *luan* (as they were called), in which the authors are seen to give the gist of what has gone before. It strikes me as mildly rhapsodical, with none of the *Sturm und Drang* which characterized the last three paragraphs. It is as if it were composed after a few days, when Lu Chi had had time to cool down. Also, I feel that there is a strong Confucianist ring to it, part of which impression comes from the last three words of the section: "and daily it [should be] new." These words "daily new" (*jih hsin*) were taken from the very Confucianist work *The Great Learning* in the *Record of Rites*. In fact, the work is so highly moralistic, and the passage was so entirely familiar to the merest schoolboy, that its use as the final word of the poem strikes one at first as complete bathos. But then, notice that Lu Chi gives it a quirk of its own. He jumps from inscriptions on monuments and its flowing through music to—just that. If moral conduct requires to be daily new, so also does real writing.

Couplet 1. "Utility": there were two other candidates here for the meaning of *yung*, "function" and "value." There is no question in my mind that by mid-Han times the idea of "function" with its biological associations was familiar to good thinking minds. Compare, for example, the *Yao Tien (ku wen)* chapter in the *History Scripture*[22] and elsewhere there. But I doubt whether Lu Chi would have said *wei yung*, as he does, if he had meant "function" here. As for "value," it would be a most right and proper rendering, were it not for the modern philosophical associations which go with it. Value, in the sense of "being of high and holy use," is of course exactly what Lu Chi had in mind.

"Endorsed": *yin* (literally, followed out by). *Yin* in Han times was predominantly used, if not entirely so, as a verb, indicating a cause-effect relationship. But I think it is wiser in our present state of knowledge to avoid rendering it by any very precise cause-effect term (cf. comment on II (*a*), 1). Not that the idea of causing was not clear to Han scholar minds and to the late Chou naturalist philosophizers: there is any amount of evidence of that. The odd thing is that Chinese thinkers did not use *yin* or any such uncolourful, abstract expression as a noun to express "cause," until the Buddhist scholars

[22] Cf. Legge, *The Chinese Classics*, Vol. III, Part I, p. 25, and elsewhere in that chapter.

with their *karma*-conditioned minds used *yin k'o* as the translation for *hetu phala*. After the Buddhist influence had made itself fully felt in China, *yin k'o* became part of the general language; but it had not reached that point in Lu Chi's day. To envisage "causing" as a process at work is one thing, to pin down "a cause" as an abstraction and give it a generic title is another, as is also to go on to thinking—or trying to think—of "causation" and "causality."

"Principle": the Chinese word is our old friend *li,* which I have so often rendered as "reason" or "reasoning." In this last instance of the use of *li* I am not drawing back from my stand for "reason" (in the mediaeval sense), but in this particular paragraph, with its rhapsodical note, "principle" seems to me nearer to Lu Chi's meaning. "Principle" without any qualifying adjective such as "functional" or "moral" is rather blurred as compared with "reason" and "reasoning." It can, indeed, be used rhetorically, as in public meetings when a politician urges a point of principle. I interpret Lu Chi as being rhetorical here. At the same time, I submit that the movement in the natural sciences towards each developing its own distinctive methodology opens the door for the Western twentieth-century commentator to conjecture some such movement in Lu Chi's third-century poetic mind.

Couplet 2. You see, we cannot actually talk to a man a million years or even a generation away from us, nor can we bawl to a man a thousand miles or only a mile away. If the more youthful readers of this commentary have never had their attention drawn to what the state of affairs would be without the written word, here is an opportunity to think the matter out.

odes to King Wen, sage-king and father of the actual founder of the Chou regime in the twelfth century B.C. It looks as if Duke Chou, that other son of King Wen, and himself later reckoned as a sage, instituted a special cult of veneration for King Wen. In the sacrificial odes to him he appears as *p'ei* to *Shang-ti* (the Ruler on High): he is represented as descending to earth to inquire into the doings of his descendants and then returning on high to report. What are we to call Lu Chi's use of *p'ei* here? A word indicating that what follows is a whimsical image, or that the comparison in his mind was on a fairly strictly analogical basis? There seems to me little doubt but that the use of *p'ei* indicates the latter. But we can hardly decide without reference to *hsiang,* its opposite number in the second *chü. Hsiang* (translated "symbol" in couplet 3, here translated "image") is one of the relatively small number of real pictographs in Chinese script. Its form depicts an elephant, and elephants, be it noted, were found in north China in pre-Han times, as is evidenced by the survival of bronze representations of elephants in vessels that the experts date as belonging to the Chou era. Further, the *Mencius Book* (end of fourth century B.C.) uses *hsiang* in this meaning. Presumably, these elephants were extremely uncommon, sent as tribute or presents from some far southern potentate. The *Mencius Book* also uses *hsiang* to mean the distinctive outline of a well-defined shape. From this the word went on to denote the physical representation of a non-physical object, and, perhaps, judging by the *Hsiang* Section of the *Changes Scripture,* to denote the non-physical, in that case moral, factors, qualifying the mechanical observable results of divining. In the passage here, literature is, to borrow the language of sacramentarian theology the outward and visible sign of an intangible but very potent influence. Now, how seriously and analogically *hsiang* is used with that significance depends on the attitude of the user to transcendent spiritual forces in the universe. Lu Chi seems to me to have had a deep conviction that there are such forces. In my judgment, Lu Chi was surely a sacramentarian. For him *wen* (the artistic, poetic word) was an outward and visible sign of a world pervading reality.

"Fattening dews": cf. the "sweet dews of the Scriptures" in Part I. The basis of the idea, as Li Shan points out, is to be found in Wang Ch'ung, the second-century writer. With regard to "spirit influences," the Chinese is *kuei shen* (literally, ghosts and spirits), but Professor Ch'ien Mu has recently pointed out that *kuei shen* came to be used in quite an abstract sense, one denoting a force in or transcending Nature, which causes extraordinary events.

Couplet 7. "Virtue": *tê,* spiritual power in special persons. This high utility of *wen* is associated directly with the power of *wen* (with its artistic connotation) to be found in music. So music has practically the last word. We have had ample evidence that Lu Chi was a lover of music. There has, however, been little to show the full scope of meaning which music had to a man of Lu Chi's day, particularly to one grounded as he was in Confucianist doctrines. It must suffice to say that in the first century B.C. there had been a semi-philosophical, semi-psychological interest in music on the part of an influential group in the capital. They were men interested also in the art of government, anxious to verify its basic principles. One outcome of this movement was a book of a high standard in scholarship and good literary merit, the *Record of Music*.[23] The cultivation of music taken as a concomitant of ritual and the dancing that went with it, was exalted as a *sine qua non* of good government. Music, above all other arts, was the power which produced social harmony. Here, then, in this epilogue, where Lu Chi sets forth the relation of *wen* to good government, he winds up by associating the art of music with the art of letters.

"And daily it [should be] new": cf. the opening comment on the Epilogue. The words in *The Great Learning* are in an ethically exhortatory sense. Whether Lu Chi used the famous expression with that meaning or as a statement of fact, there would seem to be no means of knowing. The factual sense seems to me to be not improbable. If that was his meaning, then we might render, "and daily it *is* new."

[23] Cf. "Sacred Books of the East," Vol. XXVIII, pp. 92-131.

CHAPTER VI

THE READER AND THE UNSOLVED PROBLEM

ALL WELL-BEHAVED final chapters of well-behaved books should presumably be concerned with tidying—that is to say, with giving neat authoritative answers to the questions which have accumulated. So only can the painstaking reader be assured that he has not wasted his time. Unfortunately for that imaginary bundle of conscientiousness, this book, as the preface has warned him, is an experiment, and an experiment in which the reader's reactions are of primary importance. It is, therefore, for him, not me, to say what his reactions are to his study of Lu Chi's *Wen Fu,* and the most I can do for him is to assist him in clarifying those reactions. This can perhaps best be done by trying to accustom Western minds to the nature of the problems that arise from our very appreciation of so provocative a work.

I therefore begin this final chapter by raising the problem of the veritable nature of high literary art. I do this from four different angles, in each case using illustrations for the sake of greater clarity—and thus for the greater ease of my undoing, if I be wrong in my point of view.

My first illustration is the universally known and much loved passage in Keats' "Ode to a Nightingale":

Charm'd magic casements, opening on the foam
Of perilous seas, in faery lands forlorn.

These words, it is felt, represent the very perfection of poetry. I would subscribe to that, but I cannot help notic' ing that the peculiar force of "perilous" and "forlorn" is generally lost to the mass of poetry'lovers. The nightin' gale's song on that occasion in the Hampstead garden ex' cited in Keats feelings both of attraction towards "faery lands" and repulsion, the latter because "Now more than ever seems it rich to die." So to him the song of the nightin' gale down the ages has "charm'd casements, opening"— there we see the attraction (cf. stanzas 1 and 2), but the seas envisaged are "perilous" and the faery lands are "for' lorn." There we see the repulsion, for "forlorn" is used in the rather rare sense—namely, that applied to non'sentient things of being distant and inaccessible.[1] Without the reader's appreciating this and the subtle play on words which follows:

Forlorn! the very word is like a bell
To toll me back from thee to my sole self!

he cannot attach any real meaning to "faery lands forlorn." It seems to me quite clear that lovers of Keats make the assumption that because he is writing poetry, therefore what he says should not be expected always to make com' plete sense. I submit that this is the general idea about poetry, so much so that it is practically an accepted tradi' tion. Hence the juvenile Tennyson was betrayed into writ' ing in "The Poet's Mind":

Dark'brow'd sophist come not anear;
All the place is holy ground.

[1] Cf. *The Oxford English Dictionary* and its citation of a passage where cer' tain books are spoken of as forlorn and unknown, like things in a corner.

Lu Chi, faced with the development of a like tradition, disagreed with any such idea, and was convinced, as I have already emphasized, that reason must be in command. My point here is that perhaps Lu Chi was right then and is right for us today.

If such a point of view creates a sense of outrage, and the very suggestion be dubbed an offence against good taste, then all the more is the long-suffering reader ready for the next question. It is one admirably exemplified by Alfred Noyes in his study of Shelley (*Pageant of Letters,* 1940). He demonstrates how the great names in literature since Shelley's time have one after the other seized on Shelley's reputation for atheism, got themselves bemused by his constant preoccupation with the effects of light, and so have failed, with the possible exception of the young Robert Browning, to realize how this poet of light was, with the very fervour of a poet's sincerity, setting forth his credo—his reasoned faith and trust in God and truth. To be sure, his God was not the God of that kind of Victorian church-goer it is the custom to call "smug." To be sure, he could not see God's providence at work in the British social and economic order, but he at least set his poet's mind to work on the basic principles of government, and, further, also knew the question, "For what is a man profited, if he shall gain the whole world . . . ?" For him the two *miracles,* light and water, were *the* evidences of God's existence, and he was perpetually battering at that, "calling to the Silence, importunate for an answer." Yet the best part of a hundred years had gone before another poet discovered this about him. The question is what it was in our tradition of poetry that could blind people to so obvious a fact. One cannot but suspect that it was because theology was one thing in our minds and poetry another, and do not mix. *Ergo* . . .

For light on this matter I have gone to the theologians, or rather to one doctor of divinity, Austin Farrer, author of *Finite and Infinite* (London, 1943) and now of *The Glass of Vision,* the latter the Bampton Lectures for 1948, and a book packed with stimulating material for literary critics. In its third chapter, "Images and Inspiration," he makes a distinction between "images" and "concepts" (which seems to me to be as dangerous to dogmatically minded philosophers as it is true in the context in which Mr. Farrer uses it). "A single over-all conceptual analysis will be about as useful for the interpretation of the Apostle [i.e., St. Paul or St. John] as a bull-dozer for the cultiva- tion of a miniature landscape garden." Then, in his chapter on "The Metaphysician's Image," he compares a scientist at work on any mysterious phenomenon and a metaphysi- cian. Both unavoidably, as is the case with all of us, use "preconceived conceptual yard-sticks," but the metaphysi- cian who is true to the method of his trade "keeps breaking his yard-sticks," for by the very nature of his inquiry "he must not predetermine his choice of conceptual instru- ment." So Mr. Farrer comes to the metaphysician's (and the poet's) use of analogy, "the pipe-line" of "sober and appropriate images." And that is precisely what Matthew Arnold, Tennyson, Carlyle, and the rest of them could not see in relation to Shelley. Light and water were the sober and appropriate images he used, since he, the poet, is subject to the same law as the metaphysician and every man-jack of us; and that law is that "since the human mind understands in the art of discourse, and not by simple intuition, to understand will be to describe" (Farrer, *op.*

cit., p. 67). The only thing is that your real poet is more skilled in using words and achieving fine shades of cogent meaning than we more ordinary folk, including perhaps some scientists and metaphysicians, are able to achieve.

The third question arises in connection with a distinguished contemporary critic, Herbert Read, a learned scholar with a critical sense of history and endowed with a quick intelligence which makes him conscious of ruts: ruts in the literary mind and soul. In his *Reason and Romanticism* (1926), in the first chapter on "The Attributes of Criticism," he arrives, in his last paragraph but two, at this point: "But to return to the practice of criticism. There is in such a ratiocinative process little opportunity for the exercise of intuition. But people will be found to defend, under the shelter of this vague faculty, an emotional attitude which is not without its value. Literature is, after all, mainly an expression of emotional states. I would say it is mainly the control of them. But emotion is the original substance of all aesthetic forms, for even intellectual forms cannot have value as art until they have been emotionally apprehended."[2] Very interesting! What happened when he reached that point: "Literature is, after all, mainly an expression of emotional states"? Did his mind revolt against the glaring half-truth of that conventional assumption, and so out his pen came with the magnificent affirmation: "I would say it is mainly the control of them"? If so, how was it that this unrutted, untrammelled leap of his mind did not carry him one step further, so that he saw that this control is the control of emotion by thought and its concomitant, language? In his previous paragraph he

[2] In giving his courteous permission to make this quotation Mr. Read points out that his views have naturally changed in the course of twenty-five years and he would not express himself today so naïvely.

was there at the very threshold when he complained of the confused, mechanistic meaning given to reason, and urged that reason should rather connote "the widest evidence of the senses and of all processes and instincts developed in the long history of man." But no, he must needs fall back into the old rut with his "original substance of all aesthetic forms" and be content with saying that "even intellectual forms cannot have value as art until they have been emotionally apprehended." Practice in double-harness thinking might have helped him here, so that he at least might have considered the complementary proposition: emotional reactions cannot have value as art until they have been intellectually apprehended.

My fourth question takes us back to Aristotle and the Greek language, which Plato and he did so much to make the sharp-edged tool of the conscious mind. I remember in my Greek-reading days considering our modern meanings for "art," and then in good Oxford fashion going back, in my Liddell and Scott, to Plato's and Aristotle's special usages of the term *technê*. For them, as with the Chinese term *wen*, in its wider primary meaning of "patterned lines," *technê* no more applied to the fine arts than it did to the plain crafts, and was essentially a symbol for skilfully controlled patterns whereby order was made out of disorder. This provided considerable food for reflection. Equally so did *kosmos*, meaning to Homer and Pindar "ornament," "extraneous embellishment": meanings which at a like point in Chinese history came to apply to *wen*. Here Liddell and Scott[2a] tickle my fanciful Chinese mind by translating *kosmos* into the Latin *mundus muliebris*,

[2a] Seventh edition (1882). The translation is not given in the 1940 edition, but the point is upheld.

"the woman's world," so that all ornament seems to become a feminine counterpart to the solid male uncarved block on which ornamentation is laid. Classical China evolved a distinction of this sort in discrimination between what was called the *pen* and the *mo* (the root and the branches); and then the Taoists saved the situation by insisting that the Tao, the *pen,* was, if anything, feminine. So—Plato and Aristotle did their good deed by translating *kosmos* into the solid rational concept of an ordered universe. Such is the meaning it has in the English-speaking world today, and no one cares a farthing whether it meant ornament in Homer's day. Yet, it might be worth our while rescuing art, and poetic art in particular, from our proclivity to make it a *mundus muliebris;* and at the same time to take a leaf out of the Chinese book in which some thinkers came to see that extraneous, artificial embellishment is no true embellishment at all, but a falsification of the original uncarved block. But, some readers will object, that is precisely what the best philosophers of art today do insist. Quite true! My contention is that there might profitably be a more consistent application of this abstract principle in the consideration of the poet's art and the musician's art. And I am a little concerned lest the present-day appreciation of Chinese landscape-painting and T'ang poetry should deceive people of escapist tendencies into fancying that it is "all so gloriously intuitive"—as I have more than once heard it described. It is, I fear, brutal to say so, but remember those "faery lands forlorn."

These four problems illustrate the kind of thing which has happened to me through contact with Lu Chi's mind; and I have come to believe that something of the same sort of questioning wedge should be driven into the inter-

197

stices of our Western literary consciousness. That being so, the next step in this chapter is to go back to the ancient literary traditions of our race. That means going back to Aristotle, for the more a man plunges into the philosophy of literature the more he discovers the forma-tive influence Aristotle and his Peripatetics had on the growth of our tradition. Before I do so, however, I would fain protect myself against two easy misconceptions in the minds of my readers. The one is that because I venture to criticize Aristotle, therefore I see him as a kind of *bête noire*. That by no means represents my attitude to him. The other is that because the subject of my discourse is tra-ditional literature, therefore I am not alive to what is going on about me. I shall deal with this first and come to Aris-totle afterwards.

Here I must confess, as I did in my prefatory remarks about natural science, that I am a very ignorant person, unversed in much that well-educated, cultivated people in America and England have at their finger-tips. On the other hand, it was impossible to live in the world of my adult years without realizing that in the field of literature there were two revolutionary movements going on, one among the English-speaking peoples, the other in China. Through watching the latter I learned something of the former. So, when I went back to England in 1934, it was yet more impossible not to sense that a new kind of poetry had come to birth—or was in process of being born. Finally, when in 1948 the Widener Library opened its hospitable doors to me and I could study in its poetry room, I came to appreciate American literary critics—Mark Van Doren, Cleanth Brooks, Kenneth Burke, Stanley Edgar Hyman, and others—as I had not done before. I have no right of systematic knowledge to speak, for I have only sampled, but since my experiment drove me into these fresh pastures, here is my impression for what it is worth. American criticism strikes me as both more apt and less apt than the British: more apt because it is quicker off the mark, more ready to believe that something important is happening with the new poets; at the same time less apt, in the sense of hitting the bull's-eye, by reason of the sedulously fostered idea in American society that the past need not trammel its thinking and the future is almost entirely in the hands of the new generation. Of course, one must discriminate between the areas from which the literary philosophizing comes, whether from the East Coast or the Middle West. On the whole, in spite of the fact that John Livingston Lowes' *Convention and Revolt in Poetry* (1919)—against the background of his adorable Chaucer —tickles my British conservatism very sweetly, it is the Middle-Western critics who excite my deeper interest. They are learned, but not trammelled so much by learning; and that in my humble opinion is a great virtue, being as I am a little tired of the ancient-university clinging clutch. However, my main impression of the new poetry is that I am puzzled by its apparent inability to get on quicker with its job of not only getting born but also growing up. I venture to suggest a reason for this—namely, that it is so self-conscious: as if a composer sat back from time to time and said, "I know I am being an *enfant terrible*." If there be any substantial truth in this, it is of course fatal to the creative mood. You do not create: you pose. It does not worry me that the ugly and the mean should be portrayed. However abstract art may become, it cannot avoid mimesis of some sort, and if the ugly and the mean are part of our cosmos, then they are; and, after all, honey can come from a dead lion, and the lotus has its roots in unsavoury slime. So my ultimate reaction is that I wish the rebels from tra-ditional prosody would strike the heroic mood without posing a heroic pose, and thus explore further the heights and depths of poetic objectification. They have enough incentive, have they not?

Now as to Aristotle, whose influence I have the temer-ity to criticize, but whose intelligence (*dianoia*) the more I study the less I can discount. It has been part of my experiment to see how he tasted in the mouth alongside of the new flavours to which I have become sensitive.[3] First of all, as I have said already, what a miracle of perspicuity Plato and he displayed between them in their making of the Greek language a sharp-edged tool for cutting out refine-ments of meaning! We are all their debtors, and if we ignore this debt, we do despite to our minds. That must be said, although some of the constructions are so involved that language in its advance cannot but seek more vivid forms of expression. Second, it is true, is it not, or am I dreaming, that the Hellenists have departmental minds, and that the philosophical-minded are not interested in language as living in literature, and the literary-minded are not interested in language as making philosophic sense? If it is true, then surely a little mental cross-fertilization needs to be done. Third, as far as China is concerned, it has had encyclopaedic minds, but never one encyclopaedic in the sense that Aristotle was—encyclopaedic, and at the same time able to envisage a clamant need in Greek

[3] I took the *De Organon* with me to China in 1942, and then when I got back to England, I reread the *Poetics* and the *Rhetoric* and hunted round for modern appreciations of them. Finally, I made a trial run through the other writings in the Loeb Classical Library edition.

thought for a system of universals as a scaffolding for reliable knowledge.[4] So I cannot discount Aristotle, even if
I wanted to—which I do not. He is there in our world,
but for China's edification quite as much as for ours.
The question is, however, to what extent his experience of
literature was sufficiently wide to make him the sure and
knowledgeable guide he has been taken to be. For instance,
Lane Cooper, Professor of English Literature in Cornell
University, said in 1935 that although neither Aristotle
nor anyone else can be "a final arbiter" in these matters,
yet we cannot do better than digest him. "If the student
goes as far as that, he will have nothing to unlearn, and
will have a head full of real knowledge about literary art."[5]
There I must disagree, not through lack of respect for what
Aristotle achieved, but because his perspective was so narrow. He could see the Greek side of the literary mountain
and no more, just as Lu Chi on his Chinese side of the
same mountain could see what he saw and no more.

There is a problem here for conservatives and revolu-
tionaries to unite in solving—a problem arising out of the
particular nature of the English language. That language
has come through its very varied history with a grammar
and syntax in which the Greek and Latin inflections of
nouns and verbs and even the distinction between noun-
forms and verb-forms are not regarded as essential to the
communication of exact meanings. It may be urged that the
English language has thereby gained a resilience of response

---

[4] I am of the opinion that the problem of universals came up for constructive consideration in China in the third and fourth centuries A.D. in the experimental thinking done by the *hsüan hsüeh chia* (?transcendental logicians), whether with note-worthy results it is very difficult to say as yet.
This phase in China's philosophical history has not yet received the inten-
sive group study its importance warrants.
[5] Lane Cooper, *Aristotelian Papers* (1939).

to the demands of meaning which no other Western language possesses: that in its power of adaptation to new
rhythms of thought it can more effectively state whatever
the scientist and philosopher and poet have in them to
communicate. If there be any truth in this claim, there must
be times when the writers of that language must examine
their categories of literary form, and this not with the idea
of relegating one water-tight compartment of discourse to
the scientist, another to the philosopher, and a third to the
poet. Rather we should be anxious to find where the time-
honoured categories do not serve the interests of cogent
communication in all the disciplines of the mind. It would
appear that a good deal of spade-work has been done on
this during the last thirty years, and that some of it has not
been very effective. For that reason I am emboldened to
introduce Lu Chi-an considerations into the battle of the
composers and their critics. I suspect that the scientists
and philosophers are too much engrossed in their respective intra-mural affairs to be ready to accept the challenge;
but I shall be surprised if some writers and critics do not
respond.

May we say that Aristotle had a cooler judgment on the
nature of poetry and prose than Plato had. The latter was
too much occupied with the political issues of his philosopher state. He argued that the poets were more of a lia-
bility than an asset, and his arguments sound very much
like those to be found in the writings of highly moralistic
Confucianists. Aristotle looked a good deal further than
that, although he agreed with Plato in seeing the literary
art as one with other arts in being mimetic. It arose from
a desire to portray; and here Lu Chi apparently agreed
with them. He also agrees with Aristotle in maintaining

that language should be "clear and not mean" (*Poetics*, 67). Beyond that elementary point, the Greek mind and the Chinese mind parted company.

The cleavage was a far-reaching one. Whereas Lu Chi dealt with all modes of considered writing under one heading of *wen*, Aristotle wrote two quite separate treatises, showing that for him poetry came in one category of human effort, the artistic, ranking with music and painting, whilst rhetoric came in another category, the rational or scientific. True, the latter could be regarded, and was in his day widely regarded, as the art of emotional persuasion, but Aristotle set himself against this as the prostitution of what should be the exercise of dialectical reasoning. Further, although his approach to poetry was along the same line as Lu Chi's—namely, the fact of the great writings of the past—yet this drove their thoughts in two opposite directions. For Lu Chi the superb artistry of the former writers had not to any striking degree been displayed in portrayal of action but in the lyrical, the dithyrambic, and the elegiac. For Aristotle, with Homer as the father of poetry and the Athenian tragedians as his great descendants, poetry above all was the representation of action. Dithyrambic poetry with its association with music, the elegiac, and possibly the lyrical were only sub-forms, almost negligible in comparison with the epic and the drama in performing the high function of catharsis, the purgation of emotion.

It would seem that at this point the two views are hopelessly at odds. Search Lu Chi, the critic, for any concept such as catharsis, and there appears to be nothing. Yet, in the last resort that is not true, for there is something which stands in its place, namely *li* (reason), the very governing principle which Aristotle proposed for rhetoric. For Lu Chi that was what putting a mood into words should do for it: it should make it coherent and cogent, something in harmony with the order of the universe, something adumbrating, in its own "lopsided" way yet to that degree accurately, the ultimate reality behind the universe.

There was one direction in which they agreed, although it does not appear in the *Wen Fu* at all and Aristotle was not very explicit about it. That point is *moira* (fate, or fortune, or the lot which falls to the individual), in Chinese *ming*. Now, with the Greeks' adoration of the *Iliad*, it might at first sight be thought by a stranger mind that here is proof of martial patriotism as the guiding emotion in the first Western philosophy of poetry. It is there in some measure, and doubtless for many Greeks of Aristotle's day the appeal that Homer had for them was strongly tinged with nationalistic pride. But for Aristotle the *Iliad* was the portrayal of human action on the grand scale, and human action at its noblest sometimes leads to destruction. Action in the Athenian tragedies represented the same theme, man in his greatness and his littleness compassed about with the possibility of tragic fate, the *mysterium tremendum* of all human life. So also for Lu Chi, man might propose, indeed did propose or he were not man, but fate (*ming*) disposed: witness his words to his enemy who came armed with authority to cut off his life. There was purgation of emotion there, and it is impossible to read Ts'ao Chih (A.D. 191–232) and T'ao Yüan-ming (A.D. 372–427), two of China's great elegiac poets, without discovering how profoundly they exemplify this purgation, each in his own way. But that purgation was in terms of reason. However much their experiences "departed from the square and skulked away from the round," in the end they "completed a shape and perfected a portrayal," an ordered shape, a rational portrayal. For Lu Chi, the Confucianist poet, this was the logic which was to be found in poetry. Aristotle, the Greek philosopher, did not see it that way. He took the matter outside the field of logic[6] and saw it as a moral force operating at the highest level of human imaginative effort. Which of the two critics has the truth of the matter?

It becomes clear that the two traditions in criticism, the Greek and the Chinese, different as they are, do not stand at opposite poles, are not what the logicians could describe as disjunctively antithetical. As phenomena they are comparable, even though the hot-headed romantics and/or hard-shell dogmatists on both sides should claim the vital, if not the whole, truth for their own tradition.

What shall we say of the Latin critics, from Horace to Longinus? Space does not permit of any close examination, nor would it be productive of any great value. Horace, a lyrical poet if ever there was one, yet lived under the shadow of Aristotle's overwhelming authority, and the upshot was, when he wrote his *Ars poetica* (in prosodic form, as Lu Chi did), he was cumbered with the idea of writing tragic drama: a sentimentalism on his part, so I would submit, agreeing with one modern critic who[7] describes the document as "an abortion." Horace might, therefore, with his particular poetic experience, have

---

[6] Cf. Ingram Bywater's *Aristotelous peri Poiêtikês* (Oxford, 1909). The contention there is that the mediaeval tradition that Aristotle never forgot his logic when writing the *Poetics* is wholly misleading.
[7] A. Y. Campbell, *Horace* (London, 1924), p. 235.

forged a closer link between the two views of poetry. But he did not. Dionysius of Halicarnassus, of the same generation as Horace, is useful to us, for he embraced all forms of writing within his rhetorician's purview and thus gives us a literary situation closely akin to the one which Lu Chi summarized. So also with his higher appreciation of beauty in language than Aristotle had: his detailed treatment of rhythm and changes of harmony remind one of the section in the *Wen Fu*. The only thing is that he did not care about reason as Lu Chi did. Lucian (*c.* A.D. 120–180) revolted against this. "Sacrifice first of all to the Goddess Clearness and to the Graces by whom you are quite deserted. Bid avaunt! to bombast and magniloquence. . . . Nay, you have another fault . . . that you do not first arrange the meaning of your expressions . . . but if you can pick up anywhere some outlandish locution, or invent one that seems pretty to you, you . . . are miserable if you cannot stuff it in somewhere though it may have no necessary connection with what you have to say."[8] We can almost hear Lu Chi speaking these words, but not quite. He had his satirical vein, and a sentence here and there shows it, but in the main he is constructive as Lucian was not: he knew at first hand the agonies of discipline a poet had to go through to attain to objectivity of mind. Last of all, Longinus (A.D. 213–273), most learned of critics and an old-fashioned Platonist: he took all literature as his province and had some very discerning things to say on the techniques of commissioned language—e.g., the need for ordering of paragraphs. But from Lu Chi's point of view he vitiates the function of poetry by thinking of it primarily

[8] George Saintsbury's translation in his *History of Criticism and Literary Taste in Europe* (1900), Part I, Chapter 5.

in terms of rapture. Poetry for him existed to "transport" the reader.

In a word, the Latin critics enable us to see the wealth of detailed comparison which lies awaiting exploration. Whether, because the two periods happen to be syn-chronous, these comparisons are the more worth compar-ing is not by any means certain, but there is enough *prima facie* reason for making them the subject of examination. But, most of all, these critics show clearly that the gen-eralizations Aristotle so naturally and sanely made, though on too narrow a range of observation, could in the minds of lesser men become dangerous illusions. Poetry could ap-pear to be no more and no less than an exotic form of sentimentalism. In that respect the Chinese poets of the third to the seventh century could also offend against good sense and good taste, in their case by combining sentimen-tality with virtuosity. But perhaps the most striking ex-ample of this mystification of poetry's noble function, whether after the Aristotelian pattern of thinking or the Lu Chi-an, is to be found in the French symbolists at the turn of this present century. As Mr. Bowra has shown in such masterly fashion,[9] *poésie* for them was the ivory pal-ace of their dreams, the more so because in them it occupied the place which religion had in the hearts of their Catholic friends. Granted that the composer may at one point be, as Lu Chi put it, "swimming in the pool in the heavens with its peaceful flow." But the general tenor of Lu Chi's argu-ment is that a composer has to get past that stage, if he is to create Being out of Non-Being. My unsympathetic mind envisages the symbolists as swimming in the enjoyment of

[9] C. M. Bowra, *The Heritage of Symbolism* (London, 1943), Chapters 1 and 2.

their self-centred imaginings: a psychological state which I conceive as quite able to alternate with agonized fits of self-conscious questioning.

From Longinus to Mallarmé is a matter of sixteen centuries, and a vast amount of water could flow under the literary bridge in that space of time: in fact, a prodigious amount did flow, since there came the rise of the literatures of the European language-areas. Coupled with that large-scale phenomenon came, quickly enough, the psychological phenomenon—the discovery of a new heaven and a new earth. Galileo and Columbus (to name two men to be representative of the discoveries of all the other scientists and explorers) had, of course, as revolutionary an effect on the lusty young languages as on any other department of human activity. In literature, the art pre-eminently of intercommunication, that meant not only vigorous exploration of the new problems of knowledge but also opportunity for comparing one language's literature with another's. This form of intellectual activity has developed with ever-increasing acumen. Nevertheless, even today, with the semanticists well in command of their special studies, we understand little enough of the amazing new areas of consciousness which these new implements of communication opened up. We can discuss one language's particular genius as compared with another's, and by this means saner, wider-visioned literary criticism can be born; but we are still too much at the mercy of our nationalist prejudices to be able to focus critical problems in anything more than rather myopic fashion. Not that any language-area and its criticism should, indeed can, ever afford to ignore its own roots and the soil of its begetting; any such course is patently absurd. Yet consciousness of the other literatures

—for example, the appraisement of their strong and weak points, the appreciation of their distinctive appeals, the realization of the discipline their poetic forms impose on the vagaries of thought and emotion—these, in relation to the literary capabilities which we suck in with our mothers' milk, must today become more and more recognized as sources of new inspiration. They are in fact doing so, giving new and sharper cutting-edges to the mind whilst correcting the drag on imagination which arises from insular emotions.

It is this movement which sets the stale old critical problem of classicism versus romanticism in a new light, and thus enables us to envisage more intelligently certain root-sources of intercultural misunderstanding. There is, on the one hand, the Aristotelian view of poetry as concerned primarily with the portrayal of great action. There is, on the other hand, the current Chinese view of it as concerned primarily with the portrayal of intense emotion. With the help of the Chinese basic concept of *hsin* the heart-mind, one to which the science of psychology gives new meaning, we can go forward with Aristotle's immortal discovery of a catharsis of the emotions and on to a catharsis of thoughts and ideas. Since the natural scientists, by their own confession, are not concerned with values, and the scientific historians can only provide the raw materials for a generation's judgments of the past, and since the *poiêtês*, whether he be versifier or not, is the man who sees undiscovered connections and throws them into relief, i.e., expounds them in memorable language, it is to him that we look to keep our ears attuned to "what the spirit saith." And since it is his words which have wings, it is of vital importance that we investigate what Lu Chi, Chinese of the Chinese and yet more praised than followed in his own country, had to say on the art of letters as the art of reasoning.

With this background to our thinking on poetry, we come back to our friend with the earnest inquiring mind who wants to know what this book proves. I cannot tell him: I should be a fool if I tried.

There is much evidence today that the idea of a pictographic, ideographic language, like the Chinese is supposed to be, has so knocked on the door of our Western language prepossessions that inevitably the intelligent reader will expect a study such as this to throw light on the situation. There, I fear, a disappointment awaits him. What light there is today in sinological studies is more of the ultraviolet kind, not of the plain incandescent kind people expect to get. The fact is that during the last twenty years the philologists and phoneticists have come to realize that the phonetic element in the Chinese script from Han times on is much larger than Chinese and foreign scholars had been assuming. One expert estimates that about eighty per cent is so. That must be a great shock to those whose minds have been so stimulated by the idea of a language which "got across" by pictographic and ideographic appeal. It ought also to be a shock to those who (somewhat unconsciously) feed their parochial predilections by assuming that, because the Chinese language is so, therefore it is basically and incurably an intuitive medium of communication—in a word, it cannot be strictly logical. With the Western dominant ideas about the nature of art and poetry, one can see how that idea comes. If, however, the Chinese language is eighty per cent on a phonetic basis, what happens to this idea?

Two points must, in my humble opinion, be made. The one concerns that estimate of about eighty per cent. Justice has not been done to the immensely qualificatory influence that the pictographically based classifiers must have had on the minds of those using those same numerous phoneti- cally based graphs. Many other perplexing problems pre- sent themselves in the matter, but the chief difficulty is that as yet we have very little idea as to how far the great pre-Han philosophizers (sixth to third century B.C.) (*a*) found that the new terms they wanted could most easily be made on a phonetic basis, and (*b*) used classifiers in making the script a sharp tool for the carving out of ra- tional ideas. In both cases we may assume that they did to a certain extent. But no trustworthy answers can be given to these questions until a lot more higher critical work has been done on certain key books about whose date of pro- duction and general integrity of text we can feel fairly confident. I submit that there is no need to be pessimistic about the possibility of great progress in this direction, but it is certain that such progress can only be won step by step, with many a mishap on the way.

The other point is that we need at the same time to work from the Han end of the problem. Assuming, as we cannot avoid doing, that many of the supposedly pre-Han works are really straight from the pen of Han thinkers, I submit that the next step is to try to assess more accurately what the effect of the unification and standardization of the script had on the minds of reading and writing people. From the grammarian's side (and here he and the logician work hand in hand), why should we not be able to ascer- tain what the First-Han and what the Second-Han achievements were in developing precision and expressibility in the use of the particles (prepositions, conjunctions, and so on)? Why should not good semantic method— technical and philosophical—enable us to discriminate more and more finely between the earlier and later mean- ings of words? Something has, of course, already been done (a great deal when we take Ch'ing scholarship into full account), but I do not see why we should not get on a little faster than we do, both in and outside China.

The above seems to be a no-trespassers sign to the non- sinological scholar, warning him to keep right out. It is not meant to be such, but only as a *caveat* to those who think the Chinese script is entirely ideographic. Theorizing along that line will get you nowhere. On the other hand, for those who find, for example, such a study in words as this present one both stimulating and mentally cathartic, I would urge that their co-operation in this Chinese side to comparative word-study is of strategic importance. For instance, in the writing of this book on Lu Chi, the knowl- edge that I was aiming to present all the data at the bar of the reader's critical intelligence was throughout a rowelling spur—that is to say, both a discipline and an encourage- ment. The point to note is that in so much that has been treated, problems have emerged which are of vital concern to any one who wants to think clearly and express himself cogently. On those problems every serious-minded, de- cently educated man has an opinion worth having, even the man who has taken up the intellectually dangerous pro- fession of party politician. How much more valuable would be the considered reaction of good literary critics, classical scholars, semanticists, and philosophers! (I put the phi- losophers last, because I know a little about them, and they seem to me to be so inevitably engaged in drastic springcleanings in their own house that they can hardly be expected to turn their attention just now to the border-line problems which must, however, ultimately concern them very closely.)

I confess I have been encouraged by this special study I have made. For me it has thrown new light on the riddle of the impact of the Chinese script on the minds of those who used it from the second to the fourth century A.D. I speak subject to correction, but it seems to me that as our study of Lu Chi's art of letters went on, we found more and more instances of his being able to think with extraordinary clarity and force for the very reason that he had before him (i.e., in his mind's eye) a rich variety of ideational symbols which (*a*) had in themselves a hard core of intrinsic meanings, physical and metaphorical, popular and technical, and (*b*) in combination with other symbols, or according to their strategic positions in sentences, had a wider range of meaning. Now, whether this is owing to some peculiarity in the Chinese language, I do not know. In fact, I think that my unavoidable absorption in Lu Chi's Chinese mind actually precludes my having good judgment in the matter. The question, therefore, comes up before the bar of the mind which has not been absorbed in this fashion—that is to say, of the mind which can view Lu Chi's mind and its communicatory contours as a *that*. Do the experts to whom I have referred find anything worth their attention in these data which have been amassed? If they do, to what generalizations do they find themselves drawn? Does Lu Chi appear to them as having thought ideographically?

In conclusion, I have in Chapter I been guilty of making some brash remarks about formal logic. Those remarks do

213

not represent my whole mind in the matter. I have, however, felt warranted in making them because, in spite of
the whole-souled devotion in the West to deductive and
inductive reasoning, a large proportion of the writings
devoted to the exposition of some theorem, whether in
philosophy, theology, law, literature, or even perhaps some
of the natural sciences, has not been written on the conscious pattern of the syllogism. I do not mean that this is
a case of professing belief in God and at the same time being
comfortably disposed to say the General Confession every
Sunday right down to "and there is *no* health in us": but
I do mean that for all the healthy discipline Aristotle's
great invention has exercised on Western thinking processes, it has not been possible to conduct forensic reasoning
(in its widest sense) along that strict line. The Western
mind burst its formal swaddling-clothes long ages before
the Vienna logicians and F. C. S. Schiller got to work.
Francis Bacon, of course, helped on the bursting process,
as did John Locke a century later. If this contention be
anywhere near the truth, then what have been the essentially deductive methods employed?

Alongside this question, almost as part of it, lies the
question: on what foundation of intellectual clarity and
cogency have the great poets conducted the arguments in
their writings? For that many of them did argue, and argue
with ability, is surely incontrovertible.

In order to further the examination of this question, I
have, at the risk of causing offence to lovers of Sir Thomas
Browne and Wordsworth, subjected two specimen passages from their works to a double-harness analysis. The
opening paragraph of the *Religio Medici* appears then as
follows:

214

For my religion,
though there be several Circumstances that might persuade the
    World I have none at all,
as the general scandal of my Profession, the natural course of my
    Studies,
the indifferency of my Behaviour and Discourse in matters of
    Religion
(neither violently Defending one,
nor with that common ardor and contention Opposing another);
YET, in despite hereof, I dare without usurpation assume the
    honorable Stile of a Christian.
NOT that I merely owe this title to
the Font, my Education, or the clime wherein I was born, as being
    bred up
either to confirm those Principles my Parents instilled into my
    unwary understanding,
or by a general consent [to] proceed in the Religion of my Country;
BUT that having, in my riper years and confirmed judgment, seen
    and examined all,
I find myself obliged, by the Principles of Grace, and the Law of
    mine own Reason, to embrace no other name but this:
NEITHER doth herein my zeal so far make me forget the general
    Charity I owe unto Humanity,
as rather to hate than pity Turks, Infidels, and (what is worse)
    Jews;
rather contenting myself to enjoy that happy Stile,
than maligning those who refuse so glorious a Title.

To refrain from going into over-much detail, the following strike me as the constituent elements in this marvel of
prose writing.

1. Although the author uses "I," he is objectified in his
object of attention, namely, the religion of a physician: his
emotions are thus held in restraint.

2. There is appeal to reason, but reason set to work on a
series of balanced pictures which by their discrete balancing demonstrate the intellectual sincerity of the author
and so call for the exercise of the same quality in the
reader.

3. The paragraph as a whole divides itself into three

sub-paragraphs, with three couplets each given to the first
and second, and two to the final one.

4. The main conclusion is, from one angle of approach,
one which he *"dares,"* from the complementary angle of
approach, one which he finds him "self *obliged* . . . to
embrace."

5. The third sub-paragraph, being only a corollary to
the main conclusion, consists of only two couplets.

6. The minor complementalities, thrown in by the way,
so to speak, point to this double-harness handling of the
subject being native to his habit of mind: he does this
almost unconsciously.

May we say that this is art, premeditated but not self-
conscious?

Turning to Wordsworth, I choose the following poem:

There was a Boy;
ye knew him well, ye cliffs and islands of Winander!—

many a time, at evening, when the earliest stars began to move along
    the edges of the hills, rising or setting,
would he stand alone, beneath the trees or by the glimmering lake;

and there, with fingers interwoven, both hands pressed closely
    palm to palm
and to his mouth uplifted, he, as through an instrument,

blew mimic hootings to the silent owls, that they might answer
    him.—
And they would shout across the watery vale, and shout again,
    responsive to his call,—

with quivering peals, and long halloos, and screams,
and echoes loud redoubled and redoubled; concourse wild of jocund
    din!

And, when there came a pause of silence such as baffled his best
    skill:
then sometimes, in that silence, while he hung listening,

a gentle shock of mild surprise has carried far into his heart the voice
of mountain-torrents;
or the visible scene would enter unawares into his mind with all its
solemn imagery,

its rocks, its woods,
and that uncertain heaven received into the bosom of the steady lake.

This boy was taken from his mates, and died
in childhood, ere he was full twelve years old.

Pre-eminent in beauty is the vale where he was born and bred:
the churchyard hangs upon a slope above the village-school:

and, through that churchyard when my way has led on summer
evenings, I believe
that there a long half-hour together I have stood mute—looking
at the grave in which he lies!

I find a great deal of this complementary vision in
Wordsworth. One, of course, comes on places where it
does not apply, and on odd words like the "he" in "he, as
through an instrument" which appear to affect the com-
pleteness of the contrast. In this case, as a matter of fact,
the "he" is all right, since the "and there, with fingers
interwoven, both hands pressed closely palm to palm,"
describes the posture of the hands in themselves, and the
"and to his mouth uplifted, he, as through an instrument,"
brings them into full position, both pictures being concerned with what the boy does in preparation.

The interesting thing is that the relation of main clause
to subordinate does not seem to have much to do with the
clarity and relative force of one picture as set alongside its
complement. The main effect is as follows:

Couplet 1. (a) There was a Boy. (b) Nature *in re*
the Boy.

Couplet 2. (a) Nature at the specific time. (b) The
Boy in his specific place.

Couplet 3. (*a*) The Boy's hands assuming specific posture. (*b*) The same finally in position.

Couplet 4. (*a*) What he did. (*b*) What the owls did.

Couplet 5. (*a*) Extra detail *re* owls. (*b*) The echoes therefrom.

Couplet 6. (*a*) Pause due to owls. (*b*) The Boy's response, listening.

Couplet 7. (*a*) Influence of Nature on him as sound. (*b*) As vision.

Couplet 8. (*a*) Extra detail *re* vision. (*b*) The reflection.

Couplet 9. (*a*) Introduction of death. (*b*) The Boy still young, alas!

Couplet 10. (*a*) The lovely place he lived in. (*b*) The position of the churchyard.

Couplet 11. (*a*) How Wordsworth came into the picture. (*b*) What he did and felt *re* the Boy.

In general appraisal after such an analysis the following items strike me:

A. The mental picture as a whole, with one possible exception, is drawn with great economy and suggestiveness, and with admirable accumulative effect.

B. The art in the description consists in the ordered contrast of different small pictures delineated in pairs.

C. The central significance of the whole picture is a double-visioned one (see couplets 4 and 5, and couplets 7 and 8), and each of these two pairs of couplets gives extra detail from a double angle of vision, thus giving the stress required to what is the most important part of the poem.

I am very dubious as to whether couplet 11 is not entirely wrong in vein, and whether it is not an instance of that touch of posing as a poet which came to be so marked in Wordsworth. If he had realized sufficiently that he was "embodying an object," or, to put it more stringently, had been objectified more completely on the object of his attention, he would have left that sentimental couplet out, and thus have avoided the bathos in "I believe" and the frilly "summer evenings" and "long half-hour" and "mute." Bless the man! Would his readers have expected him to be singing? No—that is bad art, drawing attention to the POET in a slouch hat.

Thus Sir Thomas Browne and William Wordsworth, the latter capable of muddling his objective description by the obtrusion of the egotistical "I," the former with his scientific habits of thought achieving a constant stream of well-balanced images. He is the double-harness writer *par excellence* in the history of English literature, the judicious mind functioning with a double angle of vision. But, if we turn to the Shakespeare of the plays *and* the *Sonnets,* we find clear traces there, as, for instance in the meditation on "To be or not to be," and the one on cosmic chaos in relation to social disorders in *Troilus and Cressida.* So, too, I would say, do we find it in Pope, with his neat antitheses confined to the neat measure of his lines. Blake is the really fascinating study, for in him we find the craftsman-artist and the etcher of sentences in such intimate combination. On the one hand, his streak of classicism filled the eyes of his imagination with looming mythical figures which line and chiaroscuro could so barely reduce to the order of co-herent design. On the other hand, the strait-jacket of con-ventional prosody enabled him to say what he had to say in extraordinarily clear word-pictures. How far is a double angle of vision to be found in his poetry as the key to this clarity?

The question is not merely historical: it is vital in rela-tion to contemporary movements in poetry and in science. The latter field is not within our sphere of observation at the moment, but modern poetry very definitely is. The movement there has been described as a "Copernican revolution" taking place, by which, for example, "sub-jective idealism has been replaced by an absolutism in which the thoughts of a single soul are the thoughts of the Whole."[10] The words were written of Paul Valéry when he broke the chain of his symbolistic youth. As-suming that they are true of him, a French poet, and that in the France and Europe of the first World War, it does not necessarily follow that they are true of poets who have composed since in the English language and to whom absolutisms do not come naturally and easily. Yet, Valéry's influence is potent. May it be that the Coper-nican revolution here is the use of a new talent for "a double angle of vision," a talent for engrossing the com-posing self in the world beyond its eyebrows, and also engrossing that world in the self which, however great its power of extrovert imagination, never loses for long its sense of self-identity? In a word, does the new poetry reveal a man conscious of the universe's experimenting with him and of his experimenting with the universe? And

[10] Bowra, *op. cit.*, p. 24.

since language and meaning are inextricably intermingled, may it be that here is the key to the breaking of the bonds of conventional prosodic form, the poet being far too anxious to get his images into the right juxtaposition, with this stress laid here and that laid there, with the result that he cannot afford to follow the rhythm of an even line? If so, then, these experiments are profoundly significant, inchoate though some of them are, for they delineate experiments in the mind subjected to the discipline of patterned communication.

The question then resolves itself into one which takes us back into history—the history of Chinese thought and expression. This new question is whether the double-harness style was more suited to a dogmatic mind or to an experimental one. Syllogistic reasoning is regarded from the vantage-point of today as having been in history the most admirable tool of dogmatic minds arguing from the fixed point of the existence of God and the revelation of ultimate truth to His servant the Church. Was the *p'ien wen* (double-harness) style something of the same sort for Chinese thinkers? Here is a challenge to the scholars in the Chinese field, and I shall only say that as far as my study of later *p'ien wen* developments take me, I find evidence going both ways. That the dogmatist found it useful cannot be doubted, because the Eight-Legged Essay of the Ming and Manchu eras was the nephew, if not the very child, of the Sung-era double-harness stylists.

Also Han Yü, the enemy of romanticism in religion and literature, staunch upholder of the Confucian tradition in an age which "went a-whoring after strange gods": Han Yü, for all his opposition to the double-harness stylists of his day, yet couched his stately dialectic in sentences which were double-harness in meaning if not in precise form. On the other hand, Liu Hsieh, the greatest of literary critics, who developed Lu Chi's ideas with an immense attention to detail, in chapter after chapter of his *The Literary Mind and Its Carving of Dragons* is just as plainly experimenting with his data. I submit that he and Lu Chi between them establish a *prima facie* case for double-harness as an admirable tool for experimental ratiocination. I also submit to the philosophers, amongst whom are both the Roman and non-Roman neo-Thomists, that the Angelic Doctor contributed to the world not only a great body of dogmatic reflection but also an experiment in reasoning from a double angle of vision.

The next question arises in connection with the sleight-of-hand which is found in all literatures and by which the composer communicates in the third person, that is to say, through the speech of one or more interlocutors. It would seem to be a device to which scientists are particularly prone, since they describe their experience in impersonal language. They imagine themselves as Mr. X., the completely detached and impartial observer, and proceed calmly on their way from their initial hypotheses to their finally achieved conclusions. Yet, if Whitehead is to be believed, some of them need to take a leaf out of the grammarian's book, and still more out of the poet's book. Their imagined Mr. X. is not always so cogent and concise as the subject-matter requires. Mr. X., however, has been of the utmost value to them, as he has been to the poets. The question is, then, whether in the production of compositions both "copious and concise . . . true to principle [?reason] and adapted to the occasion," there has not been a very striking measure of success achieved by this impersonalizing method. Does it not contain the secret of the drama's appeal to the mind as well as to the emotions? Does not Shakespeare's "To be or not to be" achieve more depth of meaning and more universal cogency from the fact that its author first envisaged one Hamlet and thereby discovered the idea, the idea which shaped itself in that particular pattern of words? The interesting thing is that some philosophers found that they needed to do this—Plato for one, Bishop Berkeley, for another, in his *Alciphron,* and, for another, that acute and wayward philosophizer on men and society, Bernard Shaw. Obviously, the device is capable of gross misuse at the hands of a dishonest practitioner, one practised in deceiving himself, as is the case with some of the people who make God their interlocutor. But the device stands today as one of the great achievements of the human intellect: the intellect at its peak of imaginative energy, and possibly most so when a modest, shrinking Jeremiah forces himself to say, "Thus saith the Lord, the High and Holy One of Israel." A whole battery of questions emerges. What has the scientist to learn from the poet in this matter? What has the poet to learn from the scientist? Is this skilful use of the device to be regarded as a rhetorical sleight-of-hand in which the quickness of the hand deceives the eye, or is it one of the foundation-stones on which the proud house of reason may be erected?

We come, finally, to the artist pre-eminent, the painter and the sculptor, who in their respective ways set out to portray. They cannot be ignored, if only for the reason that the era in China which produced the double-harness mind in literature also produced great sculpture and within two generations of Lu Chi produced Ku K'ai-chih, the greatest of the early scholar-painters. With my amateur knowledge in this field, I speak with bated breath. Two questions, however, thrust themselves forward. The one is: since with the growing influence of Buddhism in China the art of sculpture became more and more subject to theo-logical pressure, what was it in landscape-painting which escaped in part that pressure? The other is: how do the experts account for the fact that when that Buddhist pressure was relaxed in the eleventh and twelfth centuries (Sung era), landscape-painting reached new heights of expression in portrayal whilst sculpture never again took a new lease of life? I ask because I suspect that in regard to both questions the main answer lies along the line that the double-harness habit of thought and composi-tion had a free expression in landscape-painting and that in sculpture it had not. The endless curves in T'ang sculpture, entrancing as they were, led literally and sym-bolically to nowhere. The rational scholar mind had been trained to see straight lines as well as curves, to require contrasts of light and dark, to look down and to look up. In this way the art of making patterns in sentences led on to the art of finding patterns in nature, in an ordered interweaving of man's life into visible nature and visible nature into man's life.

These are great questions, necessitating comparative treatment if they are to be adequately examined. Amongst them is not included any question dealing with intuition as a peculiar gift of the artist in language or the artist in painting. This is not because I fail to recognize the element of the incommensurable in man as in Nature, but because it seems to me nonsense to assume that the poet has it and the scientist not. The same applies to the exercise of the imagination.

Many of the problems outlined above, particularly those connected with the controversy between the poets and the philosophers-*cum*-scientists, cannot in my humble opinion be profitably investigated unless the investigators have a pretty clear idea as to what their basic presuppositions are with regard to knowledge. To illustrate the force of this, everybody in the West knows that Descartes achieved for himself the basic presupposition, *cogito ergo sum,* "I think, therefore I am." To this hypothesis I conceive an ingrained double-harness thinker replying, "All right, so far so good, but ought you not to work out the implications also of *sum ergo cogito,* 'I am, therefore I think'?" Further, the question still remains to be asked whether we should not be well advised to add on another pair of complementary hypotheses—namely, "I feel, therefore I am," and "I am, therefore I feel." This, as a matter of fact, is exactly what Chuang Chou, the Taoist philosopher of the fourth and the third centuries B.C., advanced as the primary line of inquiry. To give his own words:

Delight in and anger against, grief and joy, planning ahead and looking back with regret, a state of sexual excitement and a state of sexual lassitude, these ebullitions which are constantly alternating, are [like] music coming out of emptiness, [like] damp heat producing mushrooms. Day and night the one follows on with the one before, but there is no knowing what makes it spring up. Enough, enough! With our morning and evening obtaining a *this,* from what source does it come to be so?
Without a *that* there would be no I: without an I there would be nothing to take hold of [the *that*]. This is near enough [to the truth], but we do not know what sets this acting. [Logically] there must be a True Director, but we cannot get even a glimpse of him.

That he might have a physical form is believable, but we do not see that form. He has actuality but no form.[11]

In the light of that statement, one with which all thinkers and writers were familiar in Lu Chi's day, and in relation to the entirely evident genius of the Chinese people in the realm of art, particularly that of landscape-painting, there would seem to be extremely good ground for accepting Professor Northrop's thesis in *The Meeting of East and West*. That thesis is that the East works by intuition and emotion trained along aesthetic lines, whilst the West works by reason and the intellect trained along scientific lines. The pragmatic conclusion which he draws is that East and West stultify themselves by over-emphasizing one method to the exclusion of the other, and therefore each has to learn from the other. That final exhortation must command the hearty support of all intelligent world-minded people—indeed, it does command very wide assent. On the other hand, Mr. Northrop, whose book is so admirable in its serious and learned efforts to face the situation and to ask the right questions, does in the last resort go astray: so I would urge from my point of view. He has failed to appreciate the philosophical approach to the problem of knowledge as set forth in the quotation from Chuang Chou. It is basic to Chuang Chou's affirmation that there should be an "I," and that that "I" should retain its self-identity and self-consciousness. Without this, there would be nothing which could take hold of the emotions and "the world beyond ourselves." That being so, the whole point of the two landscapes that Mr. Northrop reproduces (his Plates XIII and XIV) is *not* "the oneness of knower and object in the aesthetic continuum," *nor* "the

[11] *Chuang Tzu Book*, Chapter II.

226

undifferentiated continuum," but the existence of the "I" and its ability to sit on a bank or in a boat and contemplate the distant scene and the near at hand. As Lu Chi might have said, art does not consist in losing one's self in the infinite sea of phenomena or emotions or language, but in pinning down some specific intelligible impression of them. Actually, what Lu Chi did say was, "taxing Non-Being to produce Being, calling to the Silence, importunate for an answer." Taxing is surely a highly denotative operation. So also, an answer is no answer unless it be adequately denotative.

There I leave these problems for more able and more learned minds than mine to examine and evaluate.

APPENDICES

APPENDIX I

A Discussion about Literature
by Emperor Wen of the Wei Dynasty (third century A.D.*)*

(a) *Men of letters have regarded each other lightly; and this has
been the case from antiquity down, and naturally so.*

*Fu Yi and Pan Ku were in the relationship of elder and junior,
but Ku made little of Yi, and in a letter to his brother Chao
he said:*

*"Fu Yi on the ground that he can write is a palace recorder,
but now when he starts writing he does not know to stop.*

Men in their own eyes are good [at writing],

*But since literature does not consist of one style only, there are
very few who are good all round.*

*The result is that every man, because of that in which he excels,
despises that in which he comes short.*

*There is a rustic saying, "My family has a worn-out broom:
we offer it for a thousand pieces of gold."*

Surely there is danger of egotism!

(b) *The men of letters of today are K'ung Yung [Wen-chü][1] of
Lu Kuo, Ch'en Lin [K'ung-ch'ang] of Luang Ling, Wang
Ts'an [Chung-hsüan] of Shan Yang, Hsü Kan [Wei-
ch'ang] of Pei Hai, Juan Yü [Yüan-yü] of Ch'en Liu, Yin
Ch'ang [Te-lien] of Erh Nan, and Liu Chen [Kung-kan]
of Tung Ping.*

*These seven gentlemen are in no respect lacking in learning,
and in their diction they do not borrow.*

*Each of them regards himself as a racer of a writer, like [the
famous steed] Chi-lu, good for a thousand miles.*

*We look up to them all alike as competent writers, and as
equally good gallopers;*

*and this is the reason they have such difficulty, difficulty in
bowing before each other.*

[1] These secondary names are the familiar names of the persons concerned
as distinct from their courtesy names. The practice of giving both names
arose from the need for precise designation.

231

> *Since the man of breeding judges himself in order to estimate others, therefore I can avoid being enmeshed [in this failing] and compose this discussion of composition.*

(c) Wang Ts'an's strong point is in the phrasing of fu poems, and Hsü Kan, although at times he has the Ch'i peculiarities, is his equal.

Thus Ts'an in his Beginning of Taxing, his Climbing a Tower, his Japonica, and his Thought on Taxation, and Kan in his Black Monkey, his Round Fan, his Orange Tree,

although in these they are not surpassed by Chang Heng and Ts'ai Yung, yet in their other writings they are not in the same class.

Lin Yü's elegant memorials and letters are recorded as the outstanding products of today:

Yin Ch'ang's [compositions] display harmony, but they are not virile:

Liu Chen's [writings] are virile but loose in thought.

K'ung Yung's special force of style is elevated and subtle, has a quality by which he surpasses other men;

but he is unable to maintain an argument, his reasoning does not control his diction,

to the point where he mixes in sarcasm and joking; but at his best he is mate to Yang Hsiung and Pan Ku.

The ordinary run of people prize things from a distance and despise things from near at home, are attracted by reputation and turn their backs on what is real:

they also are anxious lest they unconsciously give themselves away and lest they blow their own trumpets.

(d) Literature as a whole comes from the same root, but in its lesser details it displays great difference.

Memorials and imperial decisions should be elegant, letters and discussions should be well reasoned:

memorial tablets and eulogies of the dead should stick to facts, lyrical poetry and fu require to have symmetry.

These four classes being different, the result is that those who have ability with any one of them are lopsided, and only those with comprehensive talents can perfect their style.

(e) In literature esprit [ch'i] is of first importance, the cleanness or muddiness of [a man's] esprit has its own embodiment, and it is impossible to get anywhere by main force.

232

By way of illustration, take the music in singing, the intervals in the tune may have been evenly adjusted, nevertheless the rhythm of the stanza likewise [requires] control [which is by no means a mechanical task].

With regard to variation in expression of esprit, the skill or clumsiness go by what is basically in a man:

although a father and elder brother have [the genius], they cannot convey it to a son or younger brother.

(f) *In making the warp of a country's institutions literature is the greatest of possessions, is a flourishing undertaking which never fades.*

Great age has its limit, the time comes when it ends; glory and pleasure are restricted to one's own person:

these, indeed, are bound to come to the limit of their continuance, in this being unlike the limitless [? the eternal] quality of literature.

Hence the composers of antiquity lodged their selves in their brilliant writing [literally, ink], and displayed their ideas in chaptered books.

They did not borrow their diction from good histories, nor did they rely on that fleeting thing, political power;

yet their name and fame have in themselves been handed down to later generations.

Hence when King Wen was in prison he expanded the Changes Scripture, whilst Duke Chou, when he was in the public eye, made the order of the rituals.

[The one] was not hampered in his task by being obscure and in straitened circumstances, [the other] had no use for pleasure and more and more gave himself to thought.

That being so, the men of old despised their foot-long sceptres and esteemed their inch-long shadows, were afraid lest time should pass them by.

Yet men for the most part cannot force themselves:

if they are poor and of low degree, they are fearful lest they be hungry and cold;

if they are rich and of high degree, they let themselves go in idleness and pleasure.

In consequence, [both kinds] are engaged in the duties before their eyes, and let slip the achievements [which will bring fame for] a thousand years.

Above, the sun and moon pass on their way; below, these men's bodies go to ruin:

233

*suddenly they along with all the beings in nature are trans-
lated hence—the consummation which chiefly exasperates
the scholar of ambition.*

*K'ung Yung and the others are now dead, only Hsü Kan is
still writing and has made a school of composition.*

Appendix 2

The Literary Mind and Its Carving of Dragons
by Liu Hsieh (sixth century)

[In spite of Liu Hsieh's dating more than two centuries later than Lu Chi, I append this opening chapter of his *Wen Hsin Tiao Lung* (*The Literary Mind and Its Carving of Dragons*). This book is the next outstanding landmark in the field of Chinese literary criticism, and its fifty critical essays on every branch and every characteristic of literature are in direct descent from Lu Chi and his *Art of Letters*. Understanding of Liu Hsieh's ideas on literature is not vital to the understanding of Lu Chi, but to the reader who is ignorant of Chinese *belles-lettres* there is perhaps a gain in this addition, for the *Art of Letters* is not left suspended in the thin air of seventeen centuries back.

[Not only so: this essay of Liu Hsieh's serves as a demonstration of the way in which matured double-harness thinking went. Note, for example, the extraordinary care with which a double angle of approach to a subject is engineered. (See my division of the essay into three sections, A, B, and C.) In this connection it is important to realize the fervour of Liu Hsieh's adoration of *wen*. He links it with the primordial power which evolved the universe in the Very Beginning and keeps that universe running in all its glory of ordered pattern. Here is a veritable philosophy of art, giving art a cosmological standing. That being so, are the contents of this chapter to be taken as the outcome of a fantastically intuitional kind of mind? Personally, I cannot survey Liu Hsieh's argument here in that light: it is too closely and deliberately reasoned on its dualistic basis, too patently dependent on observation plus history, the two planks of empirical thinking. And yet, of course, the actual writing is shot through and through with emotion, emotion born of the sublimity of the idea which has come to him, and which he essays to prove.

[It were as well to note for the scholar that, impelled by poverty, Liu Hsieh was for ten years (more or less) the inmate of a famous Buddhist temple in the capital, coming to have the position of sub-librarian. Then he was given a post in the imperial library, where he composed this book of essays. With regard to his veneration for

235

Confucius, as shown in this Chapter I, he records in Chapter L that at the age of seven he had a dream in which he "followed Confucius going to the South," and that when he awoke, he was immensely happy. In his middle years Liu Hsieh lost by death his patron and friend, the heir apparent, Chao Ming. Later the state fell into confusion owing to invasion by barbarians, and Liu Hsieh again retired to a monastery. This time he became a monk and took the name Hui Ti (intelligent about earth). (See Liu Hsieh's biography in the *Nan Shih*.)]

CHAPTER I. The Basic Tao

[Paragraphs A, 1-4: Observation and Theory Therefrom]

A. 1. *Great is the spiritual power comprised in* wen [*the art of composition*]; *it is something born with the birth of heaven-and-earth.*
   How can this possibly be the case?
   With the dark and the light there is variegation of colour; with the square and the round there is distinction of form.
   The sun and the moon are duplicating jewels wherewith are hung to view the signs which quarter the heavens: the mountains and rivers are gleaming silks whereby are displayed the forms which make order in the earth.
   Here is the artistry [wen] *in the Tao.*

2. *Looking up, we observe the belching forth of brightness, looking down we descry the patterned beauty contained there;*
   with high and low [*thus*] *fixed in their relative positions, the outcome was the existence of the Yin and the Yang.*
   Only man could make a third term in this [*dualism*], [*man*] *who is compounded of his nature and his soul:*
   here, as we speak of "the Three Powers," it is man who is the fine flower of the Five Physical Forces, man who actualizes mind in heaven-and-earth.
   Once mind was in existence, language was born; once language was born, wen *the* [*art of composition*] *revealed itself.*
   Things came like that of themselves.

236

Appendix 2

3. *Turning to the things alongside* [*in* Nature], *all animals and plants have* wen [*artistry*].
   The dragon and the phoenix by the adornment of elegant [*lines*] *reveal their* [*distinctive*] *auspiciousness; the tiger and the leopard by their fiery colouring give shape to their* [*distinctive*] *carriage:*
   the sunset clouds etch in their colours beyond all the cunning of the painter [to reproduce]; the plants and trees paint their blossoms without waiting for the embroiderer's genius.
   This is no adornment imported from without: all this is naturally so.

4. *And then we come to the woodland pipes and the echoes knotted up with them, making harmony like the tubes and strings* [*of man-made instruments*];
   fountain and stone striking out a rhythm in tune like the chiming of jades.
   Hence with the coming of specific forms comes patterned writing, with the emittance of sounds wen [*literary art*] *is born.*
   Since with things without intelligence there is this rich efflorescence of beauty, shall the tool with mind behind it have no wen *to it?*

[Paragraphs B, 1-5: The Evidence of History]

B. 1. *The beginnings of man's* wen *date from the T'ai Chi,* [*for*], *as occult revelations of numinous influences* [*at work in the universe*], *the emblematic figures of the* Changes Scripture *came first in time.*
   Pao Hsi lined out the rudimentary stage [of these symbols], Confucius gave wings to the final stage;
   and so the Ch'ien and K'un, these two [abstract] relations, are the one controlling interest in the Wen Yen [Patterned Dicta].
   Wen *in speech, Mind in heaven-and-earth!*

2. *As for the* River Chart, *it was conceived in the womb of the* Eight Hexagrams, *whilst the* Lo Book *took its substance from the* Nine Divisions;
   and these have been engraved in gold on solid tablets of jade and beautified by scarlet tracings on a background of verdant green.

Who but man could master this achievement, [for] here is
nothing less than inspired reasoning [such as is found in
sages]!

3. From the time bird-claw markings took the place of knotted
   cords, the graphs began to sparkle [with communicating
   light];
   the first Sage Kings[1] handed down [knowledge of] events,
   these being recorded in the San Fen books:
   but the tally of the years is so remote that the distinctive
   notes of those ages cannot be discerned [by us today].

   Then came the patterned writings of Yao and Shun's day,
   the first development of brilliant literary form:
   for then was composed the Yüan Shou poem, and the fashion
   for chanting began;
   Yi and Chi, ordering their words of counsel, made the tradition of [written] memorials to the throne.

   With the coming of [Emperor] Yü, the business of composing was exalted as of high public utility:
   for the Nine Services were rendered as songs, and [thus]
   meritorious virtue was the more emblazoned.

4. Coming down to Shang and Chou times, the artistic side
   [wen] became victorious over the raw material [of bare
   meaning to be conveyed];
   what is conveyed in the Ya and Sung Odes is beauty constantly becoming new.

   King Wen in his time of distress set forth the splendour of
   his Yao Judgments:
   [here] the tallying variations [in sound] were doubled and
   concealed, the fine shades of meaning were made firm and
   deep.

   Again, through Duke Chou's versatile talents the glowing
   beauty in language was enhanced, [more] odes and sacrificial eulogies were chiseled forth and hemmed together:
   elegancies of diction were axed out, and sentences were
   grouped together.

5. We arrive at the Master [Confucius], the inheritor of all
   the sages; the fine flower of all former thinkers.

---

[1] The text is "Yen Hao," Yen being identifiable as Shen Nung. Hao I
have failed to identify by dictionary or quotation; in the *Tso Chuan* (Duke
Chao, twelfth year) the *San Fen* is mentioned, and the K'ung Ying-ta commentary quotes K'ung An-kuo (Han era) as making Pao Hsi, Shen Nung,
and Huang Ti the authors. Since Pao Hsi is not mentioned here by Liu
Hsieh, he may have had some variant of the legend.

*Casting and moulding the Six Scriptures, insistent on golden
sounds and jewelled expressions,*
*he carved and polished man's natural feelings, made woven
patterns of his injunctions.*

*The wooden clapper sounded and a thousand miles away
responded, the virtue in him [literally the precious stone
on his mat] came into action:*
*he wrote down the glory of heaven-and-earth, he enlightened
the senses of the common man.*

[Paragraphs C, 1-2: *Résumé* of Above Arguments and
Final Conclusions]

C. 1. *Making a survey from Pao Hsi down to Confucius,
the Mysterious Sage created [the first] scripture, the King
in Fustian [Confucius] recorded and interpreted what
had been handed down:*
*and every one of the sages, being grounded in the Tao mind,
set out to serve the cause of patterned beauty; each grind-
ing out his inspired reasonings and so establishing his
systematic doctrines.*

*There being the distinctive formulae in the River Chart and
the Lo Book, and man's lot in life being sought by means
of the milfoil and the tortoise,*
*they [the sages] observed the patterns and movements of
the stars in order to comprehend the changes [impending],
and examined the patterns of human conduct in order to
civilize.*

*Thereafter they were able to map out the natural divisions
of the land, to weave together the intricate patterns of
basic laws:*
*to promote man's social enterprises, to ornament and burnish
both language and meaning.*

2. *Hence we know that the Tao through the channel of the
sages revealed [its] wen, that the sages depended on wen
[the art of composition] for comprehending the Tao:*
*that they gained understanding on all sides [by means of
this art], and since they used it daily, did not become
exhausted [by their beneficent labours].*
*In the Changes Scripture it is written, "Those who stir the
society of man into action continue to exist through their
literary communications";*

239

that by which literary communications succeed in stirring
society is the wen in the Tao.

[Epilogue]

How profound is the Tao mind! Inspired reasoning establish-
ing truth!
Light in all its variation in [Confucius], the Transcend-
ing Sage, who glorified benevolence and filial piety.
The Dragon Chart giving substance, the Turtle Book lend-
ing form!
Herein we see the wen of Heaven, hereby the common man
has an example he can follow.

APPENDIX 3

Some Notes on the History of the Text of the *Wen Fu*, Together with Some Bibliographical Details

As usual with famous writings of a great age in China, the history of the *Wen Fu* text divides itself into two parts, pre-Sung and later. With regard to the earlier period, it has some special features which at first sight cause the historical critic serious concern. With regard to the later period, since the *Wen Fu* was included in the greatly prized *Wen Hsüan* collection, it came in for the various printings and reprintings which the *Wen Hsüan* text underwent in Sung times, notably in the twelfth and thirteenth centuries. What recensions the several Sung editors relied on we do not know, but there was better understanding at that time than there was in Europe of the disconcerting way in which discrepancies occurred, even in well-guarded works, copies of which were in the imperial library. The Sung editors catered for a public which wanted to understand the difficult works in the *Wen Hsüan*, so the two famous T'ang commentaries on the *Wen Fu* were reprinted with their notes *in situ* on variant readings. There was at least one new critical examination of the text, that by the good scholar Yu Mou (1127–1194), and his work, the *Wen Hsüan Chu K'ao Yi*, is to be found in the *Ch'ang Chou Hsien Che Yi Shu*. Lo Hung-k'ai, in his list of editions at the end of his *Wen Hsüan Hsüeh* (Shanghai, 1937), gives two other Sung editions of parts of the *Wen Hsüan*. He also lists one Yüan critical edition available in a Japanese reprint, and five Ming reprints with revised commentaries. The two T'ang commentaries were also reprinted in those two eras.

Thus the eighteenth- and nineteenth-century Ch'ing scholars had a comparative wealth of material on which to exercise their minds both as to the variant readings and as to exegesis. Mr. Lo (*op. cit.*) cites fifty-five of these works of one sort or another, one of them, by Yen Shih-chen of K'ang-hsi's time, specially devoted to the *fu*. Yet, for complete editions of the *Wen Hsüan* the *Ssu Ku Ch'uan Shu* editors confined their critical remarks to the two T'ang commentators. Of the two they attached the greater importance to the Li Shan commentary. Like the great body of the Ch'ing scholars they had a dislike and mistrust of the Five Ch'en. Thus, the best collation of variant readings we have—that by Ku Kuang-ch'i under Hu K'ê-chia's name, published in 1809—is attached to a reprint of the Li Shan commentary.

Since then the chief events in the history of the text of the *Wen Fu* have been the photolithographic reprint of the *Six Ch'en Exegesis of the Wen Hsüan* published in the *Ssu Pu Ts'ung K'an* series on the basis of the best Sung printed edition the (Shanghai) Commercial Press editors had, and the photolithographic reprint in the same series of the *Lu Ssu-heng Wen Chi,* likewise on the basis of a Sung printed edition.

That is how the situation stands today with regard to the text of the *Wen Fu.* Since the Hu K'ê-chia collation was based on the three Sung reprints, mainly on one dated 1127, and the Commercial Press reprints are based on two other such reprints, there is both need and scope for a really scientific collation of variant readings. Pending the accomplishment of such a task, the tentative yet strong impression I have gained from the use of the standard editions just mentioned is that the margin of variation may rightly be described as of manageable proportions. That is to say, there seems no serious question as to whole couplets having got left out: the only questions are with regard to single words, and in many of these cases the argument is as to which of two classifiers was in the original text. That being so, the textual problem, to all practical intents and purposes, becomes one of exegesis—namely, what, on the basis of internal evidences and earlier usage of the phrases, Lu Chi was really meaning to say.

We come now to the pre-Sung history of the text. That divides itself into three periods: first, from A.D. 302 to about 525; second, from 525/30 to the end of the sixth century; and third, from the seventh to the ninth century (Sui-T'ang era). In the first of these periods the *Wen Fu* can only have existed in manuscript copies of Lu Chi's writings preserved for their own sake: in the other two periods it existed as part of the *Wen Hsüan* and as such was under careful court protection. I submit that whilst this was great good fortune, yet it was not unmitigated good fortune. Some of the works included in the *Wen Hsüan* were highly recondite, euphuistical to a high degree of virtuosity. The exegesis of such might well daunt a pundit. Hence, although commentaries were made on some pieces,[1] it was not until the more peaceful days of Sui and T'ang that the task as a whole was attempted. The consequence was that the systematic exegesis of the *Wen Fu* was delayed for three centuries.

For the period 302–525 we have only the statement by the T'ang

---

[1] There are some to be found in Li Shan's edition.

compiler of the *Tsin History* that at the end of Lu Chi's life the
number of his writings which were current in his generation and
after ran to "over three hundred pieces." To the critical mind that
is very poor evidence on which to base a belief in the authenticity
and reliability of the *Wen Fu* text, particularly as, so far as I have
been able to learn, there is no evidence in extant literature of those
days of references to the *Wen Fu*. On the other hand, we know
that from mid-Han times on, works of distinguished writers were
carefully preserved in the imperial library and the great families
prized the possession of copies of these works. The balance of probability comes down on the side of the authenticity of the document
we possess today. That probability, taken with the present state of
the text as outlined above, allows of the situation being regarded as
considerably more healthy than at first sight appears. It must, however, be borne in mind that we have no information as to the fateful
year 317, when Loyang was abandoned to the Hsiung Nu and the
court and its supporters moved south to Chien K'ang on the
Yangtze. How much of the imperial library was transported, and
how much of other libraries and how much if any of Lu Chi's
writings were included, these are questions to which history has no
answer.

Coming to 525/30, our confidence is reinforced. Hsiao T'ung, the
heir apparent to the first Liang emperor, found a considerable number of Lu Chi's poems in the imperial library. So also did two other
scholars of his day, Liu Hsieh, that prince of literary critics, and
Chung Yung, the student of poetry. Hsiao T'ung, commonly known
by his posthumous title, Chao Ming, made his collection of famous
fu, verse, and prose in thirty *chüan* (eight hundred pieces from
over one hundred and thirty authors), and in it gave pride of place
to Lu Chi, including his *Wen Fu* and fifty-nine other pieces: a
larger total than for any other author. Liu Hsieh, in his *Wen Hsin
Tiao Lung*, gave illuminating appraisals of Lu Chi (see his chapters
27, 32, 47) and made other references to him. Chung Yung, in his
Shih P'in, gave one of his neat (but not necessarily reliable) appor-
tionments of praise and blame. To both these writers Lu Chi was,
if not the most outstanding writer of the Six Dynasties era, at any
rate one of them. Unfortunately, whilst we have every reason to
suppose an intimate relationship between Hsiao T'ung and Liu
Hsieh, there is no information on the extent to which the former's
literary taste was influenced by the latter.

From Liang times to Sui-T'ang, the fortunes of the *Wen Fu* text
were bound up with those of the *Wen Hsüan*. In this connection
it is well to note the general opinion of the eighteenth-century
scholars as expressed by Wang Shih-han. In the *Ts'ung Mu Wang
Shih Yi Shu*, *chüan* 6–8 are entitled *Wen Hsüan Li Hsüeh Ch'üan*

Yü (The Beginnings of the Rational Study of the *Wen Hsüan*). In these sections the critic works out his theory that before T'ang times the *Wen Hsüan* was prized more for the music of the poetry in it: the scholars were not concerned with understanding the precise meanings in those poems. Alongside this judgment, which might be true but might, on the other hand, be seriously tendentious, there might be placed the suggestion that the said scholars, being themselves writers in the direct double-harness tradition, had perhaps a better understanding of the poems than later scholars could have, and therefore did not need a commentary on a work, for example, such as the *Wen Fu,* the meanings in which were for the most part clear enough to the readers of that age.

In the Sui-dynasty time one of the best scholars of the day, Ts'ao Hsien, was the forerunner of a new enthusiasm for the *Wen Hsüan,* this being the "beginnings of the rational study" referred to above. He wrote a commentary which has not survived, but three of his disciples—Hsü Yen, Kung-sun Lo, and Li Shan—produced three separate works, of which Li Shan's alone has survived. Li Shan's *piao* submitting his commentary to the court scholars was written about 628, but he spent the rest of his life studying and teaching the book, and our present work seems to contain the fruits of his mature reflection plus those of his son, Li Yung. In regard to the *Wen Fu,* it is an admirable work, admirable for the multitude of ancestors to Lu Chi's smelted and trimmed expressions which Li Shan's industry and learning discovered, admirable for the modesty with which he proffered his suggestions. In this he is in direct contrast to a group of scholars in the eighth century known as the "Five Ch'en,"[2] namely Lü T'ing-tsu, Liu Liang, Chang Hsien, Lü Hsiang, and Li Chou-han. By their bumptious way of trying to override Li Shan, they well merit the dislike the Ch'ing scholars had of them and inevitably create suspicion about the textual variants which they propose. Nevertheless, their work also is valuable to the present-day student of the *Wen Fu.* With these two commentaries to guide them, the T'ang literary connoisseurs had the essential materials for fruitful study.

With regard to bibliographical suggestions, it is of course necessary to go to the official histories, that of the Three Kingdoms and the *Tsin History* with its very instructive commentary, the *Tsin Shu Kao Chu.* Then the thesaurus of classical and early mediaeval *belles-lettres* by Yen K'o-chun (1762–1843) is a great boon both because it brings all the extant material together under the particular writer's name and because it tells where Yen got that material—for example, the *Yi Wen Lei Tsü* (T'ang era) quotes the

[2] Their *piao* is dated 718.

whole of the *Wen Fu* from beginning to end. In this connection it is of great interest to note what Professor Ch'en Shou-yi has been so kind as to point out to me—namely, that in the *T'ai P'ing Yü Lan* (Sung era) there is only one quotation from the *Wen Fu* (see *op. cit., chüan* 586). Coming to contemporary scholarship, Professor Lo Keng-chê's *Wei Tsin Liu Chao Wen Hsüeh P'ei P'ing Shih* (Chungking, 1943) and his subsequent volume on literary criticism in T'ang times blaze a new trail with most illuminating results. The earlier volume is indispensable. Equally so, though in a more dry, statistical fashion, is Professor Lo Hung-k'ai's *Wen Hsüan Hsüeh* (Shanghai, 1937; second edition, 1939). There is also Professor Ho Li-ch'üan's *Lu Ssu-heng Shih Chu* (Tsinan, 1932). For the dating of the composition of the *Wen Fu,* Professor Ch'en Shih-hsiang's very able article in the periodical *Sinatica* is important. Professor Ch'en Shou-yi has also drawn my attention to the first issue of the Wu Han University *Wen Pao* and the article there, *Lu Chi Nien Piao,* by Professor Chu Tsai-jun.

With regard to Western literature bearing on the *Wen Fu,* there are four items to be noted. The first two are Dr. Georges Margouliès' *Le Fou dans le Wen-siuan* (Paris, 1926), with its translation and notes; also his learned *Le Kou Wen chinois* (Paris, 1926). The third item is a translation in German by E. von Zach reported to me as contained in the proceedings of Richard Wilhelm's China-Institut at Frankfurt (an earlier section of proceedings which was only issued to members of the Institut). The fourth item is Basile Alexeiev's brilliant *esquisse dogmatique, La Littérature chinoise* (Paris, 1937).[3]

In conclusion, my search for Chinese editions in British and American libraries makes it clear that for an exhaustive assembling of all extant material available for closer study it would be necessary to oscillate between Peking and Paris, and perhaps Leyden and Moscow. There being certain practical difficulties about such a course of action, I venture the following personal opinion in the hope it may be of some use to serious students. I confess that those Ming and earlier Ch'ing editions which I have been able to see leave me a little cold—with the exception of Hu K'ê-chia's textual apparatus, compiled with the aid of the two expert textual critics, Ku Kuang-ch'i and P'eng Chao-sun. This coldness of attitude has arisen from the growing impression that the revival of interest in *fu* poetry during the Sung era was to a certain degree romantic in temper, and

---

[3] I have recently been informed that M. Alexeiev has now published in Russian a study of the *Wen Fu* in relation to Horace's *Ars poetica.* I have no details to hand and have not heard of any review of the book—doubtless an illuminating and provocative piece of work, not to be missed by the student.

that the strengthening of this temper of mind in later generations of scholars tended to make their researches less rather than more imbued with historical good sense. For the student my advice is to eat, drink, and sleep with the Li Shan and Five Ch'en commentaries and get to know Lu Chi's and Lu Yün's writings and those of their contemporaries. Then, with the *P'ei Wen Yun Fu* for guide, companion, and friend, see what comes. Only after that turn to the later scholars, whose ingrained antiquarianism may make them but dubious guides.[4]

[4] It is my misfortune that owing to the uncertain postal arrangements between China and America, Professor Ch'en Shih-hsiang's *Literature as Light Against Darkness* (National Peking University Semi-centennial Papers, No. XI, College of Arts: pp. 71ff.; Peking, 1948) did not come into my hands until my manuscript was prepared for the printer. Professor Ch'en informed me in June, 1949, that he himself had not received a copy. I see that Professor Ch'en makes special reference to three later critics whose works on the *Wen Hsüan* are in the *Ts'ung Shu Chi Ch'eng*. He adds, however, "Their bearing on our discussions will be only indirect and therefore will be referred to as little as possible." A cursory perusal of Professor Ch'en's important contribution gives me no right to say more than that he and I are obviously in agreement as to the intercultural significance of the *Wen Fu*.

Appendix 4

Note on the Frontispiece
by Ch'en Shou-yi

The frontispiece here in my friend Professor E. R. Hughes's book is the first of nineteen pages in which is given a transcript of the complete text of the Wen Fu. To be precise, the frontispiece is a photograph of a collotype issued by the National Palace authorities in Peking in 1934. This collotype is a beautiful facsimile reproduction, exact to size, of the original calligraphic masterpiece which has been preserved in the Imperial Studio. Although the original is unsigned, connoisseurs from the thirteenth to the seventeenth century, working on the problem of the authorship, came to the decision that the calligraphy must be that of Lu Chien-chih of the first half of the seventh century. Detailed comparison with the extant specimens of Chien-chih's styles—for he was versatile and could compass more than one *genre*—discloses intrinsic resemblances. Further, the calligraphic standard achieved is such that the artist could not have been unknown to history; yet in the centuries from T'ang through Sung there is no other known artist on whom the achievement could be fathered. Thus its aesthetic standard and particular stylistic qualities combine with certain external corroborative circumstances in compelling agreement with the decision of the earlier connoisseurs. I can see no adequate ground for doubting that the transcript was made by this famous calligraphist in the early decades of the T'ang dynasty.

Lu Chien-chih was the nephew of Yü Shih-nan (A.D. 558–638), an even more famous calligraphist. Besides benefiting from the instruction of his illustrious uncle, he seems to have been influenced by the style of Wang Hsi-chih (A.D. 307–365), the first and by many regarded as the greatest of the scholar-artists who brought calligraphy to the pitch of a high art. The record of Lu Chien-chih's life, as given in the Wu Hsien Chih and elsewhere, shows that he was a native of the district in which Lu Chi and his family had their home in the third century. We may assume, therefore, that Lu Chien-chih was a descendant of that family.

On the first leaf of the transcription there are the impressions in red of ten monograph stamps. Two of these are imperfect: the one in the top right-hand corner being completely illegible, the one in the middle below it being half blurred and revealing only two char-acters meaning "sons grandsons"—i.e., male descendants generally. Of the two oval-shaped impressions, the right-hand one records "treasured under the imperial observance of Ch'ien Lung" (reigned 1736–1795). The impression on the left is Chia Ching's seal (reigned 1796–1820). The oblong seal below the oval Ch'ien Lung stamp reads "Expertized by His Imperial Majesty at the Studio of the Three Rarities"—a studio built by Ch'ien Lung to house his priceless collection of the calligraphic albums of Wang Hsi-chih, his son, Wang Hsien-chih, and their cousin, Wang Hsün.

The remaining five impressions on the right-hand edge of the page are in two cases only half revealed on the mounted sheet, but these two can be reconstructed from other impressions of them else-where in the album. Beginning with the top one, they read as follows: (1) "The Sun Family," indicating that the original was in the possession of Sun Cheng-tsai (1592–1676); (2) "Treasure"; (3) "True Recluse of Yüan Chiao"; (4) "Mountain Studio Emu-lating Tsin [Dynasty Tastes]"; (5) "Perpetuating Loyalty and Filial Piety in the Family." These last three inform us that the transcript was in the possession of the connoisseur and collector, Li T'i, early in the fourteenth century, being a treasured item in his collection.

As Liu Chi (1311–1375), the Ming writer-statesman, remarked, "The album which contains the *Wen Fu* of Lu Chi and the callig-raphy of Lu Chien-chih is a combination of two rare beauties."

INDEX

abstract, in art, 199-200
admonitions, Lu Chi on, 100, 134-135
ai, 156
Alciphron (Berkeley), 223
Alexeiev, Basile, 245
  Littérature chinoise, La, 245
Analects, 65, 115, 122, 143, 162n., 163
analogies, 7, 8
analogues, 163-164
Annam, 72
antithesis, disjunctive, 123, 141
An-yang "oracle-bones," 61, 63
Areopagitica (Milton), 123-124
Aristotelian Papers (Cooper), 201n.
Aristotelous peri Poiêtikês (Bywater), 205n.
Aristotle, 4, 7, 19, 21, 163, 196, 197, 198, 200-205, 206, 207, 209, 214
  De Organon, 200n.
  Poetics, 200n., 203, 205n.
  Rhetoric, 200n.
Arnold, Matthew, 194
Ars poetica (Horace), 138, 205, 245n.
art, Han, 74-75
  meaning of, 196-197
Asoka, King, 27
astronomy, 25

Bacon, Francis, 214
Bampton Lectures, 194
Beginning of Taxing (Wang Ts'an), 232
Berkeley, George, 223
  Alciphron, 223

Bible, 24, 73, 145
binoms, 115, 136-137
Black Monkey (Hsü Kan), 232
Blake, William, 92, 219-220
book distribution, 22
Bowra, C. M., 207, 220n.
  Heritage of Symbolism, The, 207n., 220n.
British Museum, 132
Brooks, Cleanth, 198
Browne, Sir Thomas, 16, 214, 219
  Religio Medici, 214-216
Browning, Robert, 193
brush, writing with, 69
Buddha, 23, 27, 29
Buddhism, 18, 27-28, 29, 86n., 133, 159, 160, 161, 182n., 185-186, 224
Buddhist Conference (A.D. 489), 138
bureaucracy, 29, 37, 68, 89
Burke, Kenneth, 198
Bywater, Ingram, 205n.
  Aristotelous peri Poiêtikês, 205n.

Caesar, Gaius Julius, 8, 76
  De bello civile, 7
calligraphy, Chinese, 59, 61-65, 68-69, 71-73, 247-248
  Egyptian, 62
  Greek, 62
Campbell, A. Y., 205n.
  Horace, 205n.
Carlyle, Thomas, 194
catharsis, 203-204, 209
Ch'an (Zen) Buddhism, 182n.
chang, 70-71

First Emperor, 29, 37, 68, 69, 71, 76, 125
Five Ch'en, 121, 122, 147, 149, 168, 175, 182, 187, 242, 244, 246
"Five Emperors," 28, 30
"five-word" prosody, 89-91
Fo T'u Teng, 27-28, 28n.
Fogg Museum, 139
forewords, 109
Fou dans le Wen-siuan, Le (Margouliès), 12, 245
Four Quartets (Eliot), 10-11, 114
  "East Coker," 17-18, 120-121
four-six style, 14
"four-word" prosody, 89-90
fu, 12, 13, 14-16, 68, 69, 74, 76, 77, 78, 79, 81, 82-90, 93, 109, 116, 133-134, 143, 150, 173, 184, 232, 245-246
Fu Hsi, 24
Fu Yi, 231

Galileo Galilei, 22, 208
Gardner, Charles S.,
  Chinese Traditional Historiography, 82n.
Glass of Vision, The (Farrer), 194
Great Learning, The, 184, 190
Great Sacrifice, 160, 161
Greek calligraphy, 62
Greek language, 196, 200
Greek vs. Chinese literary criticism, 198-205

Hamlet (Shakespeare), 92, 219, 223
Han dynasty, 15, 29, 35, 37, 51, 55, 60, 68, 69-70, 71-73, 74, 75-76, 91, 112, 134, 138, 144, 149, 157, 159, 161, 162, 166, 185, 210, 211, 243
  art, 74-75
  literature, 74-90
Han Fei Tzu, 24, 67
Han Yü, 221-222
Hangchow, 32, 125
Hao, Emperor, 33, 34
Harvard Journal of Asiatic Studies, 125n.

heaven-and-earth, 126-127
Heber, Reginald, 178
Hebrew poetry, 84
Heritage of Symbolism, The (Bowra), 207n.
hexagrams, 72, 73
historians, Chinese, 67
History of Criticism and Literary Taste in Europe (Saintsbury), 206n.
History of the First Han Dynasty, 78, 82
history of past, 23-25, 28
History of the Second Han Dynasty, 30, 47
History Scripture, 63, 63n., 178, 185
Ho, Emperor, 78
Ho Hsün, 53
Ho Kuan Tzu, 148, 152
Ho Li-ch'üan, 245
  Lu Ssu-heng Shih Chu, 245
Ho Shang Kung, 172n.
Ho Shao, 135
Ho Yen, 122
Ho Yin, 49
Homer, 4, 7, 196, 197, 203, 204
  Iliad, 204
homophones, 139
Honan, 61
Honolulu Academy of Arts, 166n.
Hopkins, Gerard Manley, 16
  Notebooks and Papers, 16-17
Horace, 205-206
  Ars poetica, 138, 205, 245n.
Horace (Campbell), 205n.
Hsi T'ien Fu (P'ang Ngo), 173-174, 175
Hsi Tz'u, 187
hsiang, 187, 188-189
Hsiang Hsiu, 135-136
hsiang sheng, 68-69
Hsiao T'ung, 243
hsin, 20, 21, 22, 209
Hsiung Nu, 40, 42, 243
Hsü Kan, 231, 232, 234
  Black Monkey, 232
  Orange Tree, 232
  Round Fan, 232
Hsü Shen, 78-79

Index

Liang dynasty, 243
library, imperial, 27, 34, 34n., 76, 85, 243
Liddell, H. G., and Scott, R., *Greek-English Lexicon*, 163, 196
Lieh Tzu Book, 130
Lin Yü, 232
"linked pearls," 124
literary criticism, American, 198-199
Literary Mind and Its Carving of Dragons, The (Liu Hsieh), 222, 235-240, 243
literary traditions, Western and Chinese, 198-209
Literature as Light against Darkness (Ch'en Shih-hsiang), 246n.
Littérature chinoise, La (Alexeiev), 245
Liu An, 76-77
Liu Chen, 231, 232
Liu Chi, 248
Liu Hsiang, 78, 87
Liu Hsieh, 132, 144, 151, 222, 235-236, 243
    Literary Mind and Its Carving of Dragons, The, 222, 235-240, 243
Liu Hsin, 78
Liu Liang, 131, 142-143, 244
Liu Te, 76
Liu Yüan, 28n.
Lo Book, 237, 239
Lo Hung-k'ai, 241, 245
    Wen Hsüan Hsüeh, 241, 245
Lo Keng-chê, 245
    Wei Tsin Liu Chao Wen Hsüeh P'ei P'ing Shih, 245
Lo River, 125
Locke, John, 214
logicians, 7-8, 213-214
Longinus, Dionysius Cassius, 76, 205, 206-207, 208
Lowes, John Livingston, 199
    Convention and Revolt in Poetry, 199
Loyang, 27, 38-39, 40, 44, 51, 53, 57, 159, 243

Lu Chi, 8, 9, 10, 11, 15, 16, 17, 19, 20, 21, 23, 24, 25, 59, 60, 73, 83, 86, 90, 91-93, 192, 193, 197, 222, 223, 226, 227, 235, 242, 243, 246, 247, 248
on admonitions, 100, 134-135
and Aristotle, 201-205
on art of letters as art of reasoning, 209-210
and Chinese language, 212
on dedications, 100
Dialectic of Destruction, The, 35, 36-37
on diction, rules of, 105-106
Discussion of the Five Grades of Nobility, 35-36
dog of, 32-33
on elegies, funeral, 100, 134
vs. French symbolists, 207-208
"Impressions of a Grave Mound," 56, 57-58
on inscriptions on monuments, 100, 134
and Latin literary criticism, 206
on letters, utility of, 108
life and times of, 26-58
on lyrical poetry, 100, 132-133
on memorials, 100, 135
on musical patterning in writing, 105-106
on obscurity in poetry, 107
on panegyrics, 100, 135
on prose poems, 100
on reasoning and wording, 101-102, 104, 105
on sacred writings, 95, 115
"Sensing of Time," 56
"Sigh over Passing Away, A," 56
on songs, licentious, 104, 157, 158
on sounds, 101
Statement on Thinking, A, 56n.
on stimulus and response, interaction of, 107
on style, 100-102
on theories, expositions of, 100
time-past, sense of, 23-25, 28
Wen Fu: see *Wen Fu*
world-space, sense of, 23, 26-27

259

Date Due

PRINTED IN U. S. A.